The Promise of Restorative Justice

Restorative justice is usually found operating within the juvenile and criminal justice systems. However, like a flower growing from a rock, restorative justice principles thrive in unusual places, often outside traditional systems.

The Promise of Restorative Justice

New Approaches for
Criminal Justice and Beyond

EDITED BY
John P. J. Dussich
Jill Schellenberg

LYNNE
RIENNER
PUBLISHERS

BOULDER
LONDON

Paperback edition published in the United States of America in 2013 by
Lynne Rienner Publishers, Inc.
1800 30th Street, Boulder, Colorado 80301
www.rienner.com

and in the United Kingdom by
Lynne Rienner Publishers, Inc.
3 Henrietta Street, Covent Garden, London WC2E 8LU

Hardcover edition published in 2010 by Lynne Rienner Publishers, Inc.

ISBN 978-1-58826-932-4 (pbk. : alk. paper)

Printed and bound in the United States of America

The paper used in this publication meets the requirements
of the American National Standard for Permanence of
Paper for Printed Library Materials Z39.48-1992.

5   4   3   2   1

Contents

Part 2 Bringing Restorative Justice to the Broader World

Foreword

At a time when individuals, communities, and governments seem so stuck in dysfunctional responses to conflict and violence, the vision of restorative justice provides a powerful glimmer of hope. Having begun in the 1970s as a criminal justice system reform effort, in the twenty-first century restorative justice has truly grown to be a social movement in the global community, a movement that has expanded far beyond criminal and juvenile justice systems. In *The Promise of Restorative Justice: New Approaches for Criminal Justice and Beyond,* John Dussich and Jill Schellenberg provide a collection of essays that bear witness to the ever increasing impact of restorative principles and practices as they become embodied in so much of the fabric of human life, in multiple settings.

Restorative practices have great potential in school communities as well as in conflictual relationships in general. Addressing the ever present problem of bullying and its related violence through restorative interventions offers a practical and effective response. Applying restorative justice to issues of elder abuse, business, athletics, politics, disaster management, and grief brings the wisdom of what has been learned over three decades into entirely new arenas. Although it pushes the buttons of some, discussing how restorative justice can relate to death penalty cases is a much-needed conversation. The chapters that address restorative justice principles in victim assistance and within a Native American tribal community provide an important grounding in the core values of the movement—specifically, engaging victims and responding to their needs and honoring the indigenous values and practices that have informed the restorative justice movement over the years.

All of these stories bear witness to the incredible strength, compassion, and resilience of the human spirit when people are given the opportunity to become engaged in a restorative process, to talk about the real human impact of the conflict, and to repair the harm as much as possible. The annual restorative justice conferences held over the years at Fresno Pacific University in California under the leadership of Ron Claassen and his colleagues provide a wonderful seedbed for these stories.

In the coming years, it is my hope that even more stories of how restorative principles and practices are emerging in other unlikely settings will be documented. This is particularly true with what has been developing in areas of hate crimes, human rights violations, and transitional justice initiatives following deeply entrenched violent conflicts, including genocide, within nations. Perhaps there will be a second edition.

In *The Promise of Restorative Justice,* the authors have done a fine job of telling the story of how restorative justice is ultimately a way of life, of how we treat each other in all aspects of human existence. It is a valuable resource to be read by all those concerned about life within and among the many communities we share.

—Mark S. Umbreit
Director, Center for Restorative Justice and Peacemaking
University of Minnesota

Preface

At a recent restorative justice conference at Fresno Pacific University in California, after having listened to two days of excellent presentations, John Dussich and Jill Schellenberg were sitting around a table with Ron Claassen and his wife, Roxanne, and Duane Ruth-Heffelbower and his wife, Clare Ann, reflecting on the topics and meanings of what we had all recently experienced. John was struck with how some of the restorative justice applications presented had been unexpectedly outside of criminal justice settings. Yet, they had been presented and had been validated as appropriate for a major national restorative justice conference. He mentioned not having ever read about these "extramural" applications. He asked the others if they knew of any publications where these somewhat new and unique uses of restorative justice had ever been highlighted. All pensively considered that question and then shook their heads. At that moment, John, thinking out loud, said how interesting it would be to edit a collection focused on the unlikely places where restorative justice was being effectively used. Those around the table were asked if they might be willing to contribute to such a project, and all quickly agreed that they would. Thus, the idea was born and a commitment was made between Jill and John to embark on a journey to create a book that would discuss where the principles of restorative justice were being successfully applied to conflict situations in unusual places, especially those outside the formal criminal justice system. Our thoughts were that a book of this type, beyond being unique, could also serve to make the important point that restorative justice is more than a tool to facilitate the ways that criminals, victims, and the community can better respond to crime. It is also an important philosophy for improving the way individuals and society respond to a wider range of human conflicts, some related to, and others not related to, the criminal justice system. In essence, we thought, why limit our focus to the criminal justice system? Why not consider the benefits and even promote these benefits in the wider community?

Like all journeys into uncharted lands, the value of the experience is judged by what has been learned along the way. On this journey, we have learned that just as criminologists and victimologists have recognized that the concept of restorative justice is an idea that is timely for the criminal justice system, it seems that the same core principles are appropriate for a broad range of social challenges. Like the flower that has taken root in the unlikely rock, the essential ingredients for it to flourish were present. Because of its inherent strengths, it has proven a unique ability to emerge and outperform other less effective attempts. It even suggests a potential to change the very nature of heretofore seemingly immovable forces and to do so simply, naturally, and with great elegance.

We would be remiss if we did not mention some of the key persons without whom this book would not have come into being. First, we owe a debt of thanks to Ron and Roxanne Claassen for their immediate and spontaneous support when we first mentioned the book's theme. Also, throughout the search for likely examples, Ron provided us with unique candidates, many of which appear in the pages that follow. Another important supporter of this work was Howard Zehr, who inspired us with his lecture at the American Society of Victimology symposium in April 2007 in Baltimore. It was at that event that we realized the similarities between the theme of our work and Howard's continuing message in his writings and speeches. He has also been a beacon of light throughout this journey. We are extremely grateful to our spouses, Edda and Tim, for their encouragement and willingness to endure our frequent absences from much family time. A special thanks to staff at our former publisher, Criminal Justice Press—especially Rich Allinson, whose frequent reminders to be simple, practical, and precise were a major influence in upgrading the overall quality of this book. We would also like to thank our proofreader and book manager, Michael D. Evans, who along the way also became our friend and valued adviser.

—John P. J. Dussich
Jill Schellenberg

1

Introduction

John P. J. Dussich and Jill Schellenberg

Viewed through a restorative justice lens, "crime is a violation of people and relationships. It creates obligations to make things right. Justice involves the victim, the offender, and the community in a search for solutions which promote repair, reconciliation, and reassurance" (Zehr, 1990, p. 118). Restorative justice

> holds that criminal behavior is primarily a violation of one individual by another. When a crime is committed, it is the victim who is harmed, not the state; instead of the offender owing a "debt to society" which must be expunged by experiencing some form of state-imposed punishment, the offender owes a specific debt to the victim which can only be repaid by making good the damage caused. (Zehr, 1990, p. 118)

The rallying concept of this book is that restorative justice concepts, principles, and practices need not be limited to criminal justice activities but can be appropriate and even advantageous to many other social situations where conflicts occur. This has been the core theme in our search for suitable manuscripts for this anthology over the past three years. We are pleased to present in Part 1 of the book chapters that personify this broader concept and to bring the powerful messages of the promise of restorative justice to victims and offenders; the chapters of Part 2 bring those same messages to the broader world. Here are the findings of our two-part journey.

Chapter 2, "Innovations in Correctional Settings," discusses society's expectations that criminals are deterred by the threat of the punishment that corrections represent; that punishment teaches criminals never to offend again and thus thwarts them from reoffending; that punishment causes offenders sufficient suffering that they strive to avoid it; and that punishment might cause those punished to change their way of thinking and feeling such that they become rehabilitated. However, the notion that something that was lost by the victims is given back to the victim or the community because of the punishing experience seems illogical. This overview by Mario Gaboury and Duane Ruth-Heffelbower is comprehensive, compelling, and mostly focused on the United States. This chapter includes sections on special courts, victim-offender dialogue, conflict resolution, offender reentry programs, victim awareness training, victim impact panels, offender family reconciliation, and restorative justice boards. When reading this chapter, one is struck by how many unusual restorative justice applications exist related to corrections and how well developed they have become. In each of these new programs, there is much hope, much success, and much conviction that, no matter what the status of the offender, using these restorative justice principles makes the lives of offenders better and also benefits the lives of their victims.

In Chapter 3, "Working with Sex Offenders," Clare Ann Ruth-Heffelbower notes that among many laypersons who first learn of restorative justice, there is the notion that its use is usually limited to situations where there is minimal involvement between offender and victim and where the offense is not serious. Thus, the perception is that prosecutors should refer only mild juvenile property cases to mediation—for example, cases of graffiti or vandalism of public property. However, the author explains in this chapter how the use of restorative justice principles can deal with the unique conflicts between victims and offenders of sexual assault. At first, she addresses the misconceptions and stigmas associated with sex offenses as a major challenge faced by those trying to resolve the conflicts between these offenders and their victims so as to help heal and restore the lives of all involved. She then explains how the resources of restorative justice are particularly well suited for the conditions involved in sex cases, especially treating all parties concerned as human beings, ultimately increasing the potential for having much safer communities compared to the process now in effect. To exemplify how restorative justice has been successfully applied to sex offenders, she presents the Circles of Support and Accountability. This is a program that originated in Ontario, Canada, in 1994 and is now being used throughout that country and in many other countries, including the United States. The main focus of this program is reflected in its name: support and accountability. Two major studies that centered on measuring effectiveness have since been conducted. Both have found not only major benefits to all stakeholders—offenders, victims, and communities—but also significant reductions in recidivism. The use of restorative justice principles in dealing with the aftermath of sexual offending, despite the major challenges, has proven to offer significant benefits to restoring peace to all involved.

In Chapter 4, "A Community Responds to Elder Abuse," Arlene Groh reflects on a restorative justice view in the long search to find solutions to the complex crime of elder abuse; on a Canadian community that came together to identify, respond to, and prevent elder abuse; on the ripple effect of restorative justice as a way of life; and on the ways the pillars of restorative justice values and principles empowered the community to imagine new ways of being, to problem-solve on a deeper level. This chapter views, from a restorative justice perspective, the importance of understanding the multiple and complex root causes of elder abuse, such as a possible history of difficult family relationships, including past abuse, a history of emotional or psychiatric problems, substance abuse, the abuser's emotional and financial dependence on the "victim," or difficulty in caring for the dependent older person. This author highlights how collaborative agencies have helped elders find emotional and physical safety using restorative principles that include victims, family members, and the community. The stated goal of these agencies is to end the cycle of violence that often damages and destroys families in elder abuse cases.

Chapter 5, "A Victim with Special Needs: A Case Study," argues that because of their vulnerabilities, both obtrusive and unobtrusive, handicapped persons represent a large and persistent group of potential crime victims. These vulnerabilities are greatly magnified after their first victimization, because their experience confirms to them and to those who care for them that their ability to protect themselves is significantly weaker than that of nonhandicapped persons. For most handicapped victims, increased helplessness is a major part of the victimization impact. This chapter is author Jill Schellenberg's personal story of her daughter's brutal rape. She recounts how she (and her family) reacted to this victimization from a Mennonite faith perspective, which emphasizes peace and reconciliation in relationships. This moving account also takes the reader to the very heart and soul of her struggles with the religious issues of forgiveness in the face of anger and hatred toward the offender and relates her (and her family's) attempts to cope by using restorative justice as a resource to achieve restoration and reconciliation, at the same time trying to be true to her daughter, her faith, her family, her profession, and herself.

In Chapter 6, "Recovery and Restoration in Victim Assistance," John P. J. Dussich challenges the reader to consider whether the phrase "one would think that victim services and restorative justice are natural partners" is a myth. Yet, there are differences between these two camps that have rarely been elucidated, and perhaps therein is the truth. The author lays the foundation of restorative justice by giving the history of victim services and explaining why it was started and what its mission is. Combining restorative justice—which has traditionally been seen as being offender-oriented—and victim services, which has its own history of being victim-focused and sometimes antioffender, can be difficult to reconcile. The author notes that the basic challenge of victim assistance is to understand both the behavioral and legal paradigms and to find a way to operate within these two different orientations, ultimately bringing the victim to a point of recovery *and* restoration. This chapter challenges present and future efforts to create victim service models that are entirely focused on helping victims so that they can be restored and recovered, facilitated by the unique characteristics of restorative justice principles.

In Chapter 7, "Restorative Options for an Offender's Spouse," Shannon Moroney relates a poignant personal experience with restorative justice from her perspective as the wife of a serious sex offender in Canada. Zehr's definition that restorative justice sees crime as fundamentally causing harm to human relationships is true in Moroney's case. Her life was profoundly altered as a result of the crime her husband committed—a crime in which she played no part. She was torn between the loyalty she felt to her husband and the realization of how deeply he hurt his victims. She found that every relationship in her life was affected by the crime he committed. The criminal justice system does not really address the issue of offenders' family members also being victims. How do these indirect victims cope with the system, with their family member, and with their own shame by association? Restorative justice seems to offer the possibility of fostering the needed healing for these family members. Restorative principles seek to restore all who are harmed—that is, everyone who is affected by the crime. The author experienced the ripple effects that crime creates in the lives of families—families that suffer from guilt by association. However, she was able to emerge from the experience a stronger and wiser person, equipped and willing to help others in similar situations.

Chapter 8 speaks to the often-excluded American discussions about criminal justice among Native American people, who also deserve a place at the table of justice, especially with restorative justice. Author Julie C. Abril's words in "Applications in Native American Indian Tribal Communities" reflect the compelling problems that native people encounter, considering that their traditional system was originally more restorative in nature than the current retributive criminal justice system. This juxtaposition of restorative and retributive systems is particularly problematic in native communities. The author notes that when tertiary mechanisms of social control—for example, the police—attempt to control behavior, they often will fail if they are not accepted by the indigenous community. The tribal community engages in a negotiation of power between community members and the formal justice system. One such negotiation relates to having the police respond to spiritual matters because the tribal community demands that the police "do their job." Most Indians in the community cited felt that the police were responsible for responding to community problems. The chapter elaborates on the complexities of the two conflicting systems and the ways each system can learn from the other.

Chapter 9, "Mediation: The Case of Bulgaria," presents restorative justice in a small country relatively unknown to many. According to author Dobrinka Chankova, restorative practices associated with large developed nations are gaining acceptance around the world, including in smaller countries such as Bulgaria. Chankova cites some interesting statistics related to the recognition of restorative and mediation practices among the criminal justice system and the general public in Bulgaria. She states that it is a common belief that mediation cannot and does not attempt to replace traditional criminal justice but rather aims to complement it sensibly. One cannot possibly believe that all deficiencies of justice administration will be set off by introducing mediation. However, as an integral element in the criminal justice system, mediation can indeed bring better results—namely, satisfactory compensation for the victims of crime, faster procedures, elimination of excessive procedural formalism, and reduced use of imprisonment. Bulgaria seems poised to implement restorative justice at all levels in its criminal justice system.

In Chapter 10, "Restorative Justice and the Death Penalty," the irrevocable character of the term *death penalty* seems antithetical to the concept of restorative justice, at least for the offender. However, despite the major emphasis on the victim's needs and restoration, using restorative justice principles in death penalty cases can also provide an important benefit for the offender. Although the chapter focuses on what is perhaps one of the most victim-centric of all restorative justice programs, it is not exclusively about victim restoration. Author Howard Zehr presents the history of a program that started in 1995, a relatively recent creation within the "restorative justice movement." He identifies the beginning of the program with the bombing of the Alfred P. Murrah Federal Building in Oklahoma City and the subsequent trial of Timothy McVeigh. This initiative is called defense-initiated victim outreach (DIVO). Two key restorative justice principles form the foundation of DIVO: "the importance of victim/survivor needs and choices and, to a lesser extent, the principle of encouraging offender accountability." In a critical way, DIVO fills an important gap in the way justice is traditionally provided—that is, with virtually no constructive communication between the victim and the defense attorney. Hence, it is appropriate to use the metaphor of a bridge to describe the role of the victim outreach specialist (VOS), a person who is specially trained for the DIVO program to serve as a link between the interests and work of the defense attorney and the concerns and needs of victims. However, the VOS, although an advocate for the survivor, does not become involved in the issue of the death penalty. The DIVO program has produced *Principles of Practice,* guidelines that provide a basic orientation to how this process functions. After more than ten years of experience, DIVO has proven itself and has received high grades by those involved. The American Bar Association, as early as 2003, recognized the value of this program and has published guidelines for defense counsel functions. Other pioneer applications that have legitimized this program have been the federal defender system's JustBridges project and the Defender Services Committee, as well as the state of Georgia's Council for Restorative Justice. Although unique in its legal venue and its recent application, as Zehr points out in his ending paragraph, the three fundamental values of restorative justice are appropriate for DIVO: (1) "respect for everyone involved," (2) "humility about the limits of what any of us can know," and (3) "the importance of approaching this work—and all of life—with a spirit of awe or wonder."

In Chapter 11, "Restorative Politics," Arthur Wint provides vivid examples from all over the world—from Northern Ireland to North and South Korea to South Africa—of how international crises could be handled restoratively.

The author notes that the world had expected the most ghastly bloodbath to overwhelm South Africa, but that has not happened. Then the world thought that, after a democratically elected government was in place, those who for so long had been denied their rights, whose dignity had been trodden underfoot, callously and without compunction, would go on the rampage, unleashing an orgy of revenge and retribution that would devastate their common motherland. Instead, there was this remarkable Truth and Reconciliation Commission to which people told their heartrending stories—victims expressing their willingness to forgive and perpetrators telling of sordid atrocities while also asking for forgiveness from those they had wronged so grievously. This chapter dramatically and compellingly illustrates the international possibilities for using restorative principles in politics.

Chapter 12 asks the question: Who would imagine that a setting like business might find the principles of restorative justice applicable? However, as author Duane Ruth-Heffelbower succinctly states, "Restorative justice finds its application any time one person does not feel respected by another, whether or not the other person knows it." This chapter, "Solutions for Business Conflicts," is written in a straightforward style based on direct consulting experiences. It provides an overview of the typical conflicts that exist among the employees in any business and then presents the simple logic of how the three basic movements of restorative justice—"acknowledge injustices, restore equity, and clarify future intentions"—can be applied. These will help achieve what he refers to as restorative practices to remove references to "adversarial legalism" and facilitate resolving conflicts in business settings. This chapter also includes a well-written appendix that contains the section of the Faculty Handbook from Fresno Pacific University relating to the termination for cause, which the author uses as his main reference for working in an employee/employer business setting.

Chapter 13 makes including children as stakeholders in a restorative justice proceeding seem appropriate. The formal procedures of restorative justice have mostly been used with adults in conflict, so the prospect of considering children is unusual. We often think that children are the most vulnerable citizens, cloaked in innocence and with limited understanding. The application of restorative justice would seem to require an advanced level of understanding, a degree of maturity not normally expected of children. In this chapter, "New Skills for Children and Schools," Marian Liebmann from the United Kingdom writes about the use of restorative justice for children, especially in schools in her country where it started in 1981 with a conflict resolution program called the Kingston Friends Workshop Group. The term *restorative justice* was first used in a restorative conferencing model for young offenders by the Thames Valley Police in the 1990s. The same police department began using this model for schoolchildren with techniques learned from Australia, and it was referred to as "restorative justice in schools." In schools, these techniques can be used not only for obvious wrongdoings but also for the conflicts that arise between students, and between students, teachers, and staff. The opportunity to use restorative justice in schools has one major advantage over working with adults, in that children have less to unlearn. They can easily be taught to deal with conflicts, and what they learn will be useful for the rest of their lives. The three key principles in using restorative justice at schools are as follows: (1) "providing all those affected by a conflict or a problem the opportunity to air their experiences, their feelings, and their needs, and to feel heard"; (2) "involving everyone affected in finding a mutually acceptable way forward"; and (3) "ensuring that everyone involved becomes accountable for their possible contribution to the presenting incident." One of the key concepts in the use of restorative justice in schools is to adopt the "whole school approach" so that all persons involved understand and follow the principles of restorative justice. The potential for all schoolchildren to learn how to apply these principles not only at school but also in their daily life is a powerful idea that offers promise to all children in all parts of the world.

In Chapter 14, "Adolescent Bullying: The Whole-School Approach," Dennis Wong from Hong Kong tackles the problem of bullying prevention using restorative principles. He points out that it is well established in the bullying prevention literature that a punitive approach, such as reprimanding bullies, calling parents to school, and suspending students, is ineffective. The punitive approach, which values establishing blame and individual accountability, not only cannot resolve conflicts but also makes the relationships between bullies and victims much worse because of the interactive effect of various types of reinforcement among bullies, victims, and bystanders during bullying episodes. This chapter compares and contrasts the zero-tolerance strategy of conflict management in schools—such as punishing the offenders through demerits, suspension, and the involvement of parents—with restorative justice practices offering another means of minimizing the negative consequences of social control interventions and maximizing the opportunity for empowering proactive interventions. The author points out that children who exhibit aggressive behavior may continue a progressive developmental pattern toward severe aggression or violence. To stop the negative spiral effect of school bullying, the restorative justice practice seems to be a well-balanced strategy that could involve the victim, the offender, and the stakeholders in the community in a search for solutions that promote repair, reconciliation, and reassurance. This author gives statistically strong reasons why schools should go through a process whereby all parties with a stake in bullying come together to resolve collectively how to deal with the aftermath of the bullying event and its implications for the future, leading to the development of a positive climate that makes students less vulnerable to proactive as well as reactive aggression.

Chapter 15 asks us to consider discipline in schools in a different light. The prospect of punishing someone, especially for noncriminal behavior in an academic setting, is, for most teachers and school administrators, unpleasant and incongruent with the ideals of pedagogy; it is also frustrating when realizing that it is usually counterproductive. The conversion of a major social structure, in this case the method and structure of applying discipline at a major university, is usually difficult to achieve and causes the school culture to take notice, especially if it is successful. This program at Fresno Pacific University was a bold and creative change that came about by the honest realization that the existing retributive system did not produce acceptable outcomes and by the availability of experts in restorative justice, a model that had been tested and proven to be effective in other settings. This chapter, "Dispute Resolution in Higher Education," by Ron Claassen and Zenebe Abebe, gives further support to the idea that a sound principle for conflict resolution and restoration can be successfully used in more than criminal justice settings. This new practice shows how creativity, courage, and wisdom can be applied to resolve one of the many important challenges in the administration of learning.

In Chapter 16, "Restorative Discipline in Athletics," Dennis Janzen writes about restorative justice in sports. Sports is probably one of the least likely places to find restorative justice, yet in this chapter Janzen brings restorative principles logically and naturally into the athletic realm. He asks, "Does the typical athletic social structure of accountability based on punitive consequences achieve the optimum results we want to believe come from the competitive athletic experience?" This chapter examines the tenets of restorative discipline and justice relative to the social structures and traditions of our organized sports culture. When an alleged violation suggests the need for a disciplinary response, restorative discipline and justice uses an approach that focuses primarily on the development of agreements that can restore a sense of moral balance and "rightness" between the relationships of the offending member and the rest of the group or team members. Furthermore, restorative discipline and justice incorporates both a commitment to personal accountability for all members and compassion for the individual whose behavior has strayed outside the agreements of the group, team, or community. The judgment of the "rightness" or "wrongness" of an individual's behaviors is largely determined on the basis of what has become acceptable behavior within a specific sport's culture. Remembering that restorative discipline and justice still focus on the maintaining of previously agreed-upon behavioral standards (i.e., the rules), the restorative model may actually be a well-suited disciplinary approach for all sports because it can better recognize and deal with the marginal behaviors that so commonly occur during these special events, especially in the heat of competition and split-second decisions often made when the lines of "right" and "wrong" begin to shift or blur.

In Chapter 17, "Restorative Justice in Disaster Management," Duane Ruth-Heffelbower applies restorative justice concepts and principles to disasters. When one thinks of disasters, images of mass casualties, extreme confusion, and major trauma come to mind. Most people would not imagine conflict with an "offender" in such cases because nature is usually the source of these victimizations. However, by taking the reader through a series of vignettes, the author clearly shows how conflicts between the victims and those persons and agencies wanting to help in the recovery process emerge. The major culprit is the lack of organization among different care providers from different cultures and languages who are unfamiliar with local customs and attitudes and are usually not prepared to deal with conflicts. Basing his chapter mostly on his personal experiences and conversations with those providing aid to the victims of the Banda Aceh/Indian Ocean earthquake/tsunami disaster, Ruth-Heffelbower applies the basic principles of restorative practices to help the victims and their rescuers. He had trained some of the Indonesians trying to help those affected to cope with the multitude of conflicts that arose in the weeks and months after one of the worst disasters in recorded history. As he poignantly states, "For victims of disasters, restorative justice means being included in deciding how a project will be executed." This chapter provides insights into the conflicting situations that emerged among those desperate to replace lost property and to bring back some degree of normalcy with those individuals and organizations that assumed to know what was needed without providing the actual victims a voice in the planning and execution of their own recoveries. The basic restorative principles from Ron Claassen (2002), of having those "responsible for the offense acknowledge the hurt, work together with the offended one to figure out how to make things as right as possible, and clarify the parties' future intentions," lead to resolving even these conflicts in disaster areas. All disaster management guidelines must include information about this inevitable part of the disaster—the need to resolve the multitude of conflicts that surely will occur.

In Chapter 18, "Hope and Reconciliation with Grief," the focus is on the loss of a loved one as perhaps one of life's most devastating experiences. Coping with the unnerving confusion, the intense pain, and the sense of extreme emptiness following the death of someone dear is a major challenge. This chapter, which discusses the use of restorative justice, explains the very personal, thoughtful, and analytical approach proposed by author Bonnie J. Redfern, the result of her search for a way to recover from the grief of the loss of her son. It suggests how, after loss and grief, a unique partnership between the transformative mediation of restorative justice and the companioning model of grief therapy can bring about reconciliation and peace. The hope of her new model is offered through restorative justice, especially in its peacemaking features. What had been created to confront the conflicts, confusions, and pains of victimization has been sensitively crafted into a viable philosophy for dealing with the unlikely event of loss and grief. Anyone who has suffered similarly or worked within the field of grief therapy will connect with the depth of her feelings and her ability to synthesize therapeutic wisdom, at times practical and at times spiritual, through the use of restorative justice principles.

PART 1

Bringing Restorative Justice to Victims and Offenders

2

Innovations in Correctional Settings

Mario Thomas Gaboury and Duane Ruth-Heffelbower

Correctional settings are both an obvious and an unusual place to find restorative justice processes. Obvious because of the increased prevalence of restorative processes in the criminal justice arena generally, and unusual because restorative processes and programs most often operate as alternatives outside mainstream correctional programming. Obvious because of the ready availability of the offender population, and unusual due to the long-standing disconnect between the corrections arena and crime victims and survivors. This chapter has as its intention to broaden both the range of settings where restorative processes can be expected and the range of settings deemed to be correctional.

First, it is important to gauge the current status of corrections-based restorative justice programs, with a particular focus on the United States. In reviewing the relatively brief history of restorative programs in corrections in the United States, one finds that there were few programs until fairly recently. For example, one basic form of restorative justice programming in corrections is the "victim awareness" program, sometimes referred to as "impact of crime on victims" or "empathy education" programs. If we use this as a benchmark, the relative newness of corrections-based restorative programs is evident. In 1989, the first known national survey of victim impact programs in the United States (Seymour, 1989) found that only 10 percent of states had victim impact programs in place. In 2004, 73 percent of US jurisdictions reported that they conducted these programs aimed at educating offenders about the impact of crime on victims (National Institute of Corrections, 2004).

Keywords: impact of crime, restorative justice, corrections

Indeed, the National Institute of Corrections study survey cited found a significant level of a variety of restorative justice programs throughout the United States (National Institute of Corrections, 2004). This survey also found that by 2004 there was widespread utilization of restorative justice processes in US corrections departments. The responses from forty-seven state-level departments of corrections indicated victim impact education/empathy programs were provided by 73 percent of the departments, restorative/reparative work benefiting victims or communities by 62 percent, victim/offender mediation/dialogue by 52 percent, and family group counseling by 15 percent (National Institute of Corrections, 2004, p. 10).

Given this prevalence of restorative justice activities in correctional settings, one might ask if there is still a disconnect. Has the traditional, exclusive offender focus of corrections yielded to the more inclusive tenets of restorative processes? This would indeed hold promise for the ever increasing utilization of restorative processes in correctional settings. Next, one might ask whether these restorative processes are providing positive outcomes. According to a review of the research literature, this seems to be the case (Gaboury and Ruth-Heffelbower, 2007).

However, resistance to the notion that restorative processes—particularly with their requisite involvement of victims and survivors—are a positive development may impede progress in this area. Biermans (2002, p. 62) notes that

> some people think that restorative detention is a contradiction in terms. Some people fear that it could be used as a new legitimization for the whole idea of prison. Apart from these objections in principle, many people believe that detention is a very problematic and possibly unsuitable context to implement restorative methods and models.

Also, even what the term *restorative justice* means, both philosophically and programmatically, is subject to question. This dilemma often befalls those collections of programs that may represent an example of the underlying concept or philosophy (e.g., this is often a criticism of the term *community policing*). Restorative practices are spreading worldwide in many different settings, often losing the *restorative justice* label in the process (Van Ness, 2005).

To shed some light on the current status of restorative processes in correctional settings, this chapter looks at several examples of restorative justice programming in a variety of settings considered to be "correctional" in the broadest sense (i.e., not limited to institutional corrections). These restorative settings include those found in prisons as well as community-based correctional settings and as alternatives to traditional institutional corrections. These include special courts, victim-offender dialogue (in and out of prisons), offender reentry programs, conflict resolution (inmate-to-inmate and inmate-to-correctional officer), victim awareness training, victim impact panels, offender family reconciliation, and restorative justice boards.

Special Courts

Drug and mental health courts are new additions to the set of restorative processes available to judges. These special courts were started in response to growing prison populations and increasing levels of recidivism. Mental health courts now number about 175 nationwide (Schwartz, 2008). The premise of these specialty courts is simply to divert appropriate offenders away from traditional incarceration into treatment programs and related supervision for a set period of time. Results from a multiyear study of a special court in Pittsburgh found that only 10 percent of 223 graduates were rearrested, which was well below the 68 percent national average for all defendants (Schwartz, 2008). These types of courts have grown in number because they are successful in avoiding recidivism and are typically much less costly than incarceration. These courts are more than just novelties and often receive "buy-in" from both victims and offenders. Not only are fewer victims being created through this approach, but also many offenders are able to function outside custodial settings with appropriate assistance.

Restorative justice includes any process where victims and offenders are built up instead of being further damaged by whatever system is handling the case or otherwise addressing the situation. Any systems designed to correct problem behavior are deemed correctional settings for purposes of this chapter. In the case of mental health courts, the needs of victims are addressed through restitution orders and other conditions, which is similar to what is possible in the traditional court setting. However, there are major distinctions that affect both victims and offenders. For victims, restitution is more likely to be ordered and collected, as this is a focal point of these programs and their focus on offender accountability. Also, conditions of release or supervision are more likely to be tailored to the needs and reasonable requests of victims.

There are also major distinctions in the special court approach to the offender. Offenders in these courts are not simply given a measured dose of punishment. The root causes of the problem behavior are identified, and a plan for working with the causes is developed, implemented, and monitored. These courts are not just reactive. Their proactive approach to identifying criminogenic factors and providing appropriate intervention, along with victim involvement and protection, makes these special courts restorative.

The US Department of Justice has published guidelines for these courts. The report says that

> in courtrooms across the country, judges, prosecutors, and defense attorneys are seeing increasing numbers of defendants who have serious untreated mental illnesses charged with committing low-level crimes. Traditional court processes do little to improve outcomes for many of these people. They cycle again and again through jail, courtrooms, and our city streets. (Thompson, Osher, and Tomasini-Joshi, 2007, p. 11)

The term *restorative justice* is not used, but the recommendations clearly show the recommended process to be restorative.

Victim-Offender Dialogue
as an Alternative to Incarceration

Victim-offender dialogue (VOD) is known by many alternate names such as mediation, reconciliation, conferencing, and circles, among others. This process allows a victim and an offender to interact and learn from each other how each one experienced the event and subsequently decide together what needs to happen to make things as right as possible, clarifying future intentions (Claassen, 2002).

In the United States, VOD programs developed approximately thirty years ago as volunteer efforts sponsored by agencies with limited budgets. More recently, publicly supported (i.e., taxpayer-funded) entities have more often funded these programs. Outside the United States, taxpayer-supported entities have usually been at the forefront of the restorative justice movement (O'Brien et al., 2003). These programs have also resulted in the development of more rigorous empirical research and evaluation demonstrating program efficacy.

The most common use of VOD processes worldwide is in juvenile property crimes. These crimes are seldom prosecuted with vigor, and that has allowed openness to trying something different. With the first case being handled in 1974 in Canada and many thousands completed since then, there is little question that good results flow from this method of approaching an offense. Many VOD programs are located in juvenile justice settings, and confidentiality rules there have hampered research efforts; however, with few exceptions those studies show that youthful offenders are much less likely to reoffend after a VOD process and that those who do reoffend do so at a lower level (Miers et al., 2001).

One study compared seven programs using a variety of practices and serving both youth and adult offenders (Miers et al., 2001). The study found that direct dialogue between victim and offender that did not affect sentencing was more cost-effective and satisfying to participants and had a significant impact on reoffending. Legislative attention in the United States has been somewhat more focused on state-level efforts to determine best practices. Another study compared six California victim-offender reconciliation programs at the behest of Gov. Pete Wilson (Evje and Cushman, 2000). The authors reported that as compared to juveniles not participating in these programs, offenders participating in the Victim-Offender Reconciliation Program (VORP) paid more restitution and reoffended less, and that all participants (i.e., victims and offenders) were more satisfied with the program.

Umbreit, Vos, and Coates (2006) reviewed eighty-five studies of VOD programs and compared them on eight factors: participation rates; reasons for participation; participant satisfaction; participant perception of fairness; restitution and repair of harm; diversion; recidivism; and cost. This meta-analysis demonstrated that offenders who participate in VOD processes are less likely to reoffend and are more likely to pay restitution, and that those who do reoffend do so at a lower level.

In many countries, such as New Zealand and England, VOD measures that started in juvenile settings have been extended to adult offenders as well. In South Africa, community peace committees were formed to assume responsibility for crime prevention and resolution in localities where there was little confidence in the justice system. Recently, however, a pilot project was initiated to form a partnership with the police. Although disputants may still go directly to the community peace committee, they may also go to the police, who will refer appropriate cases to the community peace committee (Van Ness, 2005).

The lower the level of an offense, the more likely it is that a restorative justice process will be an alternative to incarceration. As the seriousness of the offense rises, the likelihood of a restorative approach following or being concurrent with incarceration also rises. We discuss these processes further in the next section.

We briefly discussed alternatives to incarceration in an article on correctional settings because these cases usually involve probation, which we consider a correctional setting (Gaboury and Ruth-Heffelbower, 2007). The life experience and range of choices of a person on probation are different from the experience of most people. Where the restorative practice results in an agreement that is then included in an offender's conditions of probation, a correctional setting is clearly established.

Restorative practices seek to be noncoercive to the extent possible. It is well established that people will keep agreements that are voluntary to a greater extent than they will those where coercion is felt (Claassen, 1996b). Even so, there is a general understanding that whenever criminal behavior forms the basis of an event, some amount of coercion will be felt as the matter is dealt with (Johnstone and Van Ness, 2006).

Even in low-level crimes, restorative practices are usually seen as an alternative to retributive practices, and retributive practices are the expected default response to an offender's failure to cooperate with a restorative process. In low-level cases, it is unlikely that there will be a follow-on retributive response to a refusal to cooperate in many jurisdictions, but the offender has no way of knowing whether that will be his or her experience. This results in a feeling of coercion to some extent.

In-Custody Victim-Offender Dialogue

Once thought to be impossible, pressure from victims has opened prison doors in most states to allow victim-offender dialogue with inmates (Ruth-Heffelbower and Gaboury, 2008). Victims want answers, and the offender is often the only one who can give them. The resistance to allowing inmates to meet with their victims may have made sense at one time, but that time is past. The prevalence of VOD programs has created a large pool of people who can help with such projects, and victims have begun to learn how healing such encounters can be when they are professionally managed and victim initiated.

The story of one such VOD is told in the newspaper article "From Tragedy to Forgiveness, with a Stop at San Quentin" (Wolfe, 2009). This story describes the transformation possible when questions are answered and the offender is no longer objectified. The victim in the story has gone on to participate as a representative victim in the San Quentin program described by Dison (2007). In this case, the offender is serving a fourteen-year sentence. If VOD had not been available in prison, it probably would never have happened.

Umbreit and others report no US examples of statistically significant increased reoffending for those participating in victim-offender dialogue (Umbreit, Vos, and Coates, 2006). This raises the significance of the difference between three basic VOD practices. The key difference is in who facilitates the meeting. In New Zealand, a trained social worker facilitates the meeting. In Australia and England, it is more common to have a police officer or other criminal justice system official act as facilitator. In most US studies, the facilitator is a community volunteer or staff member of a private nonprofit organization.

Offender Reentry and Restorative Practices

Many corrections departments in the United States are now taking a positive approach to restorative processes, particularly as they support the principles of offender reentry programs. One clear example of this is the State of Vermont's Department of Corrections website, which notes that restorative justice is the law in Vermont. This is a reference to Vermont Statutes Title 28, Chapter 1, Section 2a, on restorative justice, which states that

> it is the policy of this state that principles of restorative justice be included in shaping how the criminal justice system responds to persons charged with or convicted of criminal offenses. The policy goal is a community response to a person's wrongdoing at its earliest onset, and a type and intensity of sanction tailored to each instance of wrongdoing.

The statute goes on to list multiple points in the criminal justice and correctional system where restorative justice is mandated and describes some program components. Some of these junctures are alternatives to incarceration and others deal with offender reentry.

Offender reentry has been a major programmatic thrust of significant correctional organizations, such as the American Parole and Probation Association (APPA), which, along with federal and state government leadership, has resulted in a major push to improve the return of offenders to the community. Although traditional work on offender reentry has been active for some time, the new focus, and that which makes it restorative, is meaningful involvement of victims in reentry programs. For example, the APPA has posted on its website a "Community Response Manual" with significant programmatic detail on the development of reentry programs that involve victims in significant ways.[1] Also, Lehman et al. (2002) published an article that focused on what they referred to as the "Three R's of Reentry"—reparative justice, relationships, and responsibility—which heavily emphasized the appropriate role of victims in offender reentry and our collective responsibility to ensure that victims are accorded a significant role in these important programs.

Inmate-Inmate Conflict Resolution

Prisoner environments are oftentimes filled with conflict and violence. This situation is exacerbated by prison overcrowding. In August 2009, the 9th Circuit Court of Appeals ordered California to reduce its prison population by 40,000.[2] This reduction would leave 110,000 inmates in facilities designed for 85,000. Triple-decker bunks in gymnasiums have been common in California prisons. California is appealing the order.

Different prison populations have different codes of conduct, but prisoners with violent histories and sentences too long to be concerned about lengthening them may have a tendency to resort to violence in response to any provocation. The result is a population that does not express emotions other than anger and in which a willingness to negotiate can be seen as weakness and exploited. Violence and assaults are part and parcel of prison life (Edgar, O'Donnell, and Martin, 2003). Prisoners with sentences short enough that they can think about paroling in the foreseeable future are much more interested in nonviolent conflict resolution. Prisoners in special-needs yards are also interested (Crowe, 1997). Rather than concerning ourselves with those who are not interested in cooperative conflict resolution, we propose to offer training and support to those who are interested.

In our experience, correctional officers generally tend to see the training as useful among themselves but are not much interested in applying the techniques to relationships with prisoners. Teachers immediately see the benefit of using the skills in the classroom. Correctional officers express mixed feelings about helping inmates peacefully resolve their conflicts. While it is generally a good thing for the inmates, if prisoners are not worried about each other, they can focus more effectively on turfing the correctional facility and neutralizing supervision efforts (cf. Carceral and Bernard, 2005). Efforts to help inmates work more effectively with conflict can have unexpected negative impacts on the institution. Inmates have traditionally formed subgroups based on ethnicity or some other similarity. The rise of gangs that operate seamlessly inside and outside prison is one of the unfortunate results of this tendency.

It is now considered normal for gangs to be the de facto government inside prisons, with business opportunities divided in a way that allows relative stability. This division of turf can be tenuous but gives some rational basis for getting along under normal circumstances. We see a role for interest-based bargaining to resolve issues between these groups without violence, while noting the awkward ethical issues created by helping people to effectively negotiate illegal activity.

Our recommendation is to focus educational efforts in restorative conflict resolution on inmates not involved with violent activity and on staff other than correctional officers, who have occasion to work less coercively with inmates.

Inmate–Correctional Officer Conflict Resolution

There is a tendency for correctional officers to avoid the appearance of weakness in ways that convey lack of respect toward inmates. We suggest that restorative techniques and practices can be used in ways that maintain clear lines of authority while maintaining an atmosphere of respect. Generally speaking, this restorative way of approaching situations requires that a respectful attitude be maintained, and that where disrespect is felt by either inmates or correctional officers, the offending party should express the intention to act in ways that are more respectful next time. Training in restorative justice principles can help correctional officers identify ways to accomplish this balance.

Where both inmates and correctional officers have received training, they will share a vocabulary that will likely work better at maintaining a respectful atmosphere. For example, the search of a cell by guards is referred to by inmates as "tossing the cell," because the inmate's possessions are thrown around in the process and a mess is left behind. The manner in which the search is done and the interaction with the inmate can be more or less respectful. We suggest that a more respectful approach will have benefits.

The appearance of disrespect by anyone toward anyone in a correctional environment can be dangerous. Inmates who feel disrespected by staff and who have no conflict resolution skills can be expected to bide their time looking for an opportunity to even the score in a negative way. Restorative practices are largely about conveying respect through both words and actions.

Victim Awareness Training in Corrections

Victim awareness programs, also called impact of crime on victims programs, have become widely used in corrections departments in the United States. These programs were designed and initiated in the mid-1980s by the California Youth Authority of the California Department of Corrections (California Youth Authority, 2002; English and Crawford, 1989). As already noted, as many as 73 percent of state correctional departments claim to have such programs (National Institute of Corrections, 2004). Until recently, these programs had not been subjected to significant empirical evaluation. The first known peer-reviewed article evaluating victim awareness or impact of crime on victims programs (Monahan et al., 2004) found that participation improved offenders' cognitive outcomes in three areas: understanding of victimization facts, knowledge of victims' rights, and sensitivity to the plight of victims. However, in a fourth area, victim blaming, no significant differences were found. These findings were replicated in a 2007 evaluation study done as part of a project funded by the US Department of Justice Office for Victims of Crime (OVC) to further develop impact of crime (IOC) programs (Gaboury and Sedelmaier, 2007). This 2007 OVC project was primarily focused on revising the IOC curriculum and providing technical assistance to corrections departments that wished to update their programs.[3]

Other previous research has supported the efficacy of the IOC programs. Schiebstad (2003) indicated similar gains in knowledge and attitudes among offenders who attended victim impact classes. Putnins (1997) studied whether exposure to victim impact classes could positively affect "sociomoral reasoning maturity" in delinquent adolescents and found significant, positive differences in the group exposed to the classes compared with the control group, demonstrating tangible improvements in delinquents' attitudes toward victims and indicating a positive change in prosocial behaviors among these adolescents. However, a recent study utilizing psychological measures (Jackson, 2009) did not find significant differences in guilt, shame, and empathy over time.

Gaboury et al. (2008) followed up the study cited earlier (Monahan et al., 2004), this time focusing on behavioral outcomes. Disciplinary infractions that occurred while participants in the study were incarcerated were studied to determine whether participation in the awareness program influenced subjects' short-term behavior in the correctional setting. Initial statistical analyses indicated that there were some differences between groups of inmates that had been exposed to the program and those in the comparison group. However, this finding was limited to one subgroup, African-American adult males. Although limited to this one subgroup, the finding is provocative and may prove useful, given that African-American males are typically overrepresented in correctional populations and given the seriousness of the offenses. Reducing the frequency of serious infractions, and as a consequence these additional victimizations, is critical to the safety of both inmates and correctional officers (Gaboury et al., 2008).

There is evidence from other studies that offenders may be more behaviorally successful after incarceration if they have had an opportunity to participate in a victim awareness program. Criminal behavior usually includes objectifying persons who are harmed, and the criminal justice system is seen as furthering this objectification (Erez and Laster, 1999; McGoldrick, Rowe, and Donnelly, 2004, p. 319).

Victim awareness training programs, or IOC programs, are now standard in correctional settings, particularly prisons and correctional institutions. One example is the Bridges to Life (BTL) program, which has been implemented in prisons in Texas, Louisiana, Colorado, and Florida. The program's 2009 report says that 8,136 inmates have completed BTL since 2000. Of these inmates, 3,234 released inmates are currently in a three-year recidivism (return to prison) study. Although the three years have not passed for all the inmates in the study, 550 have returned to prison, representing a 17 percent recidivism rate. Of those who returned to prison, 336 had new convictions (10.4 percent), 214 had technical violations (6.6 percent), and 34 of released offenders returned for violent crimes (1.1 percent). These results compare favorably to the usual experience. A commonly cited figure for overall recidivism is 60–70 percent, with many variables (Bridges to Life, 2009).

Evaluation studies of BTL credited five aspects of the program for its good results:

> 1. Participants felt impacted by seeing things from the victim's side, that is, with victim eyes, and by their increased awareness of the ripple effect of their crime on others, including their family members. Victim stories were particularly impactful because they helped offenders feel pain and break through their detachment and indifference. For many, it was as if they were seeing their own impact on others for the first time.
> 2. Participants felt cared about by victims who had been hurt by people like themselves. Victims' caring was conveyed by acceptance which left offenders feeling that they belonged, at times, to a "family," they mattered and were worth something, they were not alone in their life experiences or in their struggle to live a better life, and it was safe to trust and show feelings that were otherwise hidden or dangerous to express in the prison setting.
> 3. Participants realized that they were gaining self-knowledge as a result of personal insights and the accountability process for how they treated others. This experience required them to be self-scrutinizing about the past, their defects of character, and motivations for their behavior. As a result, they were better able to stop denying their effect on others or stop blaming others for their behavior. Self-knowledge also resulted in recognizing their self-centeredness and the need for corrective action including apologies, making amends and reconciling with those they had harmed, if appropriate.
> 4. Participants felt motivated by experiences that stimulated their hunger and drive for personal growth. They repeatedly asked for more time, longer sessions or a longer program.
> 5. Participants felt transformed by the quality of their changes. They described themselves as having a spiritual awakening due to their new awareness or feeling released from the bondage of their past. They also described having new feelings for the first time, including self-forgiveness, self-care, compassion, and altruism. This sense of a "new me" was conveyed along with

their resolve to not harm others and their hope for a better life after release. (Bridges to Life, 2009)

One program working with inmate groups at San Quentin prison, called Victim-Offender Education Groups (VOEGs), provides intensive small-group work for inmates who have been serving time for at least several years and who are interested in doing restorative work. As the program director notes:

> VOEGs have been meeting at San Quentin prison in California since 2004. They operate as part of, and with the assistance of, Insight Prison Project (IPP), a non-profit group administered by Jacques Verduin. IPP offers a number of groups, programs and projects which are designed to help inmates at San Quentin find their way to a transformed life. (Dison, 2007, p. 7)

Victim Impact Panels

Victim impact panels were designed and implemented by Mothers Against Drunk Driving (MADD) in 1982 (Rojek, Coverdill, and Fors, 2003, p. 2; US Department of Justice, 2005). Victim impact panels involve victims and survivors of drunk driving crashes sharing their personal stories and testimonials with offenders who are not those that offended against the victims or their loved ones. This is distinguished from victim-offender dialogues where the victims or survivors interact directly with the offenders who harmed them.

Although these programs have variations, the typical impact panel involves one session lasting approximately two hours where several victims or survivors of drunk driving crashes provide impact statements to groups of drunk driving offenders (e.g., up to approximately seventy-five) with high-impact accounts of the tragic aftermath of their victimization (Lord, 1990; US Department of Justice, 2005). Most impact panels occur in alternative sentencing settings, but they also take place in prisons. These programs are usually coordinated by MADD's local chapters and are conducted by the victims and the survivors themselves.

The goals of impact panels include (1) helping offenders understand the impact of their crimes on victims and communities; (2) providing victims with a structured, positive outlet to share their personal experiences and to educate offenders, justice professionals, and others about the physical, emotional, and financial consequences of crime; and (3) building a partnership among victim service providers and justice agencies that can raise the individual and community awareness of the short- and long-term impacts of crime (US Department of Justice, 2005).

Rojek, Coverdill, and Fors (2003) conducted a five-year follow-up of drunk driving rearrest rates comparing offenders who participated in impact panels and those who did not. Those findings supported significantly lower rearrests for those offenders exposed to impact panels as compared to a control group. They describe these effects as "strong" in the first two years. However, thereafter, these differences diminish greatly (Rojek, Coverdill, and Fors, 2003, pp. 1325–1335). These findings do not necessarily argue against the efficacy of these programs but speak more to the issue of the long-term effects of such programs. The positive outcome is at least two years of diminished drunk driving offenses and victimizations. This result is good for both the offenders involved and the victims and survivors who participated in the panels and does not even contemplate the many potential drunk driving victimizations that seem to have been avoided by these programs. As the quality of research in this area improves, we may be able to more accurately sort out the effects of impact programs in terms of appropriate "dosage" and the length of time the effects of these symptoms can be expected to last. Depending on the length of time an offender may be involved in community supervision (e.g., probation or parole), it may be that providing additional victim impact panel opportunities for these offenders can extend these positive benefits further into the future.

Offender Family Reconciliation

There is a direct correlation between family support and decreased levels of recidivism (Kazura et al., 2002). The difficulty with getting and keeping family support is that the process of becoming an inmate has harmed the family constellation and damaged the very relationships that are necessary to success outside. The Bureau of Justice Statistics (2007) estimates that about half of all offenders are under the influence of drugs or alcohol at the time of their offense. This is a decline from 59 percent in 1996.

It is generally accepted that families with drug and alcohol issues are less able, or willing, to provide the supportive environment a released inmate needs. The use of restorative practices such as dialogue and circles with the family can increase the likelihood of successful support. Accountability to the family was probably low at the time of the offense, and it will take a concerted effort to make agreements that will allow trust to rebuild. Drug users commonly steal from the safest people first, and those are family members. Family group conferencing and other restorative processes treat the whole family system and can be helpful in sending family members to treatment or support groups for codependency issues.

The lifers mentioned previously were particularly interested in the use of Claassen's peacemaking model as a way to work through issues with their children (Ruth-Heffelbower and Gaboury, 2008). An offender's family is an indirect victim of the offense. The expense, loss of income, and heartache caused by having a family member in prison is not usually the focus of restorative justice programs but is certainly an area where growth would be appropriate. Facilitated victim-offender dialogue between inmates and their families could be helpful. Conversations that happen in the visiting room are unlikely to be sufficient for the task, because it is easy to deflect uncomfortable lines of discussion in the absence of a facilitator.

Restorative Justice Boards

Piecemeal efforts to use restorative practices in various parts of the criminal justice system are better than nothing but could be improved by the existence of an overall implementing body. This body might be called a restorative justice board. Sherman and Strang (2007) propose this idea for embedding restorative practices in the system. Prison Fellowship International has developed its Restorative Justice City model in a way that includes such an entity.[4]

Fresno, California, home of the first victim-offender reconciliation program west of Elkhart, Indiana, where the first US program developed, has been working to establish a community group that would function as a restorative justice board. The Restorative Justice Initiative drew together representatives of criminal justice and community stakeholders to develop a plan for embedding restorative justice practices in the system.[5] This ongoing effort is beginning to bear fruit. The key factors in its success to date are the twenty-five years of victim-offender dialogue cases done by VORP of the Central Valley, engaging most stakeholders and persisting through long hours of meetings where nothing seemed to be happening.

Conclusion

Restorative principles and practices in correctional settings may be unusual in many respects, and there may remain obstacles to their full acceptance. However, it should be becoming more obvious that the time has come for widespread institutionalization of restorative practices, processes, and programs in correctional settings, including correctional institutions to community-based supervision sites such as parole and probation program sites. It should not be so unusual that restorative principles and practices are appearing in correctional settings. The sheer numbers of, and the evidence-based support for the efficacy of, corrections-based restorative justice programs argue strongly that these programs and processes should soon become part of the mainstream of progressive corrections departments, and beyond.

Notes

1. A. Seymour, "The Victim's Role in Reentry: A Community Response Manual," American Parole and Probation Association. Available at http://www.appa-net.org/eweb/docs/appa/pubs/VROR.pdf (accessed October 13, 2009).

2. See *Coleman v. Schwarzenegger,* CIV S-90-0520 LKK JFM P (2007), and *Plata v. Schwarzenegger,* C01-1351 TEH (2007).

3. These materials are available at www.ovcttac.gov/victimimpact.

4. Prison Fellowship International, "How Do Communities of Restoration Work?" Available at http://www.pfi.org/cjr/apac/how-do-communities-of-restoration-work (accessed July 27, 2009); Prison Fellowship International, "What Are Communities of Restoration?" Available at http:///www.pfi.org/cjr/apac/introduction (accessed July 27, 2009).

5. Restorative Justice Initiative. Available at http://peace.fresno.edu/rji (accessed October 24, 2009).

3

Working with Sex Offenders

Clare Ann Ruth-Heffelbower

Sex offenders are feared and despised in today's world. They are seen as monsters who, at any moment, might pounce upon their unsuspecting prey, especially children. The general perception is that sex offenders are more dangerous than other criminals. As such, they have become pariahs against whom the public seeks to protect itself. They are the lepers of today who live at the fringes of society. According to a California state parole agent, 90–95 percent of the services available to other ex-offenders on parole who are reentering the community are not available to sex offenders.[1] Sex offenses cover a wide range of crimes, from offenses usually charged as misdemeanors, such as distribution of obscene material or indecent exposure, to offenses charged as felonies, such as child molestation and rape. While definitions vary from jurisdiction to jurisdiction, an offender who has been convicted of a combination of offenses, including a violent sex offense[2] and often other crimes, is generally classified as a high-risk sex offender (HRSO). These are the sex offenders who are considered most likely to reoffend and who instill fear in the community.

Much of the public fear and the action taken in response to that fear is based on a variety of assumptions. These assumptions include, among others, a belief that sex crimes have increased in recent years, that most sex offenders target strangers rather than people they know, that sex offenders reoffend at an extremely high rate, and that new and tougher laws will reduce sexual offending and create safer communities. The reality is that sex crimes have decreased since the early 1990s, that most persons who commit sex crimes know their victims, that the rate of reoffending for sex offenders tends to be lower than for

Keywords: restorative justice, criminal justice, sex offender, reentry, parole, parolee, community integration, rehabilitation, community safety, victims, support, accountability

27

other criminals,[3] and that it is questionable whether tougher laws have made or will make a difference in community safety (LaFond, 2005).

The public outrage about sex offenders is based to a large extent on a few particularly notorious and heinous crimes. In 1987, convicted sex offender Earl Shriner was released from prison in Washington State despite his threats of committing future sex crimes against children. In 1989, he mutilated, raped, and killed a six-year-old boy. Seven-year-old Megan Kanka was abducted, sexually assaulted, and murdered in New Jersey in 1994 by a convicted sex offender with two prior convictions of child molestation. He lived in a halfway house across the street from Megan's family, who had not been told that the men living across the street from them were convicted sex offenders. These crimes and others like them have led to new laws intended to prevent further offending by persons convicted of sex crimes. It is a strategy based on "a jurisprudence of dangerousness and prevention" (LaFond, 2005, p. xiii).

Sex Offenders in the Criminal Justice System

In response to the fear aroused by a few horrible crimes, society is using the criminal justice system in a particularly aggressive manner. Many states have passed laws that are intended to inflict punishment and prevent future sex crimes.

Some states have increased prison terms for sex offenders. Others have enacted indeterminate sentencing laws with harsh punishment for repeat offenders. Many states have passed "three strikes" laws. A felony sex crime would qualify as a strike in most cases. Some states have enhanced sentences for repeat offenders. Three strikes legislation calls for long sentences following conviction on a third strike. In California, a third strike carries a sentence of twenty-five years to life. The goal of three strikes laws is to remove repeat offenders from society as long as possible, if not permanently.

When a sex offender is released from prison, he or she is subject to laws intended to prevent reoffending. California was the first state to establish a registry of sex offenders, in 1947. The identity and residence of released sex offenders became available to the public in 1995 with the implementation of the Child Molester Identification Line. In 1996, Megan's Law (named after Megan Kanka) was passed in California, making increased information available to the public. This information became available online in 2004. There are services that send subscribers regular updates on registered sex offenders who move into their neighborhoods.

Recent federal legislation has attempted to protect children from sexual abuse. The Adam Walsh Child Protection and Safety Act was signed by President Bush in July 2006. It expanded the national sex offender registry, strengthened federal penalties for crimes against children, and addressed sexual exploitation of minors on the Internet.

Following the passage of the Adam Walsh Act, many states have enacted additional legislation intended to prevent future sexual offending. In November 2006, California voters overwhelming passed an initiative aimed at preventing sexual offending. Proposition 83, called Jessica's Law (after Jessica Lunsford, a young girl raped and murdered in Florida in 2005 by a released sex offender), requires registered sex offenders to live 2,000 feet from schools or parks and lifetime GPS monitoring for some sex offenders. The public attitude and intent are evident in the title of the law: The Sexual Predator *Punishment* and *Control* Act: Jessica's Law (italics added). The Findings and Declarations that follow illustrate the dependence on the criminal justice system to prevent sexual reoffending: "The State of California currently places a high priority on maintaining public safety through a highly skilled and trained law enforcement as well as laws that deter and punish criminal behavior" (*California General Election Official Voter Information Guide,* 2006, p. 127).

When sex offenders are released from prison, they are placed under parole supervision. The intent of parole is to monitor the parolee as well as to provide services to help with his or her reentry into the community. In recent years, the focus on rehabilitation has diminished, and surveillance and control have become the main goals of parole. This is due not only to a growing number of parolees with more conditions assigned to them, which increases the caseload of parole agents, but also to decreased resources and society's attitude toward crime and released prisoners (Petersilia, 2003).

High-risk sex offenders are supervised by specially trained parole agents. Sex offenders have standard conditions of parole similar to all parolees: They must report to a parole agent within twenty-four hours of release and at designated intervals after that. They must report changes of address, obey instructions of parole agents, not break the law, not travel outside a specified area, submit to search by police or parole officers, and not associate with other parolees. In addition to these conditions, sex offenders have special conditions that are tailored to their particular offenses. If they have molested children, they are not allowed to be with minors or within a certain distance of schools or other places where children are present. They must live in a location that is at least the specified distance away from schools or parks. They are ordered to have no contact with their victims in person, by mail or telephone, or through a third party. The role of parole is to closely monitor offenders so as to protect the community from further criminal activity by parolees.

The criminal justice system identifies which laws were broken by sex offenders, determines guilt, and assigns punishment to the offender deemed appropriate to the crime. It is, as is typical of the criminal justice system, an abstract and impersonal process, focused on punishing the offender and protecting the community.

Little attention is given to offender needs, rehabilitation, or challenges during the eventual transition from prison to the community. The result is that risk is increased for both the ex-offender and for the community. Reoffense is much more likely without assistance in rehabilitation and in facing the challenges of reentry.

The criminal justice system is also not helpful to the victim of a sex offense. His or her needs are peripheral and are often not addressed throughout the criminal justice process.

Sex Offenders and Restorative Justice

If the needs of sex offenders, their victims, and the community are going to be genuinely addressed, a different approach to justice is needed. When sexual offending occurs, people are harmed. Fear is generated. Relationships are broken. There is healing that needs to occur. Restorative justice, with its focus on people, relationships, needs, and responsibilities, has much to offer to everyone touched by a sex offense.

In the restorative justice framework, offenders have an opportunity to take responsibility to make things as right as possible and, in the process, to find healing for themselves. Avenues of healing are opened for victims. Relationships can be restored. The community, by its active participation in a restorative process, creates a safer and less fearful community.

The potential of a community to create a safe and healthy community is great when it is involved in a restorative process. Nils Christie, as cited in *The Expanding Prison* (Caley, 1998, p. 168), points to the potential power that communities can have as he describes how the power is given away:

> Community . . . is made as much from conflict as from co-operation; the capacity to resolve conflict is what gives social relations their sinew. Professionalizing justice "steals the conflicts," robbing the community of its ability to face trouble and restore peace. Communities lose their confidence, their capacity, and, finally, their inclination to preserve their own order. They become, instead, consumers of police and court "services."

Where sexual offending is an issue, restorative justice processes are a tool that can make a significant difference for communities and the individuals within them. By taking on the responsibility to face the "conflict" or the sex offense and the offender directly rather than depending on law enforcement and corrections, the community reclaims its capacity to "restore peace" and overcome the fear that is rampant.

Circles of Support and Accountability: A Restorative Justice Program for Sex Offenders

Circles of Support and Accountability (COSA) is a community-based restorative justice initiative that assists high-risk sex offenders who are released from prison with their reentry into the community. It takes seriously the idea that the community is responsible for its own safety and that healing and wholeness for victims and offenders is possible.

Beginnings

Circles of Support and Accountability began in 1994 in Hamilton, Ontario, Canada. A repeat child molester, Charlie, was released from prison at the end of his term. Because he had served his entire sentence, he had no parole supervision. Charlie was considered to be at high risk of reoffense because of his history and his lack of support. A prison psychologist contacted a pastor who had earlier had some contact with Charlie and asked if he could provide support for him when he was released from prison. The pastor agreed and gathered a small group of people who agreed to assist Charlie in whatever way they could. The group, which became known as "Charlie's Angels," became his friends and helped him with his transition into the community, including practical things like finding a place to live. As friends, they were there for him as he worked with issues from his past and his present, confronting him if they thought he was at risk of reoffending. At first, the community was in an uproar when Charlie was released. Threats were made against Charlie and his "angels." Over time, the fear subsided when he did not reoffend. Charlie died on Christmas Day in 2005 of natural causes, never having reoffended after his release from prison in 1994.

A second high-profile pedophile was released from prison in Ontario a few months after Charlie. A support group was gathered for him as well, in the face of community fear and outrage at his release. This offender lived without reoffending until he died of natural causes in September 2007.

Seeing the positive results of the two circles that formed in 1994, the Mennonite Central Committee of Ontario approached the Correctional Service of Canada requesting funds for a pilot project. The request was granted and Circles of Support and Accountability was born. The Canadian government continues to fund the project, recognizing the reduction of risk that results from providing support for ex-offenders and holding them accountable for their actions. There are now COSA projects in every province in Canada. Several other countries, as well as states in the United States, are exploring COSA, with several projects established. Some are variations on the Canadian model, whereas others have worked to replicate the model in another jurisdiction.

Goal

The goal of Circles of Support and Accountability is articulated in the mission statement of the original COSA project in southern Ontario, which has been adopted by the newly established COSA project in Fresno, California, as well. The mission of COSA is "to substantially reduce the risk of future sexual victimization of community members by assisting and supporting released sex offenders in their task of integrating with the community and leading responsible, productive, and accountable lives." This mission can be simplified to two guiding principles: (1) "No more victims" and (2) "No one is disposable." It is with this dual focus on community safety and offender rehabilitation that COSA takes on the challenge of working with released sex offenders.

Composition

A Circle of Support and Accountability is made up of four to six community volunteers who gather around an ex-offender, who is called the "core member." These volunteers are in turn supported by volunteer professionals who provide advice and guidance as necessary. Robin Wilson, a psychologist who has been involved with COSA from its inception in Canada, illustrates COSA with two concentric circles.[4] The inner circle is made up of the core member and community volunteers, the outer circle of professionals who lend their support (Figure 3.1). Wilson (2007, p. 300) points out that "the learning curve for professionals is that COSA volunteers seek relationships not based on terms of professional respect and distance, but on terms of friendship." Relationships based on friendship are the key to the success of COSA.

Participation in COSA is voluntary for offenders. The program is offered to offenders being released who are considered at high risk to reoffend and who have high needs with little or no prosocial support in the community. Leaders in the COSA movement in Canada suggest that COSA should work with the

Figure 3.1 Circles of Support and Accountability

● Core member   ✳ Volunteers   ▲ Professionals

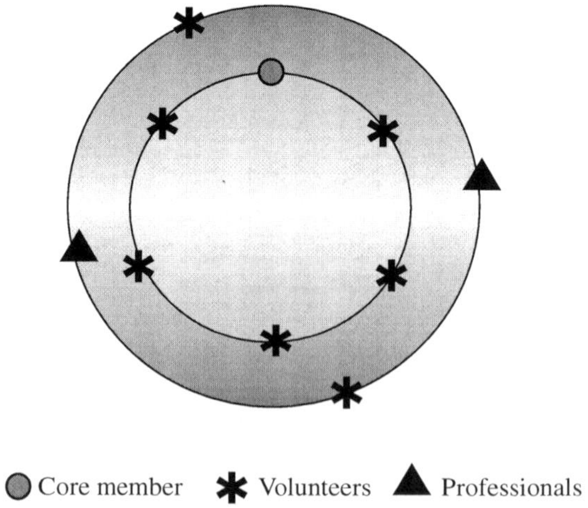

Source: Wilson, Picheca, and Prinzo, 2005.

"worst of the worst."[5] The COSA team selects participants based on risk, need, and the offender's desire to voluntarily participate in the program.

Community volunteers are at the heart of COSA. They *are* the community, taking responsibility for its own safety. Volunteers come from many walks of life and are of different ages, bringing with them a variety of perspectives and experience. They do not have special expertise in working with sex offenders. In Canada, the majority of volunteers initially tended to come from the faith community with many faiths represented. As COSA has developed, volunteers from secular backgrounds have also become involved. Volunteers are sought who have the following characteristics: stability in the community, community recognition (references are checked), maturity, healthy boundaries, availability, and balance in lifestyle and viewpoint. Volunteers are trained as they begin serving with COSA and at various points as the circle continues. Areas covered in the training include an overview of restorative justice and of the criminal justice system; an introduction to the parole system, the effects of institutionalization, human sexuality and sexual deviance, risk assessment, boundaries, the needs of survivors, conflict resolution, group dynamics, the circle model, and the circle functions; crisis response and preparing for critical incident stress; methods of working with correctional officials, police, the news media, and other community professionals; needs assessment; how to build a covenant; and how to close a circle.

Circle Functions

A COSA always keeps its focus on two aspects: support and accountability. Both are provided in the context of friendship. Support is provided as the core member works to transition from prison to the community. This support generally begins with practical concerns. The COSA might help a core member find housing and transportation, obtain a driver's license or ID, register with police, acquire clothing, or meet other immediate needs. Emotional support is provided as well as physical and spiritual support as necessary. Volunteers walk with the core member as friends through the good and bad times.

Along with support comes accountability. Circle members confront the core member about attitudes or behaviors as necessary. They watch to see if the core member is doing what is required. The circle becomes familiar with the core member's offense history and pattern of offending so that they are able to recognize signs warning of reoffending.

At times, a COSA may take on an advocacy role for the core member in interactions with treatment providers, parole personnel, and the community in general. There may be a special need for advocacy with neighbors or with victim groups. A circle can also work to mediate community concerns about a released sex offender.

Celebration is also part of the life of a COSA. A circle celebrates anniversaries and small and large victories. It might celebrate holidays together. Many sex offenders have no family connections and find themselves alone on major holidays when families traditionally gather. Those who do have family may not be allowed to join their families because of the presence of minors. Several circles may gather together for a Christmas celebration. An annual celebration may be held where the successes of all core members who are part of COSA can be celebrated.

Circle Effectiveness and Results

There are many stories of success coming out of the first thirteen years of Circles of Support and Accountability in Ontario. Many others like Charlie, the first COSA core member, have continued to live offense-free lives in the community. Two studies have been conducted to measure the effectiveness of the COSA program. The first, an evaluation of the pilot project in Ontario, was completed in 2005. The second, a national replication study that measured the effectiveness of COSA across Canada, was released in 2007.

The 2005 study looked at the experiences of core members, volunteers, professionals, and agencies connected to the project. It also surveyed members of the wider community. It found that COSA had a significant effect on all stakeholders.

Core members reported that without a COSA they would have had difficulty adjusting and most likely would have had difficulty in relationships with others, become isolated and lonely, or turned to drugs or alcohol. Two-thirds felt that they would probably have reoffended without the help of a COSA.

Volunteers reported a positive experience and felt that they were doing significant work in helping to keep the community safe. Professionals and agencies recognized increased offender responsibility and accountability as a result of COSA. The community at large also viewed COSA positively, stating that they would feel safer if they knew a high-risk sex offender in their community belonged to a COSA.

A second part of the 2005 study looked at recidivism. A group of sixty high-risk sex offenders who participated in COSA were compared to a matched group of sixty offenders who did not participate in COSA. The offenders who participated in COSA had a 70 percent reduction in sexual recidivism compared to those who did not participate in COSA. The COSA participants had a 57 percent reduction in all types of violent recidivism and an overall reduction of 35 percent in all types of recidivism. Recidivism in this case included technical violations of parole. It was further noted that in the COSA sample, sex reoffenses were less severe than earlier offenses by the same individual (Wilson, Picheca, and Prinzo, 2005).

The 2007 national replication study showed even more striking results concerning recidivism. In that study, offenders who participated in COSA had an 83 percent reduction in sexual recidivism in contrast to the matched comparison group. The COSA group had a 73 percent reduction in all types of violent recidivism and an overall reduction of 72 percent in all types of recidivism. A conclusion of this study is that "community volunteers, with appropriate training and guidance, can and do assist in markedly improving offenders' successful reintegration into the community, thereby contributing greatly to savings both financial and, more importantly, in human suffering" (Wilson, Cortoni, and Vermani, 2007, p. i).

Healing and Hope

The evidence presented in the two studies sponsored by the Correctional Service of Canada supports the anecdotal experiences of healing and hope of many of those touched by COSA. Core members experience new possibilities in life. They gain new social skills and new confidence. They form new friendships. They experience pride in not reoffending. They contribute to the community. All of this is possible because of relationships. The relationships formed between circle volunteers and the core member are the bridge to successful reentry into the community and to safe living with no more victims.

A core member of a circle in the COSA program in Fresno, California, provides an example of the healing and growth that can occur. His relational skills have blossomed as he has been part of a circle and as he now reaches out to others. He has become much more active in his search for employment. Recently, he designed and printed fliers to encourage fellow city bus riders to call and register their desire for more frequent bus service on a particular route. Thinking of a COSA holiday gathering being planned, he bought extra pies and called the members of his circle looking for freezer space to store them until the event. He is moving from being a hesitant, withdrawn, and isolated individual to becoming an active member of the community. At the same time, he is being accountable for his behavior and is committed to creating no more victims.

A core member of another circle in Fresno is enrolling in college classes with a goal of someday helping others like himself to reenter the community. He has embraced the principles of restorative justice and looks forward to a time when he can express his remorse and make things as right as possible with his victim. Still another core member in Fresno expressed gratitude to his circle. He said he found it hard to accept that people would take time out of their schedules to meet with him. "Never," he said, "in all my sixty-six years, has anyone reached out to help me like you have." He described how he had thought that he did not need people and, in fact, felt safer staying away from people. He has now realized, however, that his previous offending was rooted in his need to be valued and accepted by other people. With that realization, he now says that he knows he does need people in his life. He needs people who are friends he can trust, people who will challenge him and who are there to help him when necessary.

Circles of Support and Accountability offer hope for healing for victims and for the community as well. COSA is sensitive to the healing possibilities of meetings between victims and offenders. In the event that a meeting between a victim and an offender is desired by both parties, COSA can arrange for such a meeting to be facilitated. The community, in the persons of COSA volunteers, finds hope, and often healing as well, in the COSA experience. On a personal level, volunteers find support for themselves while providing support for the core member. They find their work with a circle to be meaningful and significant. Their enthusiasm is contagious and helpful in recruiting other volunteers. The broader community is affected by COSA as well. It finds healing as it becomes a safer place and the fear of victimization is diminished.

Circles of Support and Accountability provide an opportunity for the community to reclaim its role in making the community safe for all. By taking an active role in the management of high-risk sex offenders, COSA holds out possibilities that go far beyond keeping sex offenders at a distance with registration and residency requirements. Beyond just seeking to prevent future victimization, COSA provides opportunities for growth, healing, and hope for all who are touched in some way by the horror of a sex offense. All this is possible when the community takes responsibility and reclaims its capacity to "restore peace."

Notes

1. P. Hutcheson, Parole Agent II and SVP Specialist, personal communication, October 19, 2007.

2. Certain sex offenders are classified as "violent" whether or not the offenses are violent in a traditional sense. Offenses against children often are not physically violent but are nonetheless classified as violent offenses. This recognizes the violence of manipulation and broken trust.

3. Statistics on recidivism are complex. There are different rates of reoffending depending on the type of offense, and various studies have compiled contradictory statistics. In Hanson and Bussiere's 1998 meta-analysis of sixty-one studies, the average sex offense recidivism rate was 18.9 percent for rapists and 12.7 percent for child molesters over a four- to five-year period (*Recidivism of Sex Offenders,* 2001).

4. Personal communication, 2007.

5. A. McWhinnie, regional coordinator, Circles of Support and Accountability, and R. Wilson, professor, School of Social and Community Services, Hunter Institute of Technology and Advanced Learning, personal communication, 2007.

4

A Community Responds
to Elder Abuse

Arlene Groh

When a community can draw on and trust its own inner resources to discover the validity of a new paradigm, the community is liberated from bondage to old, embedded, fixated ways of being in the world. . . . People are empowered to imagine new ways of being, to problem-solve on a deep level. (Miller, 1996, p. 60)

Seniors in our region who experience emotional, physical, and financial abuse and neglect by someone they trust no longer need to suffer in silence. They engage in a process "where truth, justice, mercy, peace and hope are given life and interact" (Lederach, 1999, p. 80). In the fall of 1998, we were a community not so different from others. The Region of Waterloo, situated in South Western Ontario, Canada, has a population of approximately 508,000. It is a diverse ethnocultural community with three urban municipalities and large rural areas with small towns and villages. We were hearing stories of elder abuse. In our experience, however, seniors often hide this abuse and are afraid to ask for help. We recognized that the abuse of our older adults was a community problem. It was less clear what our obligations were. However, our community was willing to embark on a journey in search of solutions.

Fostering a restorative justice worldview is integral to our response to elder abuse. In 2000, a collaborative of agencies—health, social services, justice, ethnocultural, faith, and First Nations[1]—secured funding to design, implement, and evaluate a restorative justice approach to address elder abuse. This project evolved into the Elder Abuse Response Team (EART), an innovative partnership between the Waterloo Regional Police Service (WRPS)[2] and the Community Care Access

Keywords: elder abuse, restorative justice, healing, truth, justice, mercy, peace, hope

Centre (CCAC) of the Waterloo Region.[3] Restorative justice values and principles guide the team's practice. As the pioneer and coordinator of the Restorative Justice Approaches to Elder Abuse Project and a founding member of the EART, I was privileged to work with community partners to build our innovative response to elder abuse—a response that is embedded in the restorative justice philosophy—and to work directly with the people affected by elder abuse. Now, here is the story of how we conducted our long search to find solutions to the complex crime of elder abuse; of how our community came together to identify, respond to, and prevent elder abuse; of how restorative justice as a way of life can have a ripple effect; and of how the pillars of restorative justice values and principles empowered the community *to imagine new ways of being, to problem-solve on a deep level,* and to thereby find an innovative response to elder abuse.

Common Understandings of Restorative Justice and Elder Abuse

Arriving at common understandings of both elder abuse and restorative justice was fundamental to the development and implementation of the Waterloo Region's response to elder abuse. Elder abuse is "the mistreatment of an elderly person by someone that they should be able to rely on: a spouse, a child, another family member, a friend, or a paid caregiver" (WRCEA, 2008, p. 6). According to Judith Wahl of the Advocacy Centre for the Elderly in Toronto (Groh, 2003; Wahl, 2000),

> examples of abuses that are *Criminal Code* offences include physical abuse such as pinching, slapping, pushing, punching, and kicking; assault with a weapon; and forcible confinement (e.g., tying a person to a chair while the family is at work). Abuses that are offences also include, sexual assault and financial abuses such as theft, fraud, and forgery. Neglect may be a criminal offence if it involves deliberately failing to provide a dependent person with the necessities of life. Psychological or emotional abuses may include intimidation and other forms of verbal assault. Under some circumstances, mental cruelty could constitute a crime. (Groh, 2005, p. 178)

From a restorative justice perspective, it is also important to understand the multiple and complex root causes of elder abuse. To highlight a few, there may be a history of difficult family relationships, including past abuse, a history of emotional or psychiatric problems, or substance abuse; or the abuser may be emotionally and financially dependent on "the victim" or might have difficulty caring for the dependent older person (WRCEA, 2008).

Howard Zehr defines "restorative justice as a process to involve, to the extent possible, those who have a stake in a specific offense and to collectively identify and address harms, needs and obligations, in order to heal and put things as right as possible." He indicates that "the essence of restorative justice" boils down to a set of questions:

1. Who has been hurt?
2. What are their needs?
3. Whose obligations are these?
4. Who has a stake in this situation?"
5. What is the appropriate process to involve stakeholders in an effort to put things right? (Zehr, 2002, pp. 37, 38)

Susan Sharpe describes restorative justice as

> an orientation, not a type of program. It is a set of values and beliefs about what justice means, which in turn point to principles for responding to criminal harms. . . . These principles are: Invite full participation and consensus; heal what has been broken; seek full and direct responsibility; reunite what has been divided; strengthen the community, to prevent further harms. Restorative justice does not have a prescribed protocol. Different programs find different ways to carry out the five principles and many factors influence choices. (Sharpe, 1998, p. 19)

Both writers strongly influenced our journey.

Glimpses of Elder Abuse

In my practice, I was privileged to have older adults entrust me with their painful stories of abuse. A glimpse of these follows:

- A ninety-eight-year-old female lies in her bed, silently weeping. She has recently been relocated to a safe shelter. She changed her name so that her daughter could not find her.
- An eighty-five-year-old female has moved to a safe shelter to escape her abusive spouse of ten years.
- The director of a day program requests an investigation of an alleged assault of an older adult by her brother, her caregiver.
- An elderly female has not bathed for more than ten months. There is no water, heat, or electricity in her home. She is a stroke survivor. Her daughter-in-law takes care of her.

Traditional Justice and Elder Abuse

You might think that situations such as these would be addressed by the justice system, as some are offenses under the *Criminal Code of Canada*. In my experience, seniors and family members are reluctant to disclose abuse and to access the resource options available, especially the judicial system. One barrier expressed by older adults is a fear that they will lose their relationship with an abusive "trusted" person if they identify abuse or ask for help. I felt discouraged and frustrated in my work with abused older adults. Consider Mrs. Smith's story:

> Mrs. Smith (pseudonym) was an elderly widow who lived alone. With the assistance of her family, plus private and public funded services, she was able to remain living in her own home. One day she reported that her son had taken $40,000 from her bank account. Mrs. Smith was given information about community resources, including calling the police to investigate this theft. She refused. She said that her son was a good man and that he probably needed the money more than she did. She also needed him to help with her care, to buy her groceries, and to take her to church each Sunday. The relationship with her son and his family was more important to her than the $40,000.

As a case manager, I had worked with Mrs. Smith and her family for a long time. Her son was attentive to his mother. I trusted him so I was part of the ripple effect when the abuse was disclosed. Mrs. Smith's story inflamed my moral outrage and became the impetus for the Restorative Justice Approaches to Elder Abuse Project (Groh, 2003). Her situation is typical of the complexity of elder abuse that is often woven into the very fabric of relationships.

Project Genesis

A pivotal conversation with a young friend planted the seed for the Restorative Justice Approaches to Elder Abuse Project. This friend was enthusiastic about the outcomes he saw using restorative justice tools to address high school conflict and violence. If restorative justice was so successful with youth, why wouldn't it work with Mrs. Smith and others like her? I became excited about the possibilities. Could a restorative justice process weave its way through the complex fabric of relationships and find solutions that are acceptable to the people affected by elder abuse? Would the victims of elder abuse engage in this process? Would restorative justice remove the barriers to disclosure? Would it be effective? Would the community be supportive?

Fortunately, this seed was planted on fertile ground. While reading *Changing Lenses: A New Focus for Crime and Justice* by Howard Zehr (1990), I realized that I was already rooted in restorative justice philosophy. The concept of living in right relationships resonated with me. In addition, elements of restorative justice were in my practice. I was victim-focused, respectfully listening to stories of abuse and taking direction from the older adults. A restorative justice process that respects seniors' stories of abuse and respects their voice in how to resolve the abuse appealed to me.

On a community level, there was also a strong foundation for both restorative justice and elder abuse. Since 1974, Community Justice Initiatives (CJI) has provided restorative justice options for people affected by crime, abuse, and conflict. The CJI was a resource for the project development and became the point of access for the restorative justice process. Since 1992, the Waterloo Region Committee on Elder Abuse (WRCEA) has raised community awareness about elder abuse and spawned a number of initiatives: the Elder Abuse Help Line; conferences, workshops, and a resource manual for professionals; and an interagency protocol that led to an interagency case review committee. This committee provides a forum for interagency communication and problem solving related to suspected and confirmed elder abuse cases (Groh, 2003). The Waterloo Region was an ideal location to support the project.

Community Mobilization

Despite that foundation, the path from the original concept of restorative justice as a way of addressing elder abuse to a functioning project was long and challenging.

In November 1998, extensive community consultation was initiated. I talked to seniors, health and social services, legal services, and faith and cultural communities about the complex issue of elder abuse and cautiously asked about applying restorative justice to these situations. A key factor in early community mobilization was to build on our strong foundation. The process to establish an interagency protocol brought key stakeholders together to talk about what they could and could not do for victims of elder abuse. Trust was building. "Silos" were starting to come down. It was not clear to me that these partners would support a complete paradigm shift in our response to elder abuse, but there was enough trust to ask. I was amazed and delighted to secure strong support, especially the support of senior managers who were in a position to effect change.

A superintendent from the police services was one of those managers. After several failed attempts, we had finally found a champion for elder abuse within the service. I felt uneasy asking him to support using restorative justice for elder abuse for fear it would jeopardize the gains we had made. I cautiously spoke to him about my idea, and during the long period of silence that followed, I braced myself for his response. You can imagine my relief when he said that although he could not support mediation due to the power imbalance in abusive relationships, he would support using a circle process.

Another key supporter was the director of client services from the CCAC. She was a committed volunteer with the WRCEA, but using restorative justice to address elder abuse was a new concept. After hearing a detailed description of restorative justice and learning that I already had the support of a senior member of the police services, a lawyer who specializes in elder law, an employee of the Mennonite Central Committee Ontario, an employee of Conflict Resolution Network Canada, a senior, and a Native elder, she was willing to take a risk. With the backing of both of these managers and the subsequent support of their boards, we were able to proceed. The CCAC, with the director of client services at the helm, took the lead to apply for funding. In December 1999, one year later, a collaborative of seven diverse agencies was granted moneys to design, implement, and evaluate a restorative justice approach for elder abuse.

Project Development

The project began in March 2000. Our first task was to design a safe and effective restorative justice process for seniors. Despite an extensive literature review and consultation with experts, we found no models that applied restorative justice to elder abuse. We were charting new ground. This was both exciting and daunting. Due to the power imbalance in these situations, the collaborative did not support using mediation. They believed a circle process, with adequate preparation, would be effective in balancing power inequities. To further ensure the safety of older adults, Dr. Elizabeth Dow[4] and I recommended one restorative justice model that facilitators would be trained to follow. After considerable discussion, the collaborative decided to adapt the Family Group Decision Making model used by Gale Burford and Joan Pennell to address child abuse (Burford and Pennell, 1998). Fortunately, in June 2000, Dr. Dow and I attended the 6th Biennial National Conflict Resolution Conference, Interaction 2000: Pulling Together, in Vancouver, BC. Our conversations with restorative justice experts Barry Stuart, Mark Wedge, Susan Sharpe, and Rupert Ross were exciting and disturbing. Each separately was supportive of applying restorative justice to elder abuse but strongly suggested that a safe and effective process needed to be incident-driven, with values and principles guiding the practice. Not one of these experts supported a fixed model to respond to elder abuse. This was difficult for me. Further conversations with Mark Yantzi (CJI) and Dennis Cooley (Law Commission of Canada) led to the same conclusion. We needed to review how best to ensure a safe process for older adults. In September 2000, Dr. Dow and I went back to the collaborative, reported on our new findings, and reluctantly asked that they consider a change to an incident-driven process guided by values and principles. In retrospect, this change in direction was a critical step on our journey to find safe, respectful ways of addressing the complex needs of abused older adults.

Our next task was to develop core values and principles to guide the practice and to articulate a clear mission statement. Not surprisingly, this was not an easy process for a diverse collaborative. The benefit of the process was that we learned to know each other better and became even more committed to finding ways to apply restorative justice. Eventually, we reached a consensus.

Guiding Values and Principles

People have the right to the following:

1. Safety: to live in safety and security. People need to be safe and to feel safe before, during, and after a restorative justice process.
2. Confidentiality: to determine what personal information may be shared and with whom it may be shared.
3. Dignity and respect: to have personal values and preferences respected.
4. Autonomy: to determine and control their own affairs.
5. Access to information: to receive all the available information to make meaningful and informed decisions. People should understand the restorative justice process and the judicial process and should know about community resources and how to access them, or be assisted to access them.
6. The use of the least restrictive form of intervention—that is, least restrictive of the individual's rights, abilities, and personal liberties and least disruptive of lifestyle.[5]

Our mission was to provide an opportunity for change and healing to people affected by elder abuse (Groh, 2003). Putting these pillars in place had a significant impact on our restorative justice process, project development, and how the project evolved to an elder abuse response team.

The Restorative Justice Process

With their practice guided by restorative justice values and principles, trained facilitators could be flexible in their choice of a tool.[6] Adherence to values and principles was required in both the selection of a tool and the process. Considerations included the following:

Safety. Have the participants been asked what they need to be safe and feel safe before, during, and after the process? Are these needs for safety respected? What measures are in place to balance power? Has a plan for safety been clearly articulated? Does the agreement include ways to prevent further abuse?

Confidentiality. Have the participants determined for themselves what personal information may be shared? Do they understand the limits of confidentiality? For example, do they know that a disclosure of child abuse will be reported to the authorities?

Dignity and respect. Is there an understanding of ethnocultural values? Are these values respected? Are the participants' stories taken seriously? Do all participants in the process, including police, health professionals, church workers, and court officials, receive the stories without judgment? Are the victims' needs for healing respected? Are they addressed?

Autonomy. Is participation in the process voluntary? Is the older adult making as many decisions as possible?

Access to information. Do all participants understand the restorative justice process and their role in it? Do they understand the traditional judicial process and how it might affect them? Are they aware of available community resources and how to access them?

Least restrictive interventions. With support services, an older adult may no longer need the services of the person who has done the harm. Has consideration been given to a solution that makes it possible for the older adult to stay at home by providing these supports? (Groh, 2003).

In most situations, the tool selected was the circle process,[7] but other tools were used when appropriate. In one case, "shuttle diplomacy" was effective in reaching an agreement that allowed a longtime friend and neighbor to visit an older adult. The children of this older adult had moved her to a facility and had not permitted the friend to visit. In another situation, preparation for the circle process was sufficient to resolve the conflict and begin healing. In this case, a niece with power of attorney for her capable aunt arranged for an estate sale without consulting her. The aunt had moved to a retirement home, as she needed some assistance with her activities of daily living. She was outraged when she learned what her niece had done. With the assistance of a lawyer, the estate sale was stopped. The circle facilitators worked with the aunt and with the niece to prepare them for the circle. It was during this preparation that the issues were resolved. Both the older adult and her niece decided that a circle was not required. Utilizing a model that is incident-driven allowed the flexibility required to address the complex and varied needs of people affected by elder abuse (Groh, 2005).

Living Restorative Justice Values and Principles

Restorative justice values and principles also guided the development of the project, the interaction of community partners, the decisionmaking process, and conflict resolution. One ongoing dialogue was about the number of referrals to the project. We had broad community support, including the support of our ethnocultural communities, but our numbers were low. Why? The examples about ways to address this issue provide insight into how we lived restorative justice values and principles.

Some members of the collaborative believed that the term *elder abuse* was a barrier for older adults and therefore should not be used in our brochure. The Seniors Advisory Council[8] believed that it was essential to name the abuse, therefore the term *elder abuse* needed to be very visible in the brochure. There were heated discussions with both sides entrenched in their view. My efforts at shuttle diplomacy were ineffective. However, a respectful, facilitated dialogue with members of the collaborative and representatives of the Seniors Advisory Council dissipated the tension. A consensus was reached to use the term *elder abuse and mistreatment* in the brochure.

Another factor considered was the nature of community education. The Seniors Advisory Council noted that while there was extensive education and training, it appeared to be ineffective in increasing the number of referrals to the project. I found it difficult to consider changes to my education materials when feedback to the presentations was positive. However, in a respectful way, the Advisory Council kept prodding me to consider changes that would result in referrals. Their prodding was the impetus to establish the Harmony Interage Theatre Troupe, a group of seniors who are committed to raising awareness about elder abuse and restorative justice through interactive theater and "mock circles."[9] The troupe continues to be integral to our education and training, precipitating disclosures of abuse at most presentations.

There was another troubling factor about referrals. Despite a long history of restorative justice in our region, I learned that there was a lack of confidence to refer to this process. After conversations with key stakeholders, the Restorative Justice Task Force was established. This task force, with a mandate "to build a coalition of people in Waterloo Region to promote restorative justice for the benefit of victims, offenders and community,"[10] invited community partners to a forum, facilitated by Eva Marszewski.[11] Crown attorneys,[12] judges, defense lawyers, police officers, health and social services, and education came together to talk about the potential and the pitfalls of using restorative justice and how to establish safe "best practices." One step identified was a need for regional values and principles to guide restorative justice practices. Although it was a long and arduous process, the pillars are now in place to continue to build community confidence to refer to restorative justice for elder abuse and much more (*Restorative Justice,* 2005).

Project Evaluation

The challenge to increase our referrals continued throughout the project. Dr. Rick Linden, professor of sociology and director of the Criminology Research Centre at the University of Manitoba, completed an evaluation of the project. This evaluation was funded by the Law Commission of Canada and Justice Canada. His findings are forthcoming in the *Journal of Elder Abuse and Neglect* (Linden and Groh, in press). Anecdotal feedback and reflections on the benefits and limitations of the project are discussed in *Restorative Justice: A Healing Approach to Elder Abuse and Mistreatment* (Groh, 2003, pp. 57, 58). To summarize,

> the restorative justice process is a resource option that provides an opportunity for change and healing. The challenge for all of us is to find ways for legal, health and social services, and faith and cultural communities to work together with the people affected by elder abuse. We need to understand why older adults are abused, what is needed to repair that harm and to facilitate healing,

and what must be put into place by families, communities and government to ensure the prevention and resolution of abuse. (Groh, 2003, p. 65)

Transition to the Elder Abuse Response Team

An open dialogue, rooted in restorative justice philosophy, was integral to the project's evolving into an Elder Abuse Response Team. To capture this, I frame our dialogue with Howard Zehr's "essence of restorative justice questions" (Zehr, 2002, p. 38) and reference the business plan[13] that came out of our discussions.

Who has been hurt? Seniors in our region are harmed—many more than those who have come to our attention. Canadian research indicates that between 4 percent and 10 percent of older adults experience abuse by someone in a position of trust. It is estimated that approximately 80 percent of these situations remain unreported (Bain and Spencer, 2007). In our business plan, we note that elder abuse is a hidden crime that affects older members of our community from various ethnocultural groups and social backgrounds and that elder abuse will increase within the region as the population ages.

What are their needs? The needs of abused older adults are multiple, including but not limited to safety, elimination of the abuse, shelter, financial resources, and links to counseling, legal advice, spiritual care, restorative justice, or traditional justice. The primary goal for this proposed team was to commit the Waterloo Regional Police Service and the Community Care Access Centre of the Waterloo Region to an innovative partnership that would enhance the safety and well-being of our seniors by providing investigative expertise in crimes of abuse against older persons; expertise in identifying and supporting victims of elder abuse; and a restorative justice response to elder abuse and mistreatment that is fair, just, and culturally sensitive. Community partners held firmly to the vision of providing opportunities for healing and change to people affected by elder abuse. At the same time, we were exploring more comprehensive ways of achieving that vision.

Whose obligations are these? Elder abuse is a societal issue. We as a community have an obligation to build a safe place where older adults age with honor, dignity, and respect. Our business plan reflected this. We believed that it was necessary to address the abuse of older persons in a manner that is effective, preventive, and sustainable and that a partnership between the Waterloo Regional Police Service and the Community Care Access Centre to form an Elder Abuse/Restorative Justice Resource Office and Intervention Team was an important next step in meeting the increasing needs of seniors in our community.

Who has a stake in this situation? "Among other things [elder abuse] is a health, human rights, justice, family violence issue that requires complex, multiple and integrated responses from a very wide range of sources at individual, institutional, societal and global levels" (INPEA, 2007, p. 6). In our business plan, we noted that a range of options is available when a holistic approach involving a case manager and a detective is used. No single agency can meet the complex needs of people experiencing abuse. Police officers and health care providers working in concert to identify and prevent the abuse best serve the community. Everyone has a stake in this societal issue.

What is the appropriate process to involve stakeholders in an effort to put things right? Although our numbers were low, there continued to be strong support for the restorative justice process. We believed that "certain conflicts, particularly those involving family can best be resolved by repairing relationships and controlling risks rather than simply punishing offenders" (Nerenberg, 2008, p. 57). The Project taught us how essential it was for legal, health, social services, and faith and cultural communities to work in partnership to address this complex crime; that when we raised awareness about elder abuse, we needed to have frontline resources to respond; and that this is a community issue that requires core sustainable funding. The proposed Elder Abuse Response Team, with a mandate to support and develop an interagency, interdisciplinary response to elder abuse, was a way to involve stakeholders in an effort to make things as right as possible for the people affected by elder abuse.

From my perspective, the "essence of restorative justice" was integral to the project evolving into the Elder Abuse Response Team and to the team's practice. However, Dr. Linden, in his evaluation, indicates that the project partners arrived at a "conflict management system" to address elder abuse. He states that the best way to deal with conflict is to establish systems for conflict management where diverse agencies and organizations work together to address elder abuse. There are multiple points of entry and multiple options for conflict resolution (Linden and Groh, in press). While he accurately describes the Waterloo Region's response to elder abuse, at the time we did not name what we were doing. We simply forged ahead. A business plan was drafted and submitted to the chief of police and the chief executive officer of the CCAC. In retrospect, our proposal for responding to elder abuse was a "conflict management approach" that also captured the essence of restorative justice.

The Elder Abuse Response Team

In November 2004, the WRPS and the CCAC of the Waterloo Region launched the Elder Abuse Response Team. This team, consisting of a detective constable and an elder abuse restorative justice resource consultant, was housed at Police Headquarters. A memorandum of understanding was signed by both agencies articulating our mission, respective roles, core funding, and ways to resolve conflict. It clearly states that restorative justice values and principles are to guide our practice, that we are to refer to restorative justice when appropriate, and that the team's mission is "to prevent and respond to elder abuse by working in partnership with the community and by providing an opportunity for change and healing to people affected by elder abuse, thereby enhancing the safety and well being of older adults."[14] We are mandated to provide consultation, community development, training, education, and direct intervention. Direct intervention includes conducting joint investigations, facilitating linkages to community resources, and managing situations until resolution or a linkage with a community agency is completed. We provide service, whether or not a charge has been laid. When a charge has been laid, our Crown attorney designated to elder abuse cases determines if restorative justice is appropriate. Anyone can call our line. There are multiple dispositions for situations of abuse.

Dr. Linden, in his evaluation, states:

> The elder abuse program now seems to be on a very sound footing. Referrals are no longer a problem, an intensive community and professional education program continues, and a very effective network has been established involving the EART and its community partners. In its current form, the program has evolved from a restorative justice program to a much more comprehensive conflict management program. However, restorative justice values still guide the practice and the mandate from both sponsoring agencies is still to divert as many cases as possible to a restorative justice process. This process may involve circles, but it also may involve a broad range of other options. (Linden and Groh, in press)

He further suggests that this program

> exemplifies the development of sound public policy. . . . The agencies supporting the elder abuse initiative, particularly the CCAC and the WRPS, stepped forward with an increased commitment and the program was extensively redesigned. The new program has been very successful in increasing referrals and in ensuring that community partners work well together. The issue of the impact of the program on older adults should be assessed by further research. (Linden and Groh, in press)

Personal Observations

Before reflecting on my experience working as a member of the Elder Abuse Response Team, I would like to share my thoughts on some of the ripple effects of living restorative justice values and principles. Here are some that I am aware of. In 1999, our Crown attorney was asked for a letter in support of our initiative to secure project funding. She responded that while she supported restorative justice as a way to address elder abuse, it was irrelevant, as we had no cases coming to the courts. Today, we have a Crown attorney designated to elder abuse, who supports our mandate to divert to restorative justice when appropriate. There are elder abuse cases in the courts. At the beginning of our journey, the knowledge about elder abuse and restorative justice within our police service was somewhat limited. Now our staff sergeant tells visitors that, for this team, "restorative justice begins the moment they answer the phone." On joining the EART, one of the officers said, "I'm a cop, you are going to have to help me with this business of sitting in a circle holding hands," and "The credibility of this unit will be recognized by the number of charges laid." Today, he diverts to restorative justice when appropriate and says, "If the team has to lay a charge, we were called too late." Along our journey, we discovered gaps in services. New programs were developed to close those gaps. Seniors who disclose abuse may find it difficult after the abuser is removed from their home. To address this need, the Mennonite Central Committee Ontario, in partnership with the EART, secured funding for circles of support. Trained volunteers empower survivors of elder abuse and mistreatment by listening and by assisting with practical activities according to the needs and interests of the senior. One circle participant, who was barricading herself inside her home, is now able to walk outside and is engaged in community activities. Another recognized need was for situations of elder mistreatment to be addressed before they escalated to criminal code offenses. Although Community Justice Initiatives continues to be our point of entry for referrals, it recently initiated Elder Services. Mediation and circles are used to address conflicts around housing, health and medical concerns, end-of-life care, powers of attorney, and more. This program may well decrease the EART's calls for service. Living restorative justice values and principles seems to have a ripple effect that results in healthier seniors and stronger families in a more cohesive community.

Working as a member of the Elder Abuse Response Team was a remarkable experience. It was not always easy. We had rigorous debates over how to proceed with cases. We investigated tough situations. Adherence to restorative justice values and principles was integral in helping us find our way. In January 2006, our team moved from Police Headquarters to Catholic Family Counseling Services, the home of the Family Violence Project (FVP) of the Waterloo Region.[15] We colocated with approximately fourteen agencies, including the police domestic violence unit, a Crown attorney, victim services, family and children's services, crisis outreach, and more. We came together under one roof to provide seamless services for victims of family violence. With this move, our calls for service skyrocketed. However, we were now positioned to provide a response to elder abuse that could weave its way through the complex fabric of relationships and find solutions that were acceptable to the people affected by elder abuse. With access to multiple services in-house, plus a matrix of forty agencies committed to working with us, our team of two could have activities taking place at the same time. John Paul Lederach's perspective of what is needed in healing relationships captures our holistic response to elder abuse.

> With a systemic view, we see people and relationships within a context, a social fabric that is dynamic, interdependent and evolving. . . . We try to understand the overall system and how change in any one aspect will change all the others. . . . Like a dance, we simultaneously have activities taking place related to the past (Truth), the present (Justice and Mercy) and the future (Hope and

Peace). . . . We create a space where truth, justice, mercy, peace and hope are given life and interact. (Lederach, 1999, p. 79)

I was privileged to be a member of this team.

Back to Our Stories

The continuation of these stories further illustrates the complexity of elder abuse and our response. Not all of them have happy endings, but there are glimpses of healing and change.

My partner asked me to take the lead for our interview of the ninety-eight-year-old female who had been transported to a safe shelter. During her disclosure, she kept repeating, "There must be a reason for me to still be here." So I asked, "Are you a member of a faith community?" She said that for the past forty years, her daughter had not allowed her to go to church or to receive church visitors. She wanted to see her minister. My fear on leaving the interview was that my partner would remind me about the nature of a police investigation and suggest that I had gone off course. Instead, he said, "Wasn't that a heart breaker? Do you know where her church is? Let's go." This elderly female declined a referral to restorative justice because she was afraid of her daughter. But she was reconnected to her faith community and her grandchildren.

The eighty-five-year-old female who moved to a safe shelter to escape her abusive spouse met with me in the soft interview room located at the Family Violence Project. Although initially reluctant, she eventually agreed to have a police officer present for her disclosure. This woman decided she needed to spend time away from her husband so that she could think more clearly. We drove her to her home in an unmarked cruiser. The officer dealt with the spouse, and I helped her pack her belongings. Together, we took her to a safe shelter. That evening, both her minister and a crisis counselor visited her. One year later, I received a call requesting a visit. I did not want to go. I was afraid that she needed help, once again, to extract herself from her spouse. I was wrong. She wanted me to see her face, to see her eyes, and to see that she was no longer a victim. She was thriving. This elderly female was thankful for her new beginning and asked that I tell her story.

We investigated the alleged assault of the sixty-eight-year-old female, who was wheelchair-bound and dependent for her physical care. She lived with her seventy-five-year-old brother and his wife. A charge of assault was laid. The brother was devastated. He had promised his sister and their family that he would provide care. However, the care had become overwhelming. At the officer's request, the Crown attorney agreed to divert to restorative justice. A follow-up report indicated that both the brother and sister were doing well. The family expressed gratitude for the circle process and the resolutions reached. They continue their process of healing.

The elderly female who had not bathed in more than ten months was living in abject squalor and filth. She, along with her pets, was barricaded in one small room. Her food was unrecognizable. Yet, she had the capacity to make personal care decisions, and on our first visit she refused to leave. I spent a sleepless night thinking about how to safely extract this woman from her home. The next morning, I was greeted by a bleary-eyed sergeant who had spent the night researching to find a legally acceptable way to remove her from her inhospitable surroundings. This is a long, tragic story. Suffice it to say that working together with her and with community partners, we moved her to safety. She had no clothes other than the rags she was wearing. The officer gave her the coat off his back. Victim service volunteers brought her new shoes, clothes, and a comfort pack. Her caregiver pled guilty to a charge of failing to provide necessities. This woman asked the officer to be her son. She was grateful for the basics: food, clothing, shelter, and a hot bath.

From my perspective, we live restorative justice values and principles in our response to elder abuse.

Conclusion

As with any restorative justice process, we did not know where our journey would take us. In 1998, I was frustrated and discouraged by how ineffective we were in responding to elder abuse. In May 2008, when I retired, I was amazed at how effective we had become. I was honored to be part a team that recognizes the complex social fabric of relationships in elder abuse as "dynamic, interdependent and evolving; where simultaneously we have activities taking place related to truth, justice, mercy, hope and peace" (Lederach, 1999, p. 79). My perspective is that being grounded in restorative justice values and principles empowered us to "*draw on and trust our own inner resources to discover the validity of a new paradigm*" (italics added; Miller, 1996, p. 60). Our journey, of course, prompts questions. Does our new paradigm fit within restorative justice practice? Is restorative justice "an orientation, not a program," as Susan Sharpe suggests? Did our "set of values and beliefs . . . in turn point to our principles for responding to criminal harms" (Sharpe, 1998, p. 19)? Is our "conflict management approach to elder abuse" an innovative approach to criminal justice that provides an opportunity for victims of elder abuse to engage in a restorative justice process? Those are some of the questions I ponder. My hope is that sharing my questions and our story will precipitate further dialogue and will be a catalyst to begin other community-specific responses to elder abuse. As Howard Zehr notes,

> while the experiments, practices and customs from many communities and cultures are instructive, none can or should be copied and simply plugged into communities or societies. Rather, they should be viewed as examples of how

different communities and societies found their own appropriate ways to express justice as a response to wrongdoing. These approaches may give us inspiration and a place to begin. (Zehr, 2002, p. 62)

Notes

1. A collaborative of seven agencies defined and shaped the Restorative Justice Approaches to Elder Abuse Project: The Community Care Access Centre of Waterloo Region (now Waterloo Wellington Community Care Access Centre), http://www.wwccac .on.ca, funded by the Ministry of Health, provides information and a broad range of in-home health services. The Waterloo Regional Police Service, http://www.wrps.on.ca, provides a leadership role in crime prevention and law enforcement and is committed to working in partnership with the community. The Network for Conflict Resolution Canada (1988–2008) provided consultation and resources on conflict resolution. The K-W Multicultural Centre, http://www.kmc.on.ca, assists with outreach to the diverse multicultural community of the Waterloo Region. The Community Justice Initiatives of Waterloo Region, http://www.cjiwr.com, provides consultation and resources on conflict resolution. The Mennonite Central Committee (Ontario; MCCO), http://mcc.org/ontario, is a relief, service, and peace agency of the North American Mennonite and Brethren in Christ churches; the MCCO supported the project from its inception and had a contract with and supervised the evaluation assistants. The White Owl Native Ancestry Association Weejeendimin Native Resource Centre provides information about native traditions and consultation about the circle process. The Waterloo Region Committee on Elder Abuse (WRCEA) is composed of volunteers with a mandate to raise awareness about elder abuse and increase the community's ability to respond.

2. The WRPS provides a leadership role in crime prevention and law enforcement and is committed to working in partnership with the community.

3. The CCAC of the Waterloo Region is a government-funded in-home health service with a mandate to respond to elder abuse.

4. Dr. Elizabeth Dow, formerly from Memorial University of Newfoundland, influenced the early development of the project. She has elder abuse expertise and an understanding of restorative justice.

5. Our guiding principles were adapted from Gallager and Pittaway (1995).

6. For a detailed description of restorative justice practices and models, see *The Little Book of Restorative Justice* (Zehr, 2002, pp. 47–52), *Building Community Justice Partnerships: Community Peacemaking Circles* (Stuart, 1997, pp. 1–12), *Restorative Justice: A Vision for Healing and Change* (Sharpe, 1998, pp. 25–42), and *Peace Making Circles: From Crime to Community* (Pranis, Stuart, and Wedge, 2003).

7. Circles are a way of talking together where everyone is respected and has a chance to talk without interruption, where one can explain oneself by telling stories, and where everyone is equal. No person is more important than anyone else. The circle is useful when two or more people have a disagreement or conflict or when there is a violation of a trusted relationship. The circle is a container strong enough to hold anger, frustration, joy, truth, conflict, opposite opinions, and strong feelings. Everyone sits in chairs placed in a circle facing each other, without a table or other furniture between them. An object called a talking piece is passed from person to person around the circle. Each person has a chance to speak when they have the talking piece. Everyone else listens without interruption until the person with the talking piece finishes, and the talking piece is passed to the next person who then may speak. Respect is very important in the

circle—speaking with respect and listening with respect. The circle allows us to balance ancient wisdom about being in the community with modern wisdom (Pranis, Stuart, and Wedge, 2003; adapted by Eva E. Marszewski for project facilitator training).

8. The Seniors Advisory Council provided a voice for seniors for the project. The council reviewed and made recommendations regarding project activities. Membership included older adults from ethno-specific communities, health, business, academia, social work, and community services. See Groh (2003, Appendix 4).

9. The Harmony Interage Theatre Troupe is a group of seniors committed to raising awareness about elder abuse and restorative justice through action theater. "Anti-models" based on real-life scenarios are mimed or acted out. The actors remain in character and invite the audience to find solutions or to change the outcomes. This form of theater derives from the work of Augusto Boal. He maintained that participatory theater could transform monologue into dialogue and help people overcome oppression.

10. The Restorative Justice Task Force, supported by the Crime Prevention Council of Waterloo Region, had a mandate "to build a coalition of people in Waterloo Region to promote restorative justice for the benefit of victims, offenders and community." This group started meeting in August 2003 to address the issue of how to build community confidence in the restorative justice process. Their goals included increasing the use of restorative justice as a viable alternative to traditional justice; developing and promoting a broader understanding and appreciation of restorative justice philosophy, models, and applications in the community; reaching a consensus on principles, values, and best practice guidelines for the application of restorative justice; increasing resources for restorative justice efforts in the Waterloo Region; and providing educational opportunities in restorative justice to broaden the web of trained facilitators in the Waterloo Region.

11. Eva Marszewski of Peacebuilders International (Canada; http://www.peace buildersinternational.com) is a former litigation lawyer in Toronto who is an experienced adjudicator, mediator, facilitator, circle-keeper, and trainer.

12. Crown attorneys serve as the prosecutor in the Canadian legal system.

13. Superintendent Steve Hibbard, in partnership with Arlene Groh, project coordinator, and Kim Voelker, director of client services for the CCAC, developed a business plan, "Responding to Abuse of Older Adults." This proposal to establish an Elder Abuse Response Team was presented to the boards of the WRPS and the CCAC for their approval.

14. Family Violence Project of Waterloo Region. Available at http://www.fvpwaterloo .ca (accessed March 31, 2009).

15. The Family Violence Project (FVP; http://www.fvpwaterloo.ca/en) is a collaborative response to family violence that provides a holistic seamless service delivery with a one-stop access point for victims and their families. The collaborative partners are committed to working together to help families find emotional/physical safety and to work with the community to end the cycle of violence that so often damages and destroys families.

5

A Victim with Special Needs: A Case Study

Jill Schellenberg

Restorative justice is a broad term that can include many forms of alternative dispute resolution, along with victim and community inclusion in the criminal justice process. The United Nations defines the "restorative process" as any process in which the victim, the offender, and/or any other individuals or community members affected by a crime participate together actively in the resolution of matters arising from the crime, often with the help of a fair and impartial third party. Examples of restorative processes include mediation, conferencing, and sentencing circles (United Nations, 2000, p. 37).

Restorative justice grew out of concerns that the needs of victims of crimes were not being met. Crime is considered a violation of law rather than a violation of victims. The state becomes the victim and those harmed by crime become witnesses for the state, at best. If the victims' testimony is not needed, then their role becomes secondary or irrelevant. The Judicial Council of California, Office of the Courts, notes that the justice system in the United States has traditionally been a system that administers punishment for crime. Offenders are taken to court, receive a sentence for their crimes, and pay society back by way of fines, probation, or jail time. In this retributive system, crime is an act by an offender against the state. The system is built on the concepts that criminals should be punished for their crimes and that deterrence is the way to achieve community safety. This retributive system is not focused on addressing the needs of the victims, the community, or the offenders. Restorative justice, in contrast, seeks to repair the harm done to all parties affected by crime—the victim, the community, and the offender; to hold offenders accountable; and to improve community safety (Judicial Council, 2006, p. 1).

Keywords: restorative justice, Mennonites, rape, VORP, forgiveness, mediation

55

My Background in Restorative Justice

Fresno, California, has been an important city in the development of restorative justice and victimological issues. The first victim impact statement was created in 1976 by Jim Rowland in Fresno. The first Victim Offender Reconciliation Program (VORP) was started in Fresno in 1982 by Ron Claassen. Fresno has two universities (California State University, Fresno, and Fresno Pacific University) that teach courses in victimology and restorative justice. Perhaps it was inevitable that I would hear about restorative justice in Fresno and get involved. My first exposure was in the mid-1980s when my husband and I took a course at the Mennonite Brethren Biblical Seminary. The course was taught by Ron Claassen, and one requirement was to complete a VORP case. Bringing victims and offenders together and witnessing the healing that took place taught me that restorative justice was a process that really worked. It was a viable alternative to the retributive justice that is commonly practiced. Restorative justice principles were valuable to both victims and offenders. Victims have a central voice in the process, receive answers to their questions, and usually receive restitution. Offenders gain empathy skills, conflict management skills, and accountability for their crime.

Restorative justice also fits into my theological beliefs. I belong to the Mennonite Brethren church denomination, which believes that "believers seek to be agents of reconciliation in all relationships, to practice love of enemies as taught by Christ, and to be peacemakers in all situations. We view violence in its many different forms as contradictory to the new nature of the Christian" (Canadian Conference, 2008).

Mennonites, who have roots in the Anabaptist movement of the Protestant Reformation in sixteenth-century Europe, were instrumental in the founding and development of the restorative justice movement in the United States (Dorne, 2008, p. 167).

Currently, I am the director of the Criminology and Restorative Justice Studies program at Fresno Pacific University. Because restorative justice is considered a viable alternative to the problem of overcrowded prisons and jails and budget shortages, the need arose to educate people in law enforcement, corrections, and other criminal justice fields in proper implementation of restorative justice principles.

A Crime Is Committed

We lived in Canada for four years and then in Europe for almost ten years. Our return to the United States was a difficult transition. Searching for jobs, finding new friends, helping our children navigate the school system, fitting in to our church, and especially trying to make sense of the American culture were much more difficult than we anticipated. After all, we were returning to our home culture. We should have known what to expect, but we underestimated the difficulty. We returned to take care of my elderly father, who unfortunately died of a stroke after a short time. Our family was not quite settled back into American society when we were hit by a tragic crime against our daughter.

Our oldest child is a beautiful, talented girl, who is mentally and physically handicapped. Her diagnosis is ataxic cerebral palsy, which results in low muscle tone. She has been a joy and delight, reminding us of what is important in life. When we returned from Europe, her desire was to move into an independent living program for handicapped people. She was thrilled to have an apartment and a roommate. With supervision from the staff, she was able to fulfill her dream of having more autonomy. We were so proud of her.

One winter day, I was upstairs putting away laundry when the phone rang. It was the manager of the independent living program where our daughter lived, telling me that our daughter had been raped. I remember the scream that froze in my throat and my running down the stairs in slow motion to tell my husband and sons. It seemed as if time was standing still. That evening, in the hospital trauma unit, we learned the extent of the crime. It had been a particularly brutal rape. She had gotten off the bus after school and was walking to her apartment. She was taken by a man to his apartment and dead-bolted in. We were grateful that he released her instead of killing her. The police were able to apprehend the offender almost immediately because he probably did not think a mentally handicapped person would be smart enough to remember details. He was wrong. She was able to tell the police his street address and apartment number. There they found his bed covered in blood, our daughter's blood.

A crime does not affect just the direct victim. Our family and friends were devastated. One of our sons broke down at the hospital. He could not bear to hear what the doctor was telling us about our daughter and had to be taken home by my husband. The other son stayed the entire evening, took off school, ran errands, cooked meals, and kept very busy. I have often thought about their reactions and have decided both were appropriate.

Restorative Justice Goes Out the Window

My first thought when I heard about our daughter's rape was that the offender must be an animal. A human being could not be capable of doing this to a mentally handicapped girl. I was shocked at the depth of my hatred for this man. Pacifists should not think this way, but I wanted to strangle him. I was so angry about the crime, angry about how badly my daughter was hurt (mentally and physically), angry that we now lived in fear, and angry that all joy and happiness were drained out of our lives. Our future seemed dark and hopeless.

The first Sunday after the crime, we attended church and the sermon was about forgiveness. Forgiveness seemed to be the ugliest word in the world, and

I could not bear to hear it. How dare the pastor speak about forgiveness! The sermon had been planned long before the crime happened, but I was particularly offended. I got up and walked out of church. What happened to my faith in God? What happened to my education about how to respond to crime restoratively?

The district attorney's office handled our case. We met with our attorney, and he informed us that the offender had pleaded "not guilty." He claimed that the sex was consensual and just got out of hand. I do not think I could have been more incensed. How could he plead not guilty? My daughter is mentally handicapped and cannot even tie her own shoelaces. How could she "consent"? Unfortunately, the district attorney was not incensed. His perspective was that because she was mentally handicapped, it would be easy to trick her on the witness stand. He was not sure he could win the case. The bottom line seemed to be winning or losing the court case. He wanted to know if we wanted to proceed with the case. Of course, we wanted to proceed! What message would we give our daughter if we dropped the case? What message would we give the offender? In our minds, dropping the case was out of the question. Holding the offender accountable for the crime was the right thing to do.

Doing the right thing was not easy. There were many hearings, however, where we were not allowed in the courtroom because we had been subpoenaed. The subpoena stated that if we did not come to the courthouse, we would be arrested. The language of the subpoena seemed hurtful to us. We were rarely informed about what went on in the hearings. We started to feel totally irrelevant to the entire process. The anger inside me was building. Every time there was a hearing, we needed to recall all the details of the crime. This was painful for my husband and me, but our daughter was really suffering. She was not always capable of verbally expressing her frustration, but we saw signs of depression. She slept all the time. Rape counseling was helpful but still challenging with a mentally handicapped victim.

One day, I realized that I had become obsessed with the crime and was angry all the time. "Excessive irritability, bitterness, or anger" (Neimeyer, Prigerson, and Davies, 2002, p. 242) can be a symptom related to grief, and there was not a day that went by when I did not experience those symptoms. Joyful times were quickly replaced with the realization that we were victims of crime. I became convinced that something had to change in my life to restore the joy and happiness that were missing.

Restorative Justice Reexamined

Memories of restorative justice and the VORP cases we had completed years before reminded me that there had to be another way to deal with this crime. I called the VORP office and asked if they had any suggestions for our case. Interestingly, they encouraged me to write a victim impact statement for the end of the trial. Because this can be a restorative measure, they felt that was the way to begin. Unfortunately, no other agency suggested this—not the district attorney's office nor victim services.

Trying to craft a victim impact statement made me reexamine my theological and academic foundations. The idea of forgiveness resurfaced, but this time I was ready to explore it. Forgiveness was not as ugly a word as it had been right after the crime. If I kept the hatred inside me and refused to forgive, the offender was not suffering, I was. I asked myself questions about what type of person and what background the offender might be. My guess was that he was not surrounded with love like my daughter and our family were. After the rape, we realized how blessed with loving friends, family, and colleagues we were. The rapist might not have those close ties. What would drive a person to commit such a crime? There must have been pain and suffering in his life. These thoughts of forgiveness did not mean I thought he should not go to prison. He was obviously a dangerous person and needed to be removed from society. However, I wished that he knew love, could get rehabilitation, and could someday reintegrate into society.

The Amish school shooting in the fall of 2006 taught me harsh lessons on forgiveness. Ten little Amish girls were lined up and shot in a schoolhouse, and five of them did not survive. The Amish stem from the same Anabaptist roots as Mennonites. Although I have a similar theology as the Amish, it took me a long time to consider forgiveness, whereas the families of those victims were able quickly to do so. Donald Kraybill wrote that

> forgiveness is woven into the fabric of the Amish faith. And that is why words of forgiveness were sent to the killer's family before the blood had dried on the schoolhouse floor. It was just the natural thing to do, the Amish way of doing things. Such courage to forgive has jolted the watching world as much as the killing itself. The transforming power of forgiveness may be one redeeming thing that flows from the blood that was shed in Nickel Mines this week. (Kraybill, 2006)

Forgiveness did not seem to be woven into my faith, and I wanted to change that. I wrote the victim impact statement and gave it to the attorney to be read at sentencing. Courage failed me to deliver it myself. The offender struck a plea bargain, which is unfortunately typical in the criminal justice system. "Lack of communication about a proposed plea agreement continues to be one of the highest sources of victim dissatisfaction with the criminal justice system" (US Department of Justice, 1998, p. 16). I cannot recall if we were told about his sentence because by that time I was numb. We were never consulted on what the sentence should be because victims are not officially part of the process. Restorative justice reform is desperately needed to put victims back into a central role.

Current Plans for Restoration

Our daughter's rapist was sent to prison and registered as a sex offender. Time passed and my commitment to forgive had an added bonus. Joy returned to my life, and I no longer lived in fear. My daughter slowly recovered and is currently doing very well. This story could end with . . . *and they lived happily ever after,* but that is not enough. Recently, I found out that the offender is out of prison. Instead of filling me with fear, this news made me realize that it is time to take the next step. My husband and I want to meet with the offender in a mediation setting. We will not include my daughter in this mediation because she might misunderstand the purpose behind the meeting. We want the offender to know how much he has hurt our family. We want him to know that this should never happen again. We want to hear his side of the story. He is the only person in the world with the answers to our questions about why he did this and what he learned in prison.

Mediation should be voluntary for its maximum benefit. We have chosen a mediator, and he is contacting the offender. There should be several individual meetings between the offender and the mediator to ensure a constructive process. Having a commitment to be constructive rather than destructive is essential for everyone participating in mediation. These meetings include reviewing ground rules for appropriate behavior in the mediation. Those ground rules, which are extremely important for the mediation to succeed, include the following:

1. *Allow the mediator to lead the process.* Allowing the mediator to lead recognizes that the mediator is guiding the process and will facilitate the conversation. Sometimes people in mediations want to have control of the conversation, and this limits the mediation getting out of hand.

2. *Say if the process is not fair.* Speaking up and saying whether the process is fair is very important. The mediator or the other parties involved cannot read minds. If participants think something is not fair but do not express that verbally, they cannot expect that everyone will guess their feelings. Agreeing to express when something seems unfair makes for a smoother mediation.

3. *Listen without interrupting.* People need to commit to giving each person a chance to talk without interrupting. This is easy to agree to in advance of the mediation and difficult to abide by during the process. I usually have people write down what they want to say on a sheet of paper so that when their turn to talk comes around, they can express what is important to them.

4. *Be as honest as you can.* If people agree in advance that they will be honest, then it is easier to create a safe space where people can say what really happened. Honesty can be confused with destructive talk, so people need to be reminded of their commitment to be constructive when they are telling their side of the story.

5. *No name calling or profanity.* Name calling and profanity are not constructive forms of communication in mediation. Some people feel that profanity

helps them express the seriousness of their feelings. However, a mediation setting is not an appropriate time to use profanity, just as profanity in a court setting would not be appropriate.

6. *Be willing to summarize.* Being willing to summarize is vital in a mediation. Summarization of what people have said helps in several different ways. First, it shows that the hearer understood what the speaker said, at least well enough to be able to paraphrase. Second, it offers an opportunity for the speaker to correct misunderstandings in the hearers' interpretation of what was said. In the end, the speaker feels assured that what was said was received the way it was intended. This is important for both victims and offenders (Claassen, 2001).

When the mediator is comfortable with the offender's readiness to participate constructively in mediation, then there will be similar individual meetings between the mediator, my husband, and me. It is important for those meetings to prepare victims to articulate what they want from the mediation. This should clarify what victims hope to accomplish for themselves and what they expect from the offender. Even though I mediate cases frequently, it is time for me to set that aside and be a mom rather than a mediator. My role is not to second-guess the mediator but to trust the process.

The reason behind having mediation is to give offenders an opportunity to recognize the injustice, make things as right as possible, and declare their future intentions. The restorative justice principles are as follows:

> 1. Crime is primarily an offense against human relationships and secondarily a violation of a law (because laws are written to protect safety and fairness in human relationships).
>
> 2. Restorative justice recognizes that crime (violation of persons and relationships) is wrong and should not occur, and that after it does there are dangers and opportunities. The danger is that the community, victims, and/or offenders emerge from the response further alienated, more damaged, disrespected, disempowered, feeling less safe, and less cooperative with society. The opportunity is that injustice is recognized, the equity is restored (restitution and grace), and the future is clarified so that participants are safer, more respectful, and more empowered and cooperative with each other and society.
>
> 3. Restorative justice is a process to "make things as right as possible," which includes attending to needs created by the offense, such as the safety and repair of injuries to relationships and the physical damage resulting from the offense and attending to the needs related to the cause of the offender (e.g., addictions, lack of social or employment skills or resources, lack of moral or ethical base).
>
> 4. The primary victim of a crime is the one directly affected by the offense. The secondary victim is one who is indirectly affected by the crime and might include family members, friends, witnesses, criminal justice officials, and community members, among others.
>
> 5. As soon as the immediate victim, community, and offender safety concerns are satisfied, restorative justice views the situation as a teachable moment for the offender—an opportunity to encourage the offender to learn new ways of acting and being a successful contributing part of the community.

6. Restorative justice prefers responding to the crime at the earliest point possible and with the maximum amount of voluntary cooperation and minimum coercion, because healing in relationships and new learning are voluntary and cooperative processes.

7. Restorative justice prefers that most crimes are handled using a cooperative structure, including those affected by the offense as a community to provide support and accountability. This might include primary and secondary victims and family (or substitutes if they choose not to participate), the offender and family, community representatives, government representatives, faith community representatives, and school representatives, among others.

8. Restorative justice recognizes that not all offenders will choose to be cooperative. Therefore, there is a need for an outside authority to make decisions for the offender who is not cooperative. The actions of the authorities and the consequences imposed should be tested by whether they are reasonable, restorative, and respectful (for the victim, the offender, and the community).

9. Restorative justice prefers that offenders who pose significant safety risks and are not yet cooperative be placed in settings where the emphasis is on safety, values, ethics, responsibility, accountability, and civility. They should be exposed to the impact of their crime(s) on victims, invited to learn empathy, and offered learning opportunities to become better equipped with skills to be a productive member of society. They should continually be invited (not coerced) to become cooperative with the community and be given the opportunity to demonstrate this in appropriate settings as soon as possible.

10. Restorative justice requires follow-up and accountability structures utilizing the natural community as much as possible, because keeping agreements is the key to building a trusting community.

11. Restorative justice recognizes and encourages the role of community institutions, including the religious/faith community, in teaching and establishing the moral and ethical standards that build up the community. (Claassen, 1996a)

Conclusion

In conclusion, restorative justice seeks to repair the harm done to all parties affected by crime—the victim, the community, and the offender. The current criminal justice system tends to leave out the victims or relegate them to an insignificant role, as in our personal case. The attorneys are looking to win their case rather than see that victims are helped with healing. Restorative justice can help victims move toward forgiveness or healing and offenders toward accountability and remorse for their crime. Mediation can be an excellent venue for all of this to take place if everyone has a commitment to be constructive and agree to and abide by the ground rules.

Our mediation may never take place, but not because we stood in the way. As was stated earlier, mediation is best when it is voluntary. The offender has a choice to participate or not. He could possibly be afraid of our family and worry that we would want revenge. He might not be willing to take responsibility for the crime. Restorative justice processes depend on the offender's taking responsibility for the crime. It opens a safe space where the offender can admit what he did wrong and hopefully apologize for the wrongdoing. Our mediator will assess the sincerity of his admission of guilt, his ability to be constructive, and his willingness to agree to the ground rules. If everything looks positive, then the mediation will take place at the County Courthouse. This setting provides the security that would be important in such a serious case. There are metal detectors that everyone must pass through in order to enter. That security would probably make both parties feel more secure.

Restorative justice has already helped our family heal from the trauma of the crime. It gave us the framework to realize what we needed to recover. We needed to see the offender as a human independent of the crime he committed. Mediation has the possibility of making a difference in the life of our daughter's rapist. He would be exposed to the incredible harm he caused and also to the knowledge that we want his negative behavior to stop. We want him to know face to face that we forgive him and want what is best for him. If that happens, then restorative justice holds the possibility of saving another victim from experiencing the horror of rape. It is time for healing to continue for everyone involved.

6

Recovery and Restoration in Victim Assistance

John P. J. Dussich

What would we say about a movement that apparently forgot to invite most of its professed beneficiaries? What, if we discovered, for example, in the victims "movement" that victims were, politically, all dressed up but had no place to go? What kind of movement would it be? Would it really be a movement at all? (Elias, 1993, p. 26)

The Early Point of View for Victim Assistance

At issue in the beginning of society's reaction to victimization was the true role of the victim in response to wrongdoing. During the early colonial days of the United States, victims had much to say and do if they were wronged. There were no organized police and no public prosecutors to respond to crimes. Victims were often expected to respond by paying for their own private investigations, hiring sheriffs to make the arrests, and paying for prosecutors to take the cases to court; and, ultimately, they were usually the major beneficiaries of their efforts and investments. The core theme in responding to a crime was predominantly reparations to the victim. As much as three times the amount stolen or lost could be returned to them by the convicted offender (Karmen, 2007).

Eventually, as a rudimentary government took shape, a formal criminal justice process emerged with professional personnel: trained police; educated lawyers to serve as defenders; prosecutors and judges; and jail keepers. Amid these advancements, a constitution was created that guarded the rights of offenders against government abuses. Because the folk traditions had always favored

---

Keywords: victim assistance, recovery, restoration, justice, treatment

the victims, special rights were not deemed necessary and thus victims were not mentioned in our newly formed Bill of Rights. With the passage of time and the further development of our legal system, the victim's importance was limited to reporting the victimization, cooperating in the investigation of the victimization, and serving as the key witness during the trial of the offender. The state took on the role of having been wronged as had occurred as far back as the eleventh century after the Normans invaded Britain and King Henry I defined crimes as offenses against the "king's peace." Thus, our new nation adopted the legal traditions of retributive justice from England, and that was the foundation of our early response to criminal wrongdoings (Pollock, 1899). The state here in our country, as in England, became the offended party, and consequently the collected fines went not to the victim but rather to the state as reimbursement for the cost of administering justice throughout the land. The conflict between the victim and the offender became a formal state issue to be managed by an impersonal process of police, prosecutors, defense attorneys, judges, and corrections officials. The central theme of this new criminal justice process was no longer reparations for the victim; it was punishment and rehabilitation for the offender. The victims had largely lost control of their response to their own victimization. Their needs were no longer as important as they had been before.

About 200 years later, the American roots of direct victim assistance originated in the early 1960s primarily in the sentiments and passions of the civil rights movement, the women's movement, and the law-and-order movement. The pioneering victim assistance efforts began in the early 1970s with the concerns and effort of feminists who established the first rape crisis center in the United States. It was established in Oakland, California, in 1971 and was called the Bay Area Women Against Rape. Then, in 1972, the first comprehensive program for victims of crimes, called Aid for Victims of Crime, was founded in St. Louis, Missouri. Subsequently, more programs for victims were scattered across the United States in such cities as Washington, DC, Tucson, Arizona, and Ft. Lauderdale, Florida, followed by more pioneering efforts in other states, including Ohio, Pennsylvania, Minnesota, Oregon, New York, and Massachusetts. The primary focus of these programs was to facilitate victim cooperation with the criminal justice process and at the same time render assistance to the victims of crime. Although the programs that evolved were mostly concerned with helping victims cope with their injuries and trauma, they also helped them cope with the inconveniences, and sometimes even abuses, they might encounter in dealing with the criminal justice system. Administrative expediency often was cited as the reason victims were not treated with respect and care— "it took too much effort" and "there was not enough time."

In the mid-1970s, the National District Attorneys Association reported that many prosecutions were failing due to uncooperative victims. Programs that evolved from the distress of district attorneys were mostly created for victims and witnesses so that they would cooperate and testify against offenders. Helping to protect victims, provide them with information, and treat them with concern were offered up as the unspoken benefits for their cooperation. Victims whose offenders were not arrested were of less interest to the prosecutor-based victim/witness programs than were victims who could testify against those accused. After most trials, or if plea negotiation was used, there was not much need for victims' further participation. Often, their services were consequently terminated or, in some cases, referred to some other community agency to continue the services and help bring the victims to some level of recovery. During their involvement with the criminal justice system, often victims were tacitly encouraged to believe that "justice" was what they needed and that they could attain it by helping prosecute the offender and find him or her guilty of the crime committed against them. Thus, the main focus for most victim advocates was reflected in the concerns of the criminal justice system, namely investigating the criminal act and prosecuting the offender. In the early days of victim services (especially within the prosecutor-based victim/witness programs), the major efforts were aimed at facilitating victim cooperation with the prosecution, by explaining to the victims that their responsibility was mainly to assist in bringing their offender to justice. The objective was to provide them with information about how they could better cooperate. If they were having emotional problems, they might have been helped to receive services in the community from other agencies and given information that would prevent them from being revictimized. Concern for the offender's well-being was also an issue for some victims, especially if the offender had been in some type of relationship with the victim. Later, with more sophisticated forms of victim treatment, and especially in cases where the offenders and their victims had continuing relationships, it became obvious that a large part of the victim's recovery was linked to resolving the ongoing conflict between them. Ironically, most victim advocates were focused on defending the victims and finding ways to make their immediate situation less stressful. The long-term, larger picture of the continuing conflicted relationship between the victim and the offender was rarely discussed in victim assistance programs. Consequently, the emphasis was primarily on the needs of the criminal justice system rather than on the needs of the victim. It may seem surprising, but this had been the accepted way that victims were treated. It was and, for the most part, still is today the way of helping victims in the legal process in the United States and other Western countries.

The Early Point of View of Restorative Justice

Mostly with the use of simple forms of restitution and compensation, variants of early restorative justice practices have been found in the ancient worlds of Israel, Sumer, Babylon, and Rome, and among the aboriginal people of North America and Oceania. In the twentieth century, largely in response to the crime wave of the 1960s and 1970s, and in search of alternatives to traditional methods of dealing with the crimes of that era, experimental programs using restorative justice principles began to emerge in the early 1970s in Canada, the United States, England, Australia, and New Zealand. In Kitchener, Ontario, the first known restorative case involving two teenagers on a vandalism rampage in 1974 was responded to by a volunteer probation officer from the Mennonite Central Committee, Mark Yantzi. This initiative was then developed into the first Canadian Victim Offender Reconciliation Program (VORP) in 1976. A few years later, across the border in Elkhart, Indiana, the first US VORP was established in 1978 (Braithwaite, 1999; Ruth-Heffelbower, 2007). Since then, the popularity of restorative justice has grown significantly, and today in the United States, the majority of states' statutes contain variants of restorative justice principles. It is also being formally used in such countries as New Zealand, Australia, Canada, Colombia, and South Africa and in twenty-five European countries: Albania, Austria, Belgium, Bulgaria, Czech Republic, Denmark, England and Wales, Finland, France, Germany, Hungary, Iceland, Ireland, Italy, Luxembourg, Moldova, Netherlands, Norway, Poland, Portugal, Scotland, Slovenia, Spain, Sweden, and Ukraine (Miers and Willemsens, 2004).

Today, restorative justice is enjoying unparalleled popularity. There are more books written about it than ever before, and it is being taught and researched in many nations across the globe. Its main purported application has been aimed at the needs and roles of the principal stakeholders: victims, offenders, and the community. Its basic principle is "Crime is a violation of people and of interpersonal relationships. Violations create obligations. The central obligation is to put right the wrongs" (Zehr, 2002, p. 9). Although the principles of restorative justice profess that it is for both offenders and victims, the reality is that the majority of programs are predominantly being used for offender rehabilitation. For the most part, victims are still being neglected by most practitioners in the countries where restorative justice is used. In fact, recent authors in this field have noted that the restricted participation of victims is the most often mentioned criticism found in these restorative justice programs (Becroft, 2006, p. 2284; Green 2007, p. 171; Tkachuk, 2002, p. 8; Wright, 2006, p. 7). As with many victim assistance programs, the host agencies for these restorative justice programs exert a strong influence over their clients; consequently, it is the offender who receives the primary attention. Perhaps the reason for such an unbalanced situation is that most restorative justice programs are located within traditional criminal justice settings and within a predominantly retributive culture. This absence of an egalitarian balance between offender and victim is also seen within the three intellectual traditions that serve as the main roots of restorative justice—civilization, communitarian, and moral-discourse—most of which serve offenders (Dignan, 2005). Compared to the richness of theory and research about offenders, an equal assessment of the victim's status within restorative justice theory and research is lacking (Braithwaithe, 2002).

Between the criminal justice system and victim services, there is a strained partnership. This exists partly because they have different objectives and partly because they serve different masters: The criminal justice system serves the "punishment master," whereas the victim services system serves the "welfare master." Other differences include conceptual differences: retribution versus reconciliation, stereotypes versus behaviors, victim blaming versus victim defending, to mention a few.

Natural Disconnects Between Victim Services and Restorative Justice

In an ideal setting, victim services and restorative justice both should want recovery and restoration for crime victims. One obstacle blocking this objective would be, as mentioned, the opposing goals of the host agencies for both victim services and restorative justice programs. If either or both are embedded within the traditional retributive criminal justice setting, then the organizational objectives and politics influence the activities of these services away from victim recovery.

Yet another disconnect is that recovery and restoration are not the same. On the one hand, recovery is primarily a psychosocial concept that relates to an end-state for victims once they have regained a degree of mental health and functionality in their life after a traumatic event. This means having achieved relative freedom from the emotional symptoms to allow victims to integrate their victimization experience into the realities of the present, coupled with the ability to reenter a life of normal functioning. On the other hand, *restoration,* as used in the concept of restorative justice, is an end-state such that a victim, the offender, and the community are healed and things are put as "right as possible" to a satisfactory condition (Zehr, 2002, p. 37).

In this comparison, psychological and social recovery has little to do with justice, whereas with restoration, justice is a core component and the main objective of the term *restorative justice.* Consequently, restoration is mostly about justice, albeit a different type of justice—restorative justice and not retributive justice. The question that begs asking is, can a person who is not psychosocially recovered be restored? It would seem the answer is yes. However, if a victim achieves recovery without justice, then it would seem that she or he cannot be completely restored. But one could argue that a restored person could recover more easily and quickly because the psychosocial conditions, when things are put right, would seem to enhance one's ability to cope with the stressors surrounding one's victimization.

The comparison is further complicated by the fact that with the restorative justice–type restoration there are two other stakeholders that must be taken into account—the offender and the community—whereas with recovery, the focus is principally on the victim alone. Thus, it becomes apparent that there is a significant difference in the ultimate goal of these two activities. With victim services, the concern is mostly with healing the victim so that he or she recovers, regardless of whether things are put right for the offender or the community; whereas for restorative justice, victims must yield something to the other two stakeholders in order to achieve the desired three-way restoration even if it means hindering their own recovery. It would seem that there is an incompatibility of paradigms. The recovery paradigm addresses the process and the ultimate objective of becoming functional again independently from getting "justice." The restoration paradigm addresses the process and the ultimate objective of negotiating a compromise between the stakeholders such that all three are satisfied that their perceived needs (subjective satisfactions) are addressed and that legal and economic justice is achieved for all. This discussion is similar to the clash between the two classic paradigms that operate simultaneously in the criminal justice process: the behavioral and the legal. On the one hand, the behavioral paradigm is based primarily on the sciences of psychology and sociology, so its tools are variables that exist as continua and have as their paramount goal the explanation and manipulation of human behavior. On the other hand, the legal paradigm is based on written statutes of law and compliance with its mandates, so its tools are the procedures of jurisprudence with its goal being the moral judgment of behavior. Therein lies the challenge of victim assistance: to understand both the behavioral and legal paradigms and to find a way to operate within these two different orientations and ultimately bring the victim to a point of recovery and restoration.

Natural Linkages Between Victim Assistance and Restorative Justice

In an ideal program, the response to victims would greatly enhance their well-being if victim assistance and restorative justice would be joined. Both these activities increase the participation of victims in the criminal justice process and demonstrate high regard for victim respect, dignity, and equality. One of the important advantages of a partnership between victim assistance and restorative justice is the commitment to resolve the conflict between the victim and the offender, thereby facilitating recovery. In this sense, restorative justice could be a major multiplier in helping victims recover by first removing the risk of continued conflicts and allowing for healing to fully occur and ultimately by keeping victims safer from future victimizations after their recovery is completed. Anyone who has worked with victims, especially a victimization that resulted from a violent relationship, knows the difficulty in trying to help that victim overcome the effects of having been traumatized when the fear of revictimization remains present. One of the significant rules for facilitating recovery is to first find a safe and healing environment within which to practice advocacy, do counseling, and empower victims. In the face of a continuing conflict that promises to again victimize, healing is seriously hindered and recovery is unlikely to result. Thus, in a very real sense, deconflicting the victim-offender relationship is an essential ingredient before attempting any long-lasting healing for victim recovery. Obviously, it is critical for victim advocates who contemplate using restorative justice principles to ensure that the process for helping victims is not circumvented by restorative justice advocates who would continue the traditional momentum in favor of offenders' rehabilitation. The ideology of equality somehow must be turned into practice rather than adhering to the historical bias that still neglects the victim in most cases (NAVSS, 1984).

Restorative Justice Principles with Victim Assistance

Three examples where restorative justice concepts are working within a victim service model are the classic Victim Offender Reconciliation Program, the pure Victim Offender Mediation Program, and the Humanistic Mediation Model. Of the three, the classic VORP model was the first model and uses a relationship-driven social work approach known as case development. The VORP model involves extensive preparatory work before the victim/offender meeting. Also, this model requires at least one meeting between the mediator and the victim and one meeting between the mediator and the offender. It is usually a lengthy and time-consuming process for the victim, offender mediators, and program staff (Price, 1995). The second model, called the "pure mediation" approach, which is, according to Mark Umbreit, "settlement-driven," omits "case development" and usually does not have any contact between the mediators and the victims and the offenders before the first meeting. This model is considered to be more efficient with small claims cases and with negotiating restitution contracts between victims and offenders than the classic VORP model, but less successful at achieving the healing effects. There are two problems with this model: first, a smaller percentage of victims and offenders show up for the mediations (about 50 percent) and, second, those who do show up leave more angry and disappointed than with the classic VORP model. The third model, created by Umbreit, is called the Humanistic Mediation Model. This model emphasizes empowering both the victim and the offender, talking about how the conflict affected each person, helping each other to arrive at an appropriate solution, and promoting understanding based on compassion, strength, and common humanity (Umbreit, 1995, 2007). This "higher plane" form of mediation calls for special training for the mediators (Price, 1995). It seems that with each of these evolutions of the original VORP concept, the victim is given a better chance to recover. Political or administrative expediency is less important, and the humanity of the victim and the offender is enhanced.

Because of the importance of providing equality for all stakeholders in all restorative justice applications, we would assume that all restorative justice programs promise to offer offenders and victims healing, funds, and/or services. However, despite the use of the terms *victim* and *offender* in the rhetoric of both these programs, in practice most of the attention in most of the programs is devoted to rehabilitating the offender. In each of these three programs, restoring the victim is addressed, but disappointingly its importance is usually secondary. This glaring shortcoming with the restorative movement is best summarized by Simon Green: "If restorative justice is to take seriously its commitment to the victims of crime, it must find ways of protecting them from rhetoric and policy that has all too often been advanced in the name of the victims without actually being for the victim" (Green, 2007, p. 186).

Although victim restoration is an integral component of all restorative justice models, this cannot be claimed for all victim assistance programs, especially given that many programs do not use restorative justice principles. Moreover, because some victim service programs are mostly concerned with facilitating the prosecution of offenders, as with most victim/witness prosecutor-based programs, they usually are not focused on restoring victims. They do, however, offer a range of services that accommodate victims financially, socially, and emotionally, and they do provide a degree of satisfaction that keeps them cooperative. Whether the victims in these programs are restored or recovered as a result of their participation is another issue as yet not adequately researched. One of the compounding and contentious issues is the notion that victim satisfaction is a measure of both recovery and restoration.

The image of most victim assistance programs, regardless of who the host agency is or what other system needs are being served, is that they do offer many services that victims need, especially the reduction of suffering and the possibility of helping them recover from their psychological and emotional trauma. In an interesting empirical study in England by Kathleen Daly, it was found that 70 percent of the victims claimed that they overcame the harm done them because of the passage of time, their own resilience, and support from family and friends rather than from the restorative justice conference program in which they had participated (Daly, 2003). Of course, this suggests that restorative justice, at least in the later stages of the process, is not the solution for all victims and that there are other resources used to achieve recovery or restoration. In light of the findings of Daly and other researchers, it seems more appropriate that if we want to provide the ideal array of resources to maximize victim recovery, perhaps restorative justice principles would be a valuable addition to the traditional services now being provided by most victim assistance programs.

Taking the position of a victim advocate, it makes sense to find a model that ultimately would place the victim first in the hierarchy of stakeholders, regardless of the criminal justice system's administrative or political needs. The challenge for future efforts is to create a victim service model that is entirely focused on helping the victim to be restored and recovered. Today, because of vested organizational interests, most victim service agencies are not structured to deliver services aimed only at restoration and recovery. Tomorrow, it behooves those of us in the victim movement to foster continually newer models for enhanced victim treatment based on the most current research findings.

> The nirvana story of restorative justice helps us to imagine what is possible, but it should not be used as the benchmark for what is practical and achievable. The nirvana story assumes that people are ready and able to resolve disputes, to repair the harms, to feel contrite, and perhaps to forgive others when they may not be ready and able to do any of these things at all. It holds out the promise that these things *should happen most of the time* when research suggests that these things can occur *some of the time.* (Daly, 2003, p. 18; italics in original)

7

Restorative Options for an Offender's Spouse

Shannon Moroney

At age thirty (in 2005), my life was traumatically altered: Without warning and while I was out of town, my husband committed several violent sexual assaults on two strangers at his workplace, then kidnapped them to our home from where he later called the police. Following a lengthy court process, he was declared a dangerous offender and sentenced to an indeterminate period of incarceration, Canada's highest sentence.

This chapter details aspects of my journey from the day of my husband's offenses through to the first year following his sentencing, inviting you into three settings where restorative dialogue occurred: a prison visiting room, in my home (also a crime scene), and in a courtroom. By sharing my story, I hope to raise awareness about the often overlooked ripple effect of crime, with particular emphasis on how harm is caused to family members of an offender, and the possibility that restorative justice holds to repair damage and help people and communities heal from the effects of violence.

The Shattering

Three months after my husband Jason's arrest and incarceration, my family doctor, Sue, came to my house for an old-fashioned home visit. She knows that there are times when patients are just not well enough to go out, and on that particular day I was one of those patients. My confining symptoms were stress,

Keywords: restorative justice, dangerous offender, restorative dialogue, trauma, compassion, guilty by association, Canada, vindication, victim, offenders' families, victim recognition fear, and grief. When Sue arrived at my door, I invited her into the room at the back of the house that had been Jason's art studio. Canvases, paints, inks, and paper lay exactly as he had left them, save for any disturbance created by the police search following his arrest. As Sue took it all in, I stood next to her looking almost helplessly at the piles of supplies overwhelming the room. After a moment, she turned to me and said matter-of-factly, "I think you should do something with all this stuff."

I nodded in agreement and began mumbling about some ideas I had about donating it to charity or a school. Sue interjected, "No, I mean do something *for yourself.*"

"Oh." I replied. *For myself? What did she mean?*

Sensing my confusion, Sue quickly jumped in with a suggestion: "In two weeks, come to your next appointment with a piece of art you have created using these supplies; something which captures what you have been going through for the last three months since the crimes. Focus on your emotions: What has it all *felt* like?"

I nodded slowly in agreement, but I already felt overwhelmed. How could I ever capture the complexity of my experience in a piece of art? I considered myself a craftsperson—creative, but not an artist. Sue seemed to sense my hesitance. "You can do it, Shannon. It doesn't have to be beautiful, it just has to be real. Don't think too much, just get those feelings out. You'll feel better."

Two weeks later, I walked into her office with a large Masonite board I had spray-painted black and then covered with cutout photos, scraps of fabric, fragments of poetry and song lyrics, dried leaves, and shards of broken glass. Collage seemed an appropriate choice of media to describe the brokenness I felt. In the middle of the board I had pasted a large half-moon piece of silver polymer wrap so that it looked like a silver bowl. Inside the bowl, I placed a photo from my wedding day: all the guests standing together under the autumn leaves, smiles beaming from their faces. I'm in the front row in my wedding dress and Jason is standing behind me with his hand on my shoulder, looking proud and happy. We are surrounded by our loved ones and on the brink of a new chapter of our life together. It was October 8, 2005.

Exactly one month later, that life shattered. Early on the morning of November 8, 2005, a police officer came to the door of the hotel room in Toronto where I was staying for a professional conference. I was just finishing up a thank you card for a wedding gift and about to go downstairs for the first workshop of the day when his knock interrupted me. Opening the door and seeing the police uniform in the doorframe, my heart instantly filled with fear and dread. The officer stepped inside and I stepped back.

"Nobody has died," he said, "but I'm here about your husband, Jason—he was arrested last night, charged with sexual assault."

The words were like thunder in my ears, and I felt my body go numb while my mind began to race with questions: *What happened? What did he mean?*

Who had made these allegations? Most of all, *There must be some mistake!* A moment later, the officer told me that Jason had called the police himself, so I knew that there was no mistake. My heart fell further as my thoughts jumped to what I had known about Jason's past since his disclosure on our first date that he was on parole with a life sentence. He had committed a murder seventeen years earlier, just after his eighteenth birthday. He had served ten years in a federal prison, and I met him five years after that, early in 2003. At that time, he had been working as the coordinator and chef of a restaurant for low-income patrons for several years, and he was loved and respected by staff, clients, and volunteers alike. I had been one of those volunteers. When Jason and I began to form a romantic relationship, we were fully supported by our families and friends, as well as by corrections officials. Concern that Jason might reoffend was never raised. The focus was on the future, and with his talents, support, and loving relationships Jason had everything going for him. Now there was devastating proof that something was still wrong with him, very wrong. It was like a cancer exploding after a long period of remission, after all the experts said it was gone for good.

The officer did not know the details of the assaults because he was not from the police force in the small town where we lived, so he handed me the phone number of the sergeant and said I should call him right away. As he gave me the number on a slip of paper, he said gently, "I think you better expect that it was 'full rape.'"

My stomach flipped over, making me feel nauseous. I could only think, *What happened? What happened to you, Jason?!* Images of Jason as I had known and loved him flashed before my eyes, and nothing that was happening now made any sense. Jason was my best friend—a gentle, kind, thoughtful, and loving partner. I had never heard him raise his voice or seen him get angry. Any disagreement we had was always easily resolved. He made me laugh, and our home was always filled with art, music, good food, friends, and family. What the police officer said put me in a state of complete shock.

When I hung up the phone, I called my parents and they immediately left their home outside Toronto to come and take me to the town where Jason and I lived. I sat down in the hotel room and waited in shocked silence, the officer sitting across from me in another chair. I tried to picture the victim: *Was she someone that we knew? Was she all right?* I was not given any information about her that would enable me to picture her accurately, so instead my mind clicked to an image of someone attacking and raping me, which was terrifying. Then, as if I were watching a slideshow of violence in my mind, an image of Jason raping a nameless, faceless woman came crashing in. It was sickening.

I excused myself from the police officer for a minute, and I went into the bathroom where I noticed that I was bleeding. I will never know for sure, but I believe it was a spontaneous miscarriage caused by the shock. I remember staring at the bright red blood and feeling the most tremendous loss. I just could not comprehend how this was happening, when mere moments ago I sat in the hotel room writing thank you cards for wedding gifts and thinking that I might be pregnant.

When my parents arrived at the hotel, I burst into tears. My mother cried out, "Didn't Jason know how much we loved him?" Their faces were completely distraught. They led me out of the hotel and to the car with their arms sheltering me, but they could not protect me from what had already happened nor what was about to.

When we arrived at the police station two hours later, the graphic and disturbing details of the assaults were recounted to us in different stages. It kept getting worse and worse. There were two victims—two unsuspecting women who had been customers in the store where Jason worked. Sometime around 4 P.M., the first, a forty-six-year-old woman, entered the store. He held her at knifepoint, threatening her life. Then he dragged her into a back room where he tied her with duct tape and sodomized her violently. He took her down into the basement and then returned upstairs. He had not locked the door to the store, so when another woman came in, Jason also held her at knifepoint and threatened her, fearing that she had heard the first assaults. She was twenty-six years old. She fought him, and her hand was cut badly in the struggle. Jason overpowered her by choking her to unconsciousness. He then carried her down into the basement where he restrained her with tape and rope. When she regained consciousness moments later, Jason sexually assaulted her, too.

Following these vicious attacks, Jason rented a van and took the women to our home. By this time, night had fallen and in the darkness Jason carried the women inside our house and down to the basement in garbage bags. Their eyes were taped and so were their hands and feet, but they still tried to rehumanize him by talking to him. At some point, Jason left our house to go back to the store for a ladder and some rope as he was starting to formulate a suicide plan. When he came back, the women continued to talk with him. When Jason told them about his plan to take his own life, they showed extraordinary bravery and compassion by trying to convince him not to end things this way, even as their own lives were in his hands.

As the police told me about how the women had acted, I was overwhelmed with emotion: I was in awe of their bravery, I was grateful to them for their presence of mind, I was devastated by the violence they endured, and I also had feelings of wanting to protect them. I kept picturing them in my home and I hoped, likely in vain, that something of mine—anything—would have offered them some comfort during their terrifying ordeal. I felt utterly helpless.

I remembered speaking to Jason on the phone a little after 10 P.M. the previous night. Putting the chronology of events together with information from the police, I later realized that as I told Jason I loved him and would see him the next day, the two women were in my home, bound, bleeding, and fearing for their lives.

After our phone conversation, Jason drove to a pay phone at the bottom of our street and called the police. He told them who he was, what he had done, and he asked them to come and rescue the women from our home. Then he drove to an adjacent street to watch our house and wait for the police to arrive. After about twenty minutes, when the police had still not arrived, Jason returned to the pay phone and called them again. By this time, the police had traced his first call and put several cruisers in the area, and the officers performed what they termed a "high-risk takedown." Jason was brought to the police station, where he gave a full statement of confession and responsibility, one the lead detective said was an exact match to the statements the women gave after they were treated at the hospital.

The police laid seventeen charges against Jason that included double counts each of kidnapping, forcible confinement, assault with a weapon, sexual assault with a weapon, and several others. He was also charged with mischief after disclosing to the police that he had secretly videotaped me and others in the bathroom of our home on several occasions in the months leading up to the assaults. Later, Jason and I (through his lawyer) asked the court to elevate this charge to the sexual offense of voyeurism, because that charge entitled victims to a publication ban on their names, whereas mischief did not. I was called to identify each of the numerous victims for the Crown's list; the police had me come into the station to watch the videos, a disturbing and humiliating task. Jason himself appeared in the videos several times, his face close to the camera as he adjusted it for his twisted mission. The person I saw was a detached, robotic, and empty man—someone I had not known. I felt sick, angry, shocked, and confused. I was repulsed by the actions but could not deny simultaneous feelings of compassion for the person who had committed them. *What could be so wrong; what could have happened to someone to make him able to degrade and violate others, especially the people that loved him the most?*

As the police told us about the offenses, I switched back and forth from a state of sobbing to silent numbness. I asked where Jason was and the sergeant told us he was downstairs in a holding cell. I could only picture him as the Jason that I knew—someone who would be devastated by these acts. Did this Jason still exist? I cried in agony. I asked about the women, and the sergeant told me that they were recovering and with their families. They were described as very brave. I could only imagine what they had gone through and the state they might be in. I sat in total shock, tears rolling down my cheeks. I could not believe I was asking about two women *my husband* had *raped.* How could this be happening? The sergeant and another officer were already telling us that Jason would be a candidate for the "dangerous offender" designation,[1] which is the highest sentence we have in Canada and would mean an indeterminate period of incarceration. From my perspective at the time, it was the living death penalty. I began grieving like a young widow. I was heartbroken.

Then there were aftershocks: The crimes were reported in the newspaper and on radio and television. People began to place themselves on a spectrum, some offering love, support, and compassion, whereas others began to make accusations and judgments—not only about Jason but also about *me.* When the ground finally stopped shaking and the toll of destruction could be taken, the losses were numerous and far-reaching, leaving huge cracks and holes in relationships, dreams, and places of safety and belonging.

Just six weeks before all this happened, I had celebrated my thirtieth birthday. I remember how I felt at that time: a satisfying combination of contentedness and anticipation. I had taken the occasion of my birthday as an opportunity to reflect on my twenties. I saw a decade characterized by adventure, travel, study, and responsibility in my emerging career in community development and education. I looked ahead at the new chapter about to unfold: In just two weeks I would be getting married to the man I was in love with and considered my best friend. We already owned a little house and had worked hard on renovations for more than a year. We had a guest room that we hoped would soon become a nursery. We planned for our wedding to be a great Thanksgiving celebration that would bring everyone together, and it was. I felt as though my life was in a silver bowl—that all my experiences and the people I knew had come together to celebrate the start of a new phase ahead. I had no way of knowing that terrible and traumatic events lay just around the corner and that life as I knew it was about to come to a devastating halt.

The terrible crimes that Jason enacted turned the silver bowl of my life into a colander, shaking madly as if in an earthquake. In the aftermath of his violence, I flailed around inside that new and terrifying reality, grasping to hold on to anything while I watched people, places, memories, hopes, and dreams inexorably fall through the holes and over the sides. Eventually I fell out too, onto a broken and dangerous landscape where I crawled toward the outstretched arms of family and friends who did their best to hold and protect me.

I knew instantly that my journey to wholeness and safety was going to be long and hard, but I resolved to survive this experience, to search for meaning and peace, and to rebuild a life out of the rubble. I had always been a person with a fundamental love and appreciation for life, and that did not change. I was fortunate to be surrounded by people with the strength and love to help me sustain my resolve. None of us knew exactly how something good, just, or beautiful could ever come out of something so senseless as this, but we all believed it was possible. I knew that I would have to work hard for the possibility of such an outcome. I wanted *restoration*. I wanted my life back.

The Roots of Restorative Justice

I have been influenced by restorative justice values my whole life. When my siblings and I were children, my parents fostered relationship accountability by having us write reflections on why we misbehaved and what we could do to right our wrongs, rather than merely punishing us for our mistakes. They consistently role-modeled what it meant to be a responsible and caring community member through their own volunteer work, so in adolescence I followed their lead and took on various commitments in school and in the community. At university, I studied international development and spent a year living in a remote indigenous village in Ecuador, where community decisions and conflicts were resolved in a participatory process facilitated by a leader. My program of teacher certification was called "School, Community, and Global Connections," and it focused on participatory and experiential education methodology. When I began teaching and counseling, my assignments involved working with at-risk youth, and I found mediation and dialogue effective methods to handle conflict among students, adults, and community groups. All of these experiences contributed to developing values for open communication, truth, participation, and accountability when it came to issues surrounding conflict.

In 2004, I began to learn about restorative justice when I was given the opportunity to establish an alternative education program at a shelter for homeless youth, which was a partnership between the school board and a local shelter. The goal was to reengage students with the school system in a way that fit their unique needs. As I interviewed and registered students for my "one-room schoolhouse," I noted that about 90 percent of them were on probation or in court remand. Some had recently been released from jail. As I got to know them, it was easy to see that their lives were grounded more in relationships of power, control, and image than they were in trust, accountability, and basic human worth. I believed that many of their attitudes and offenses reflected the brokenness and powerlessness they felt in their lives. Often, it seemed that a trajectory of conflict and crime extended when it became routine to go to court instead of going to school. I understood restorative justice to be a community-based approach to dealing with harm caused by crime, and I was determined to learn more about restorative justice and bring it into my work with these young people.

I never imagined that events in my own life would soon call out for restorative justice. I would learn firsthand what it meant to be named a victim of an offense, to be additionally harmed by close exposure to violence on others, and to endure the numerous collateral consequences of crime when it is committed by a family member. My eyes would be opened to see that there is a perilous gap between victim validation and support services that must be filled, and that all victims need to be recognized so they can access help. I would experience the agony of having the reins of life taken by a criminal justice process, and facing multiple losses caused by violence and its effects. In my worst nightmares, I did not foresee becoming so acutely aware of the vast and complex ways that crime fractures the foundation of societal trust, safety, and belonging, and the need to recognize and validate all victims. When crime and violence entered my life by the actions of my own husband, shock, devastation, and grief overwhelmed me, and my safety, identity, and community status were severely harmed. As I faced judgment, stigma, alienation, and isolation from some, what emerged in me and in others was the will to find a better option than silence, alienation, and a downward spiral of victimization. What was discovered was the power that restorative justice has to reconnect people and mend relationships separated and conflicted in the aftermath of violent crime.

The Jail Visiting Room:
Victim-Offender Restorative Dialogue

At the end of the first day at the police station, my parents took me back to their house. I was not allowed to return to my own home; it was a crime scene, surrounded by yellow police tape. Officers would be combing through it for evidence over the next few days. At my parents', I cycled through feelings of grief, numbness, and then hyperactive thinking: I had so much information to process, and it was all so painful and confusing. My sense of hearing became extremely acute and even the clicking of a computer keyboard in another room made me feel nauseous. I was overwhelmed with phone calls and e-mail messages, and I began to actually feel burdened by the responsibility of letting everyone know that I was all right and of providing the details about what had really happened. Some friends had driven by our house and seen the police tape, and they became extremely worried when they could not reach Jason or me. *Had we been robbed? Had there been a death?* Then the news reports hit the radio, newspaper, and TV. There was a lot of confusion and fear and, for the most part, my distraught family and I were the only sources of information other than the media. Friends and relatives came over to visit my parents and me, and I filled them in as best I could. Part of me was still the school counselor I had been just days before, helping other people—yet now I was the one who needed help. The sudden role reversal was almost impossible to manage.

My mind created a filmstrip of all the violence, and it circled continuously in my head. I was helpless to switch it off. At night, those images formed into violent nightmares and I would wake from them gasping for air. As I realized with greater and greater depth the losses of my hopes and dreams for my life with Jason, the torture he put the victims through, the destruction he had caused to his own life, and the number of other people who were affected by his actions, I felt as though I was sinking into a deep, dark hole. As I struggled to see even a pinpoint of light, I wondered—*Is Jason also in this dark hole?* I pictured him alone in a jail cell, which was heartbreaking. I wanted to see him. I wanted to ask him what had happened. The police had told me that Jason said in his confession statement, "I never want to see my wife again." Just as I could not make sense of anything else, I could not understand why he would have said that. I felt something was wrong. I recalled the words of Sister Helen Prejean, whose work as a spiritual adviser to inmates on death row in the United States had been made into the film *Dead Man Walking.* I could hear her voice telling the man in the film as he was being strapped onto a gurney to be executed by lethal injection, "Just look at me: I want the last face you see to be a face of love." I decided that, whether or not Jason wanted to see me, I had to go to the jail and show him a face of love.

After a two-hour drive, I arrived at the jail: a huge, gray, factory-like building in the industrial area of a small town. I sat down for a few minutes in the sterile waiting area with my mother and a friend, until a receptionist called my name. I went through security. At first, it was like going through airport screening, but when I was shown into a small, steel elevator that sucked me up onto the second floor and deposited me at the entrance to a long glass tunnel-like bridge, it felt more like I had gone through a time machine. My surroundings were absolutely surreal. As I walked through the tunnel-bridge, I looked out at the small, empty prison yard below and at the barred windows of what I assumed were cells. My heart clutched. I had recently heard that one of my students was in this same jail; I thought about her as well as Jason. It was both sad and eerie to know that in fact there were close to 1,600 inmates in this institution, because from where I was it was absolutely silent and lifeless.

The long glassed-in bridge opened into a longer, empty gray hall. It sloped down slightly and led to a guard sitting at a table. I told the guard the purpose of my visit, and he made a phone call. Then he told me to continue walking straight to the first door on my right. He said I should listen for a click and then pull the door open. My heart was pounding. I had learned that Jason was being held in solitary confinement,[2] which meant that we would have a "closed" visit, sealed from each other and from other visitors and inmates; but I still did not know what to expect. The door clicked open, and I entered a tiny room with a small window. I glanced outside at the cold and gray landscape. The room was divided in half by a thick sheet of glass extending up from the waist-high steel counter. The bottom half of the divider was made of cement block. There was a small metal stool bolted to the floor in front of the counter.

I was still getting my bearings when Jason came through the door on the other side of the glass. As soon as we saw each other, we both started crying uncontrollably. I put my hands up to the glass, words of distress falling out of my mouth, "Jason, oh Jason . . ." but he could not hear me.

He pointed to a phone receiver on the wall that I had not noticed before, and he picked up the one on his side. I cried into the phone, "Jason, what happened? What happened?" and he replied sobbing, "I don't know, Shan! I don't know! I'm sorry, I'm sorry!" We stood there, each holding the phone receiver in one hand and our other hand pressed against the glass to each other's. It was hard to stop crying, but I had a million questions. The first one I asked him was the one my mother had voiced in the hotel room five days earlier. I said, "Jason, didn't you know how much I loved you? How much we all loved you?"

He replied through tears, "I'm sorry, I'm so sorry, I didn't really know." I was filled with sadness, and I felt like I was looking into the same eyes as in a picture I have of Jason when he was six years old, the school photo taken of him the year his dad died. In his eyes in that picture I always felt that I could see a profound sorrow and deep longing. These dark blue eyes were the ones I was looking into now.

"Jason," I said, "the police told me you said that you never wanted to see me again—why did you say that?" The expression on his face changed from sorrow to confusion, and after a moment he said softly, "No, Shanny—I said, 'my wife never has to see *me* again.'" That made a lot more sense to me. It felt better to make sense of even that much in the chaos of everything that had happened.

It was during this first visit that I knew, with absolute certainty, that I loved Jason as much as I had said I did in our wedding vows just a month before, even more than I would have thought I was capable of. He had acted like a monster, but he was still a human being, one filled with remorse for what he had done. I forgave him. I did not forgive his actions, but I forgave *him*. This duality—holding these feelings of love for the person and hatred for what he did— is not easy to live with. The feelings of love I still have for Jason as a human being are in conflict with the hatred and disgust I feel over his crimes. The struggle that I face, that all of us who knew Jason and still hold him in relationship face, is to integrate the Jason we knew with the Jason that perpetrated such horror and violence, and to come to terms with what we can understand and what we cannot.

The first half-hour visit with Jason went by quickly. We were still talking and crying when the phones clicked off and left us looking helplessly at one another, separated by the thick sheet of glass. We held our hands up to each other's for a couple of minutes more, and then a guard came to take him back to his cell. I felt raw and drained as I walked back up the corridor, across the bridge, and into the time-machine elevator, but I also felt relieved. My Jason was still alive, and he could and would answer for himself. Now I had to figure out who the other Jason was, how they had lived in the same body, and what had happened to cause this horrific violence.

This first visit was the beginning of what I now call our *restorative dialogue*. Meeting face-to-face, I saw that the person who harmed me was responsible, remorseful, and apologetic, and that gave me the option to forgive him and open the door to compassion and eventual healing. I needed to understand how Jason could have done what he did, and over time he was able to disclose some long-held secrets that gave at least a partial explanation (not a *justification*) that I could understand. I learned that Jason had been sexually abused by his adoptive mother and that she and her alcoholic boyfriend exposed Jason to serious sexual violence when he was a boy. In prison at eighteen, he was gang-raped. Over time, his anger and shame found an outlet in pornography, and he had developed a serious and totally secret addiction to it. Even as I felt disgusted, my heart ached for Jason, though he never asked for any sympathy or used any truths from his past to minimize or excuse his actions. I struggled to comprehend how he could have so much turmoil internally but present himself as if nothing was wrong—so loving, kind, and gentle. How could he have hidden *everything* from me?

Many nights I stayed awake reading psychiatric journals about sexual sadism, boys who murder, dissociated identity disorders, and the effects of early childhood abuse and trauma. As I searched for answers from professionals and in the literature, and even searched my own home for clues about what had gone wrong inside Jason, I was grieving like a widow, but I became afraid and uncertain about whom I could share my grief with. As I had continued to receive cards and phone calls of love and compassion, I also received messages of anger and accusation. Some said I did not care enough about the victims. One person wrote me demanding to know how *I* could have put her family in danger by bringing Jason into their home. I had to fight for my right to grieve because of the stigma that surrounds the way in which I lost my husband. Other friends and family of Jason's, also in grief, faced this kind of stigma to a degree, and some relationships came to an end. There was loss on top of loss on top of loss.

Over the nine months that Jason was in solitary confinement, I visited as much as I could. We also wrote many letters and had short conversations by phone. Jason was allowed just two half-hour visits per week and I took the majority of them, giving away about one in six to other friends or family, most of whom also entered into restorative, healing, and supportive dialogue with Jason that continues today. Often I would write down questions that I needed Jason to answer and bring them on a little piece of paper in my pocket. He answered all of my questions to the best of his ability, and I pushed him to tell the whole truth, saying to him, "Jason, I don't care how awful or disgusting your thoughts, actions, or experiences are—you can tell me. I won't judge you and I won't stop loving you, but you have to be honest with me."

There were many times when I felt angry, and because we were in dialogue I could express my rage and anger to him. There were times when I was able to offer support and understanding and, for me, being able to be compassionate made me feel strong and confident. Jason's remorse made it possible for me to offer forgiveness, and that strengthened our relationship. It was also important to me that I hold Jason accountable in a real way for what he had done. While the prison system locked him away from society in a place where he could just "shut down," I (and others) kept him connected and forced him to look at what he had done and to become aware of the consequences of his actions. Although it was impossible for him in a practical way to clean up the chaos he had left behind, at the very least he needed to know about it. He needed to understand all the ways that his actions had caused hurt and harm to so many more people than to the direct victims of his violent assaults and to himself. I was the one to tell him, and I did not shelter him from any details about what I was going through or about the price I was paying for his actions.

I could not represent or voice the experience of the victims because I did not know them, but I could ask Jason to think about how he would feel if someone had violated me like he had violated these women. I think that if he ever enters a formal restorative justice process with the victims, he will be more prepared because of the dialogue that began between us in that little visiting room at the jail.

Since that time, Jason and I have worked hard to reweave the love that we had for each other from romantic to platonic. We are no longer married, but we are friends, committed to maintaining a relationship because of the history that we share and because each of us has new dreams for the future that benefit from mutual support. We are able to put our love into supporting one another as we each face the daunting task of finding new purpose, a renewed sense of belonging, and ways of contributing to the world we live in—Jason, from inside prison, and me, in free society.

I encourage Jason to make a contribution to the outside world through his artwork, and he has completed several exquisite portraits of people who have loved and supported him through this time. He has joined the burgeoning restorative justice committee at his prison, saying that our love and friendship encourage him to face his demons and search for treatment options. He remains connected to family and friends who believe in his worth as a human being even when he does not, and this helps him stay connected. Jason has been a key editor of my writing, helping me especially during the course of my master's degree. I feel a sense of restitution in his efforts. When I began dating again, Jason encouraged me. One by one, I set new goals for myself and, as time goes on, I feel satisfaction in reaching them. Speaking out about my experience, calling for greater victim support and voice, and becoming a restorative justice facilitator for youth have all helped me transform the pain of trauma into power for advocacy. Writing a memoir of my journey is a way of reaching out to others going through relatable experiences, and the writing process also provided some personal catharsis.

I look back on the moments of desperation and grief and remember when I had wished that Jason had died. I thought then that it might be easier to imagine him living in some kind of heaven than to face the heartbreaking picture of him in a lonely and dangerous prison. I wondered if death would have been simpler. What I think of now is the dark place I might be in if I had never gone to the prison and asked Jason all my questions, or if he had not responded to them with honesty and sincerity. Participating in restorative dialogue with Jason has given me relief and respite from what could have been a stranglehold of unanswered questions and a compromised ability to forgive, understand, or come to terms with what happened. What I have instead is a profound gratefulness for life and the conviction that my only way forward from what happened was to go through it by placing one foot in front of the other the best that I could.

Healing Circle at the Crime Scene:
Restorative Dialogue Among Colleagues

Three months after Jason's crimes, I received a phone call from my colleague Barbara, who was the dance teacher at the school where I had been a guidance counselor at the time of Jason's arrest. When Barbara called, she explained that she was at home recuperating from an accident but that she had called the school to ask about my first few days back at work. It had been her understanding from school administration that I would be returning from my leave when my doctor said I was ready, and most of the staff had assumed that would be at the beginning of the second semester in February. When she called the school, she learned that I was not yet back. Concerned, she decided to phone me at home.

On the phone, I told Barbara the truth—that at a meeting held at the school board office weeks earlier, my principal and superintendent told me that I would be relocated to a different school when my doctor said I was ready to return to work. I had been invited to attend this meeting, described as a "reentry meeting," with a union representative. Well aware and sensitive to the fact that Jason's violence had affected everyone in our small community to varying degrees, I went into the meeting prepared with ideas about how my return to work could best be facilitated. As a counselor, I was one of the key caregivers in the school. I knew that if this had happened to anyone else but me, I would have organized ways to help people cope. I might have asked one of the police officers or correctional services personnel to come into the school for a staff meeting. In this safe forum, people could voice their questions, concerns, anger, disbelief, sadness, or any other thoughts and emotions they might have. I heard that my principal had accepted funding to train all the staff about restorative justice, and I saw this as a hopeful sign. I felt confident that she would see the need, as I did, to put restorative practices to work for me and all those in our school community affected by Jason's crimes.

Yet, I did not have a chance to share any of my ideas for a safe reentry to work. Any strength or preparedness I had was immediately confounded by the shocking delivery of the decision to remove me from my position. I sat at the table in disbelief, my union representative silent beside me, and tried to absorb what was happening. As I tried to collect my thoughts and mentally formulate a way to protest, I was bombarded with the issues that my employers had prepared to justify their decision. A central concern they raised had to do with a particular student who they told me was the stepson of one of the assault victims. They would not reveal the identity of the student, and as a result I suffered extreme anxiety about going out in public, especially because I lived in close proximity to the school. My principal relayed rumors and allegations that were going around the school community about me, saying that a few parents had called her to say that they did not want their children anywhere near me and that some colleagues were questioning how I could be a good counselor when I had married a man like Jason. Others were upset to learn that I was visiting him. The worst thing that she said was that I now represented something terrible, and she used this construct to ban me from entering the school without permission. I was devastated and shocked further—shunned by my professional community and the relationships I valued with students, families, and colleagues. They were severed, all because of something I had absolutely nothing to do with. I was made guilty by association.

In distress, I went to victim services at the police station to ask for help getting my job and professional reputation back, because I knew that what was happening to me was not right. I envisioned an intervention by a police representative, a victim advocate, or a corrections official. I wanted a continuation of the initial meeting at the board office, one in which I could actually voice my ideas and defend my innocence, and I needed support to bring about a vindication. However, instead of showing compassion and providing assistance, the victim services counselor said that I needed to give everyone else time and that I needed to understand the seriousness of the case, as if for one second I did not. Instead of being offered support, I was coldly dismissed. I went home, utterly overwhelmed and isolated by my worsening situation.

Soon thereafter, I was diagnosed with post-traumatic stress disorder. The trauma and losses were piling up, and without my job and the sense of purpose and belonging it gave me, I sank deeper into grief and anxiety. The harm that losing my professional position and status caused was immense, fracturing my self-concept and self-confidence and robbing me of my place of belonging. I felt voiceless, helpless, judged, and stigmatized. With all that I was facing and my health condition, the option to start a brand new job in a new school (in the same town) was unrealistic. The option I was left with was to accept an unpaid medical leave and apply for social assistance. I was not able to initiate either a restorative or litigious legal process because I was forced to focus energy and attention on supporting myself financially, facing the stress of Jason's criminal proceedings, making decisions about the legal status of my marriage, handling the strain that many of my relationships were under, and dealing with ongoing press coverage.

While I explained all this on the phone to Barbara, the dance teacher, she became upset and dismayed. She protested, "But Shannon, we all miss you! We need to see you. You didn't do anything wrong."

I told Barbara what our principal said about the rumors at school and how it upset staff to see me. Barbara said that, yes, some staff had that reaction, but that the majority were concerned, sympathetic, and compassionate. I knew this to be true because of the numerous gifts, cards, letters, and messages of support I had received from colleagues—some I knew well and others were mere acquaintances.

Barbara was very compassionate, but beyond her words, she took action. She said that people needed to see me and that it was clear I needed some kind of voice. She was adamant that human reconnection after trauma and loss is essential to healing, and she was right. At the end of our phone conversation, she asked me if she could talk to some other teachers about what had really happened. I gave her my consent and expressed my gratitude for her advocating on my behalf, because I had been silenced. Barbara promised to call back in a day or two.

When she did, she called with a plan. She told me that many people were angry to hear that I was being forced to relocate and that they wanted to see me. Barbara asked if she could take charge of organizing a healing circle—an evening of dialogue and reflection that would address our collective need to be connected during tragedy, not separated because of it. It sounded wonderful to me. At the time, neither Barbara nor I called the circle a restorative justice initiative, but now that I am more formally educated on the principles, values, and practices of restorative justice, labeling it as such seems obvious. It was a community-based approach to the harm caused by crime. It was a forum in which victims' needs could be voiced, misunderstandings cleared up, and complex emotions understood and validated rather than judged.

At first, we talked about holding the circle at Barbara's house or another venue, but my gut instinct was that it should be at my house. It had been hard for me to return home to a place where violence had occurred and where evidence had to be cleaned up. My space and privacy also felt invaded by the police search; they had gone through everything of mine, even photos. I faced some criticism about my choice to return to my house after the police search was over, but I had decided that I could not become homeless on top of everything else. There was no denying the terrifying connection to Jason's actions, but I saw my home as the place where three lives (the two victims' and his own) were ultimately saved that Jason easily could have taken. My gratefulness for these lives made it possible for me to live in my house again, even as it was veiled in stigma. I wanted this veil lifted as much as possible. When I suggested that we hold the healing circle at my house, Barbara instantly agreed that it felt right; she said we could heal the place as well as the people. We set a date for an evening a couple of weeks later.

Barbara looked after everything, from inviting staff to creating a ceremony that would establish a sense of trust and safety in the group. She was the first to arrive that evening, and we put dining room chairs in a circle in my living room to fill in the gaps between the couch and the armchair. The doorbell began to ring, and I answered it each time to find a face of compassion. Some were the faces of colleagues I could have predicted would come—people who had already been in touch with me in some way—but the arrival of others surprised me. There were colleagues I did not know that well, like the physical education teacher with whom I had had only a few interactions. The arrival of more casually known colleagues conflicted with what my principal had tried to say when I told her that I had been shown significant support. She had brushed me off at the time, saying, "Yes, well, your *friends* support you, sure." The broad spectrum of participants in the restorative circle affirmed what had been shown to me all along—that the majority of colleagues were not leveling blame on me or assaulting my character but were wanting to face what happened with empathy and compassion.

Barbara began the evening by seating everyone and setting the tone by inviting all of us to breathe deeply and acknowledge in our hearts the presence of every person. She said,

> We are all here tonight to acknowledge ourselves and each other. As we look at each other, we see ourselves. We are all aspects of the same thing, the same infinite Creator. Particularly tonight, we are all Shannon. Together, we have all loved, feared, felt sorrow, anxiety, excitement, joy, sadness, rage, blame, and compassion.
>
> I ask that we take hands and close our eyes. Bring your awareness into the present moment, into this room. Let go of all your thoughts and expectations and focus solely on your breath. In this breath, we are all connected. In your stillness, in your nothingness, imagine a gem nestled in your heart. It is a brilliant fuchsia color and it is beaming outward as well as filling you with pink light. See yourself as a source, a beacon of radiant pink light. Let the light filter through you and out to every person in this room. As your light connects in others, it shines even brighter.
>
> Now, let's all turn our gem hearts, our radiant selves toward Shannon. See that her light is perhaps somewhat diminished. There is a struggle with some strong emotions that surround her gem heart. See her joy, see her beauty, see her sadness, see her pain, see her hope. . . infuse Shannon right now in this exact moment. Nothing else exists. Recognize that we all are Shannon . . . as she becomes this magnificent, bright fuchsia source of light, energy, and love. Together now, redirect that source to Jason. See him sitting alone in his cell. See him as an aspect of creation as we all are, see him. . . . Now we send the fuchsia light to Jason. See it fill him up. As it does, he becomes fuel. His heart shines as bright as yours. Recognize yourself in him—in his truest nature, not the constructed personality that he is, or that you are. Recognize his beauty, his pain, his excitement, his suffering, his sadness, his blame, his guilt, his hope. Now we focus that fuchsia light outwards as it connects us like a web—take it out into the world so that it touches any being, especially those that are suffering in relation to Jason's actions. Infuse those individuals also. Think especially of the victims of Jason's crimes.
>
> Finally, redirect the light back to yourself. Contain it in your being like you are a vessel. Find your breath. Breathe and relax your body. Relax your mind. Breathe. Find the connected breath; the oneness of this group of friends.[3]

After the meditation, Barbara read a poem and then she passed a bowl of stones around the circle and invited each person to choose one. Each stone had a different word written on it, such as "hope," "fear," "anger," and "sadness." The words on the stones could help all those present to begin to articulate the feelings they had about what had happened. Everyone expressed their condolences to me for my losses, and I listened with an open and hungry heart. People shared their frustration and anger about what was going on at school and how upsetting and confusing it was. What an injustice to education; what a fallacy it was to everyone that our principal was concurrently expounding the virtues of restorative justice for youth, while taking part in shunning me from the community! No one knew quite what to do about it, but in our way, we were beginning a restorative process for ourselves. It was especially restorative for me. I felt safer after that. I felt validated and affirmed. I felt listened to. My home was reclaimed as a place of peace, healing, and love for me and for others.

When I told Jason about the evening and about how the circle gathered for him too, he broke down in tears. We both did. I was still floored at Barbara's brave compassion—her incredible strength at leading all of us. Later, Barbara relayed that some staff told her that they would have come to the healing circle, had it not been at my house. They could not get past the images of what they knew or imagined had happened there, and they were put off for that reason. We both had to accept their decision and respect their boundaries. We were grateful that they made the effort to say that they had wanted to come to a healing circle; that was meaningful. Several people sent greetings via those who did attend, and we were appreciative. They were there in spirit.

The healing circle that Barbara organized to address the harm caused to me by the loss of my job and its related effects on others reinforced and encouraged my belief that this type of approach—a restorative approach—would be my first choice in resolving the conflict I had with my employer when I was ready. Searching for support in my resolve was put on the backburner while I coped with immediate survival needs: applying for social assistance and pursuing counseling. I found some energy to invest in writing applications for master's degree programs and scholarships because I believed that further education would give me options for the future. A few months later, I was awarded two scholarships to study for a social work degree in England, and in my coursework and thesis I focused on restorative justice, resilience, and trauma recovery for youth. I was certain that one day my personal insight on these topics, combined with graduate-level study, would enrich and renew my career working with young people.

I left for England ten months after the crimes happened. Although the transition was highly stressful in many ways, I was afforded a sense of purpose as well as some distance and much-needed anonymity for the duration. I returned to Canada four times because of Jason's court process, but my last trip home was with my master's degree in hand. I relocated to Toronto and found a job in a children's mental health center right away, but instead of feeling excited and confident in my new position, I felt aimless and disconnected. On a daily basis, I was confronted with overwhelming feelings of self-consciousness, anxiety, insecurity, and lack of trust.

After six weeks in my new position, I took a week off to attend a training course on trauma and restorative justice at Eastern Mennonite University in Virginia, and it proved to be a life-changing experience for me. Through story-telling and listening to others, I was able to realize that my year in England was not enough to propel me past all the loss and trauma I had suffered, and that I had a lot more work to do to recover my life. I came to understand that the problems I was facing in my new job were coming from the unresolved trauma of having my position as a guidance counselor taken away from me, and from the severing of relationships with staff, students, parents, and the community. In Virginia, I met Dr. Howard Zehr, who put me in touch with a restorative justice organization in my area called Community Justice Initiatives (CJI). When I returned home, I resigned from my job to give myself the time and energy I desperately needed to move forward with the healing process. The restorative circle that Barbara held for me had helped on a collegial level, but I still needed justice at the leadership level with my former school board. I contacted CJI right away and was welcomed to come and meet with them.

At CJI, I was met with the same compassion that my colleagues in the restorative circle had offered. The facilitators, Jennifer and Judah, gave me a safe space to talk about the victimization I felt from my former employer, as well as all the other aspects of what I was going through. They had significant experience working with victims, as well as with people who offend sexually, and I truly felt I could talk about anything. We met several times over a few months, and I started to feel stronger.

We made two attempts to engage my former principal in facilitated dialogue, but both were turned down. At first, I felt angry and frustrated, and it was a daily struggle not to let these emotions deteriorate the confidence and optimism that I knew were central to my personal and professional character. Without acknowledgment of the harm caused to me, let alone an apology or an effort to right the wrong, I was able to forgive only on an abstract level and because I refused to let bitterness or resentment intoxicate me. I was challenged to move forward and restart my career in a new school board knowing that I might never experience the justice I wanted and needed from my old board. In the work that I do now writing and speaking publicly about my experience, I raise awareness about the possibilities that restorative justice can offer to mitigate the ripple effects of crime. I do not want what happened to me to happen to anyone else. However overt or covert, treating innocent people as guilty by association only exacerbates trauma and victimization, resulting in voicelessness, desperation, isolation, and hopelessness. Left unaddressed, these reactions can have devastating results over the long term that can even include violence against self and others. I believe that restorative justice can redirect the downward spiral of victimization to an upward spiral that offers hope and the ability to live to one's fullest potential in a safer society.

The Middle of the Courtroom

Twenty-seven months after the crimes, Jason pleaded guilty to all of the charges and was convicted. To arrive at this point required a Gardiner hearing[4] a few days before Christmas 2007. Because one of the victims had made some changes to her original statement, it was no longer in congruence with Jason's or the other victim's statements given at the time of the assaults. We (Jason, our family, and I) had hoped this "minitrial" could be avoided because we all disliked the idea of victims of violent crime having to recount and be cross-examined on their memories. As Jason's lawyer explained from a legal standpoint why this type of hearing had to be held, I could understand the justification. When I sat through the hearings and watched as the two women were questioned, my understanding was disrupted. To the best of my ability I put myself in the position the women were in, and it troubled me greatly to imagine going through the scrutinizing cross-examination process.

I was further upset when I saw that the cross-examination of Jason's recall put him in a position to defend himself against some specific accusations regarding aggravating factors. This resulted in his appearing detached and robotic. The analysis of the crimes became cold and clinical—the human cost and impact buried under a tangle of unfamiliar legal terminology. It was all painfully frustrating for us observers who knew Jason to be aware, responsible, and remorseful. I felt angry with Jason, and I also felt helpless and defeated by the legal system. At this point, it seemed that all the time and effort that Jason's supporters and I had dedicated to our restorative dialogue with him for more than two years would not emerge. That we had been helping him to be more than just responsible for the laws he had broken, but also accountable to the people that he had hurt, would still not be known. *Would it ever?*

As described previously, I had worked hard to make Jason aware of the harm he had done to me and to others around me since our first visit in the jail. I had also asked him to imagine what the women and the people around them were going through. Although from his prison cell he could not make any practical restitution, I believed he could—and should—face all the consequences on an emotional level. For me to continue a relationship with him, I had to know that he was facing them. In turn, I wanted others to know that I made these demands of him; that my love and support for him was neither naive nor blind but required accountability. I wanted my integrity to be known and to stand up against the false allegations that had been made against my character. I could not actively support someone who was not responsible or who did not have the courage to regain the human empathy and respect he had proven able to break when he assaulted these women. It was also the way in which I hoped I could help the women: by not allowing the person who hurt them to deny, minimize, or dissociate from the results of the violence he enacted on them.

In court during the Gardiner hearing, there was no chance for anyone to express the impact that Jason's crimes had had over the previous two years, nor for Jason to acknowledge that he had any understanding of this impact. I learned that such expression would only take place during sentencing hearings when personal statements could be made by each. If everything that legal and law enforcement professionals had told us was true about the sentencing process involving an application for the dangerous offender designation, then such a time was still two to four years away. It was harrowing to imagine this continued stress, limbo, and voicelessness.

From an early point, Jason had expressed to me and other friends and family that he did not want to contest the Crown's application for a dangerous offender designation.[5] He felt that if he did so, he would be perceived to be minimizing what he had done by trying to get a lesser sentence. He did not want to lengthen the limbo period that so many were already enduring. Furthermore, there was little reason to think that the Crown would be unsuccessful in their application. Dangerous offender designations could be applied when the Crown proved (beyond a reasonable doubt) the criteria laid out in the Canadian Criminal Code.[6] The Crown had a strong case. From all vantage points, Jason's future looked grim.

At first, neither I nor anyone who loved Jason could bear the thought of his conceding the rest of his life to an unending prison term, even though we knew his chances of release before old age, if at all, were extremely slim. Statistically speaking, less than 1 percent of offenders declared "dangerous" are paroled in Canada (Public Safety Canada, 2006). Although certainly no one wanted him to be released from closed custody as long as he was still capable of violence (including Jason himself), we did not want to throw away the key to his accessing treatment that might mean he could safely return to society one day. Beyond his physical freedom, we wanted treatment for him that would (with hard work and commitment on his part) mean he could reach the root causes of his violence and find inner freedom that might bring some peace during a life of incarceration. Knowing that Jason could access therapy might also bring some relief to those of us trying to support him from the outside, too. Typically, inmates serving federal sentences in Canada are prioritized for treatment in the last third of their sentence, so this would keep Jason interminably at the bottom of the list of prisoners waiting for treatment. That notion was hard for any of us to bear.

Although suffering through the uncertainty of legal limbo was an excruciating emotional roller coaster ride lasting thirty months, it did give us some time to start to come to terms with the concept of indeterminate incarceration for Jason and to prepare ourselves to handle this sentence we saw as the "living death penalty." Jason's lawyer took time to get to know us as a family, to understand Jason's point of view on the matter, and to come to terms with the idea of allowing a client to accept the highest sentence without a fight. At my request, she managed to arrange a time for a few of us (Jason, his aunt and uncle, my mother, and me) to meet together at the prison and discuss the "best way" (i.e., what we could live with) to proceed into the sentencing process. The experience felt akin to making decisions around treatment for a terminal illness, when patients and their families scrape for dignity and grace, trying to focus on life, not loss, through the battle. Normally, prison rules do not allow an inmate to visit with family and professionals combined, but an exception was made and it offered us some comfort at a sad time. In the end, those of us closest to Jason were able to support him as he decided to accept the dangerous offender designation without a sentencing trial should the judge allow it. We sat in a circle with our arms around Jason as he signed the papers instructing his lawyer not to protest the Crown's application for him to be labeled a dangerous offender.

Several weeks after that, we went to court for the last time. Jason's sentencing took place on a sunny day in May 2008, but inside the huge historic courthouse, the atmosphere was dark, solemn, and heavy. There were thirteen members of our family and friends there that last day, sitting in the gallery rows closest to Jason. Jason tried to make eye contact with us, but it was difficult because he had to stand or sit with his back to us so he could face the judge from the prisoner's box. He was handcuffed and leg-ironed the entire time. I found the courtroom to be intimidating and polarizing; at times, it was like watching a tragic play—if only that were true.

Though there was no viable option to sit anywhere but on the opposite side of the gallery from the victims and their families, we were there not only to hear and support Jason and each other but also to hear and support them. We could only hope they might somehow comprehend that standing behind Jason did not mean we were in any denial or delusion about the harm he had caused them; we wanted healing for everyone. After two and a half years of being alienated from these two women, accused of not feeling enough for them and of feeling helpless to do anything for them, I was extremely anxious about seeing them in court. I did not want them to hate us. I did not want them to feel unsafe. I did not want them to think that I did not hate what Jason had done to them. I wanted them to know that I did not have any expectation or even hope that they would ever see Jason as I did. I fully respected their right to recover in whatever way was best for them. Our lives had become connected by unbelievable and traumatic circumstances, and I wanted the tangle of that type of connection to be shaped into something peaceful I could truly live with.

I had no idea how any healing could take place in this intimidating and adversarial courthouse, but I had to try to at least let the victims know that I cared. I also wanted the Crown attorney and the victim services counselor to hear my story, to know how it felt to be ignored, misinterpreted, and polarized. I wanted the judge to hear how I lost my job, endured assault on my character, and had to move from our community. I wanted the press to know what it felt like to be at their mercy. More than anything, I wanted a voice. I wanted to stand up for myself because I felt as though the ordeal had put me on trial, too. My hope was that someone in the court would *hear* me. Like all victims of crime, my losses needed recognition and acknowledgment. I had some faint hope that when I explained what I had endured and continued to endure, someone with power or authority would say, "This is wrong. We have to do something to turn things around."

I asked to give a victim impact statement to express what I had gone through, and the lead detective on the case, who had shown me and my family great compassion throughout the investigation, was encouraging. He said I should take the opportunity because it might be the only chance I would have to share my story and that I should feel free to take all the time I needed in court. What gave me the legal right to make a statement was the fact that I was listed as the victim of a specific offense (voyeurism), yet the victimization I experienced by this crime felt minor compared with everything else I had been through over the last two and a half years. I considered it to be nothing compared to what the two victims of the assaults had endured, but it was the only criminal act perpetrated against me that gave me official victim status and thus the chance to formally explain the harm I endured in the fallout from Jason's actions. It took more than a month for me to write my victim impact statement and then have it vetted by both the Crown and the defense. My stress level was extremely high as I prepared to present it.

I was the first to be called to the witness box. I felt nervous and small in the huge courtroom as I left the gallery area and walked through an old wooden gate up to the witness box where I took my oath and then sat down. From where I sat, the judge was to my right and slightly behind me as I faced the whole court. I could see Jason fairly well as he was the closest, but everyone in the gallery—my family and friends, the victims and their supporters, the press, and the victim services counselor—was blurry. I began to read and I tried to look up from my pages at Jason, my friends and family, and also the victims. At one point, the older of the two victims left the courtroom for several minutes. I was worried that I had upset her, because she left during the first part of my statement, which involved describing the wonderful life Jason and I shared before his crimes. I understood how that could be very hard to hear in contrast to her experience. I had anticipated this kind of reaction, or worse, so I had already asked both the Crown attorney and the detective to let the women know ahead of time that part of my statement would involve speaking about Jason as I knew him, but that it was in no way intended to undermine their experience and suffering at his hands. Rather, this part of my statement would serve to contextualize the harm that I had suffered by giving a picture of how my life had changed.

About two-thirds of the way through my statement, the judge interrupted me and announced we would be taking a recess. I was caught off-guard by this unusual declaration, wondering if I had said something I wasn't allowed to.

Confused, I stood up and the Crown attorney ushered me back toward the gallery section, telling me that another case was scheduled to be heard and a different judge was waiting for the courtroom. I would continue later. As I passed through the little wooden gate, out of the corner of my eye I saw the younger of the two victims rise from her seat, push by her family to the end of the row, and walk quickly down the steps and across the front of the gallery to where I was standing. I turned to her and she opened up her arms and embraced me. I put my arms around her and we held each other for several moments. It felt like an absolute miracle. I had wanted to hug, protect, or comfort her for so long, and now here she was reaching out to do the same for me. She began, "It makes me so angry to hear how you have been treated! I want you to know I have never thought you were responsible for any of this."

My words spilled out along with tears as I said emphatically, "I have thought about you every day for the last two and a half years! How are you? What can I do for you?" We stood there for about ten minutes comforting and validating each other until court resumed. To date, that remains the only time we have spoken, so I cannot say how she was affected but I can say what our encounter did for me. It offered a renewal of the grace, dignity, and acceptance that others had taken away with their judgments. Through one lens, it could be seen as a victim-victim restorative dialogue; through another lens, it could be called a dialogue between the victim of assault and the assaulter's wife. Beyond labels, on that day, in the middle of the courtroom, we were two women whose lives had been traumatically altered by the same violent events. We cared about each other, and we connected on points of empathy and understanding. The excruciating alienation I had felt for so long was broken through by the reaching out of arms. The vindication process I longed for began with this simple, yet extraordinary and courageous, act of compassion.

After the other case was heard, I returned to the witness stand to resume giving my statement. This time, when I looked up at the younger assault victim, she smiled and nodded at me and I felt relieved and encouraged. I had decided to show the judge the piece of art I had created two years previously—the collage with the silver bowl in the middle that depicted my losses and trauma. I knew that it was not usual court procedure for an adult to enter artwork as part of a victim impact statement, but it was important to me that I present the most accurate picture of what I had gone through, and I believed I could do that with both words and art. The judge examined my piece for several minutes, and though he was not able to provide verbal comment, he accepted it as evidence and ordered it to be entered as a numbered exhibit. It was a significant validation of my experience, though I realized that, like all impact statements, it was ultimately used toward the sentencing of the offender, not toward helping the victim.

I finished my statement and stepped down from the stand. I walked back to my family and friends and burst into tears of relief that it was over and sadness about what I had described. Jason was also crying, but he was not allowed to turn around and look at me.

Next, my mother gave her statement. She was amazing and strong. I was crying a lot as I listened to her explain how these events had affected my dad and her, as well as our broader family. She bravely denounced Jason's actions and then announced her love and support for him, saying that she will always consider him her "son-in-love."

After lunch, we resumed with the statement of the younger victim. She described not feeling safe in many circumstances. She described how hard it had been on her family. She said that many people wanted her to hate Jason but she does not, and that has been tense and difficult. She said that she feels a lot of pressure to do something extraordinary with her life or to be very accomplished because she survived a near-death experience, but what she really feels is an inability to focus or to know what her meaning is. She described the moment before she lost consciousness as Jason was choking her—she said that her heart broke. She said she just could not believe that someone would really want to hurt her. Much of what she described were the same feelings or responses I have had even though we were harmed in very different ways. She said that her overwhelming feelings were of sadness and loss of trust.

Next was the older victim's statement. She described much of her physical pain and ongoing problems that the assaults had left her with. Because of the manner in which she had been assaulted, she had to take anti-AIDS medication and be retested for sexually transmitted infections several times until clear blood tests came back. This made her sick and afraid for her health—even her life—until test results alleviated her fears. She had endured significant financial losses as she was not yet able to work full-time in her practice as a therapist, afraid in particular of being alone with male clients. She said she never felt safe, not even in her own home. She was very emotional during her statement. She did not look at Jason. I imagine that she must have been very afraid. I just kept crying.

The last statement of the day was Jason's. Initially, he had told me that he did not want to make a statement at all. He said that he did not think that he deserved to take up any more of anyone's time, but I impressed upon him that making a statement was not about his receiving anything but about his offering something to others. It was the least that he could do, and it might be the only time he would ever have contact with the two women and their families again. Whatever newspaper article came out that day or the next might be the last, and there was a chance that the reporter would this time choose to tell the community that the offender had taken responsibility and was remorseful, and that might help me. Jason worried that whatever he said, whatever kind of apology he could offer, would sound trite or clichéd. I responded by saying that it was a chance he would have to take and that only hard work, preparation, and presence in himself would enable him to show the authentic remorse and pain he felt. I told him that I had confidence in him and that I would help him prepare his statement to the best of my ability without taking it over. His statement had to be his words in his voice. He worked on it for weeks leading up to the sentencing, and his lawyer and my mother also helped him review it. What I gained from this process were feelings similar to those I had when I talked with Jason about the impact of his actions—that I was contributing to restorative justice by encouraging the offender to be accountable. I hoped that Jason's statement of remorse might bring the victims some of the comfort that it had brought me.

When Jason was called to read his statement, he stood up and tried to turn around to face us and the victims, but he was told to face the judge. As an outsider to the justice system—a regular citizen—I understood the legal theory behind the design of criminal procedures and courtrooms, but as a victim in the actual process, I was troubled by the disappearance of the harmed to the harmer and the absorption of individual identities into "the state." In Canada, criminal cases are given titles that follow the formula, *"Regina v. (name of the accused)."* It seemed absurd to think of the Queen of England against Jason when the people he had harmed were there in the room, and we had names and faces. I thought that he should have faced *us*.

When Jason began to read, he was quickly overcome with tears, and he struggled to get out his words of remorse and regret. The courtroom was silent as he read, except that several people were sobbing, including one of the police officers. The judge and all the court officials stared intently at Jason; it seemed as though perhaps they had not heard such a statement before. When Jason finished, the court went into recess. Jason was taken back to a cell, and in our rows we just sobbed and clung to each other for the first several minutes. All I could think was: *How could this all have happened?* I wanted to embrace Jason, just to hold him: I was proud of him for being authentic and responsible, but I was also so devastated. We all were. It felt like a funeral, only the person we were mourning was still alive.

The judge came back in and we composed ourselves. He reviewed the facts of the assaults, and he also made a statement about the strength of the victims. He noted the incredible compassion and humanity they showed as they tried to convince Jason not to take his own life that night, even as their own lives were in his hands. He said the case was "remarkable" in this way and in the outstanding support shown to Jason by his wife, family, and friends. He said that Jason was talented and intelligent but that he had a great capacity to fool people and to enact violence, that he lacked empathy, and that he was unpredictable. He sentenced Jason as a dangerous offender, and that was the end.

When the End Is Not the End

In the days and weeks following Jason's sentencing, I felt very depressed. The "survival adrenaline" that kept me going through so much of the turmoil seemed to have run out, and I felt drained of energy. A lot of people seemed to expect that I would feel relieved that everything was finally over, but instead I felt as though I were under a heavy fog: exhausted and empty. On that final day in court, so much pain and loss was described, not only by me but also by the victims, my mother, and Jason himself. Yet, at the end of the day it seemed like all that happened was that one person was sent to prison for the rest of his life and everyone else was just sent home. It did not feel like justice to me.

Reflecting on that day now, I often wonder how the future paths of each person in that courtroom that day would be different if the key questions of restorative justice had been raised and addressed in a continued forum: Who has been harmed? What are their needs? Whose obligation is it to fulfill those needs?[7]

I imagine if the judge could have said something like, *I hear you. The court hears you. The court laments your pain and losses. The court appreciates the responsibility taken by the offender. The next step will be to ask each person affected by these terrible crimes what he or she needs in order to recover and feel whole and safe again. We cannot undo what happened, but we can look to the future of the individuals and the community. Time will be taken and facilitators provided for this dialogue. Resource people from the community may be called upon to assist the process, as well as representatives from the various systems involved. Together, it will be decided how the needs can best be met and by whom. We will begin with the victims, their families, and Jason's family. We will invite people from the community who also feel scared, angry, or unsafe. We will include Jason because he has a responsibility to try to repair the damage he has caused, and he will need help in doing so. We will turn to our partners in the Correctional Service to help Jason by creating a meaningful plan for his rehabilitation that includes involvement from his supporters if they so choose.*

Although I have not yet figured out exactly how this could have taken place (or might still), what I am certain of is that the desire for this reconnecting and rebuilding type of justice existed throughout the two-and-a-half-year court process, and it still exists. My certainty arises from the evidence presented to me by individuals and groups who recognized the need to repair relationship conflict that arose in the aftermath of Jason's crimes. This assuredness also comes from places inside me: those that are still broken or fractured by what happened and that long for healing and redemption, and those that have been repaired through dialogue, understanding, acceptance, and forgiveness. The idea of starting in a courtroom is just that: one idea of many possibilities. It came to me because I saw that over two and a half years, the courtroom was the only place where all the stakeholders were brought together.

Conclusion: Living Restorative Justice

I had many material needs in the aftermath of Jason's crimes, but my greatest need was—and is—to have trust, safety, and acceptance and belonging restored to my life. Every relationship that I held at the time was affected by his actions. Many family ties and friendships strengthened significantly as individuals rose to answer the call for deep and lasting compassion; some broke apart completely, while others fractured and needed to be examined for the possibility of repair. These negotiations put significant demand on my energy reserves and were a daily battle against fear, anxiety, and isolation. The confident relationship I normally had with myself was also affected as I was forced into circumstances and emotions that were completely unfamiliar to me. I had to act as my own best friend, yet sometimes my grief, stress, anxiety, and anger made self-love and compassion difficult to sustain.

Consistently choosing healthy coping mechanisms such as exercise, writing, and spiritual practice over substance abuse, violence, or reclusiveness was not easy. For months, I searched for support from organizations and professionals that I thought might have some experience working with people in circumstances similar to mine, but the results were discouraging. I remember thinking that with roughly 14,000 people serving federal sentences in Canada, there must be others "out there" who were going through something similar to what I was experiencing. Where were they? What were their stories? Had they found any help?

I began to think that one day I would have to do something to raise awareness about what families of offenders go through so that help could be made more available to us. This process is now unfolding as I have begun to speak out about my experience, and especially as I am able to advocate for restorative justice. I explain to audiences that although it took more than two years to find an agency that could assist me in seeking formal and facilitated restorative justice, it was only a few days before the restorative principles of dialogue, reconnection, understanding, and compassion emerged in and around me. These laid out a foundation for continued renewal to unfold along my journey. I share what I discovered: that restorative justice is not a prescribed process but a way of living.

I did not get a choice about what happened to me, but I did have a choice about how I responded to it, and that choice involved making a commitment to allow this experience to shape my life but not to control it. I have to make that choice each and every day in how I care for myself and in how I interact with others. Early on, I recognized the powerful potential for my hurt and anger to eat away at me and make me someone who could actually hurt others. I knew I did not want this result, and so I maintain an intrapersonal restorative dialogue, asking myself questions: What do I need to do today that will nurture me? What can I do to address my wounds so that I do not run the risk of wounding others? What opportunities for celebration, joy, and contentedness can I find and embrace, and whom can I share them with? Is there someone who needs me to reach out?

Since surviving the earthquake that Jason's crimes caused, and all the devastating aftershocks that followed, I have worked hard to put my life back together and find renewed meaning and purpose. It felt like running a marathon every day because of how exhausting and overwhelming it was to rebuild a life after so much loss: Whether with a potential friend, colleague, or employer, each new relationship I formed involved making difficult decisions around disclosing this part of my life. With no one to ask who has experience in this exact situation, I have had to figure things out as I go along in this painstaking process. It has been a struggle to protect my vulnerability while at the same time working to integrate my experience of the last few years with the person I was before and the person I am now. I allow my tears of grief to flow out when they push up from the well in my heart. At the same time, I work hard to keep this heartline open in both directions so that joy may find a way in—and it does, more and more.

I still long for vindication, especially from my former employer. Reestablishing my professional life and feelings of trust and belonging in a workplace was no easy task. In 2008, I began working in public education again as a substitute teacher for a different school board—far from the position I used to hold as a guidance counselor. The flexible schedule allowed me time to write and to travel for speaking engagements, and in the early days it was important when I needed to attend court or other meetings regarding Jason's legal process. By 2009, I had increased my responsibility and commitment to a full-time position and loved being able to work with teenagers again. My school administrators support and value my work in restorative justice and arrange release time so that I can accept invitations to present my story to various groups. Their attitude has served to rebuild my trust and confidence in educational leadership. I have built a community in the great city of Toronto and have learned to accommodate a space in my heart for the loss of the town I had to leave, visiting it occasionally with less and less anxiety. I am grateful every day for the love and support of my family and friends and the bravery of individuals who took action and reached out to address harm with integrity, imagination, mindfulness, and confidence. The experiences of restorative dialogue that I have shared in this chapter have served as nourishment along the way for me, and I believe that they have had a strengthening effect on all those who shared in the conversations.

At first glance, the actual places where these conversations took place may seem surprising: in the visiting room of a jail, at the scene of crime, and in a conventional courtroom during sentencing hearings. However, looking deeper and seeing crime fundamentally as restorative justice asks us to see it—as an assault on human relationships of trust and respect—we can understand that the places are merely backdrops. What is extraordinary are the relationships in which conflict was overcome by applying restorative principles: between victim and offender, between a victim of assault and the spouse of the assaulter, and among colleagues separated and silenced by the stigma of crime. What moves me forward with hope for sustained and expanding justice now is the solid evidence I have that many people affected by violent crime want reconnection, compassion, accountability, forgiveness, and dignity. They want to listen, to speak from the heart, and to be heard.

Such evidence is in contrast to much of what I see the media focusing on or expecting: rage, vengeance, and a call for tougher action on crime and harsher punishments for criminals. *I* am outraged by crime and I want a tougher response too, but from my point of view I see that response as involving restorative principles, values, and practices to the fullest possible extent. From what Jason tells me, it is a lot harder to actually face up to what he did, to search for answers, and to be accountable to others than it is to just "do time" in prison. On my end, I often hear the expression "time heals all wounds," but I have found that it is what I *do* with time that makes the difference. For me, growing and expanding restorative dialogue is a challenging and rewarding way to live the life I am so fortunate to have.

One of the last cutout images that I placed on that first art collage is a picture of a salmon pushing up out of the bottom of the piece where all the rubble lies—the scraps of photos, pieces of broken glass, and words such as "loss," "empty," and "suffering." For me, the symbol of the salmon is a powerful one, proof of the many miracles of life and rebirth on our planet. Every year, salmon swim a thousand kilometers upstream in search of their original birthplace, where they lay eggs for new life. It happens every year; it is a cycle we can count on. From the very beginning, I had some sense that I would have to swim upstream for a long time to create newness and rebirth, and I am both humbled and amazed by where that river has led, and the place of wholeness I find myself in once again.

Notes

I wish to acknowledge the following people for their support as I wrote this chapter: Connie Baran-Gerez, Barbara Dametto, Susan Gleeson, Brian Yealland, Paul McCarthy, John Dussich, Jeff Morgan, Michael Baird, and especially Patricia Moroney, Lisa McDonald, and Jason. Your insight, expertise, and guidance are deeply appreciated.

1. The Dangerous Offender provisions of Canada's Criminal Code are intended to protect the public from the most dangerous violent and sex predators in the country. Individuals convicted of these offenses can be designated as a dangerous offender during sentencing if it is shown that there is a significantly high risk that they will commit future violent or sex offenses. If the court finds a person to be a dangerous offender, it imposes a sentence of detention in a penitentiary for an indeterminate period. Further information is available via Public Safety Canada (www.publicsafety.gc.ca) and in Section 753 of the Criminal Code of Canada.

2. Also called "segregation" or "protective custody." It is common practice in Ontario and many places to place high-profile or violent offenders in this type of lockup to protect them from being harmed by other inmates or from harming others or themselves. The conditions normally mean that inmates are locked in single-bunk cells for twenty-three hours and forty-five minutes per day; they receive meals through a slot in the door and are permitted fifteen minutes of fresh air per day on a balcony or a small yard.

3. This excerpt has been included using the original notes prepared and presented by Barbara Dametto, with her permission.

4. When the Crown wishes to rely on disputed aggravating factors that go to the gravity of the offense, it must prove the aggravating factors beyond a reasonable doubt in a Gardiner hearing. This finds expression in the Canadian Criminal Code, s. 724(3)(*e*), which provides that "the prosecutor must establish, by proof beyond a reasonable doubt, the existence of any aggravating fact or any previous conviction by the offender." See also *Regina v. Gardiner* (1982), 68 C.C.C. (2d) 477 (S.C.C.).

5. Crown attorneys serve as the prosecutor in the Canadian legal system.

6. Section 753 of the Criminal Code of Canada states that the designation of dangerous offender may be applied when the court determines

1. That the offence for which the offender has been convicted is a serious personal injury offence . . . and the offender constitutes a threat to the life, safety or physical or mental well-being of other persons on the basis of evidence establishing

   i. a pattern of repetitive behaviour by the offender, of which the offence for which he or she has been convicted forms a part, showing a failure to restrain his or her behaviour and a likelihood of causing death or injury to other persons, or inflicting severe psychological damage on other persons, through failure in the future to restrain his or her behaviour,

   ii. a pattern of persistent aggressive behaviour by the offender, of which the offence for which he or she has been convicted forms a part, showing a substantial degree of indifference on the part of the offender respecting the reasonably foreseeable consequences to other persons of his or her behaviour, or

   iii. any behaviour by the offender, associated with the offence for which he or she has been convicted, that is of such a brutal nature as to compel the conclusion that the offender's behaviour in the future is unlikely to be inhibited by normal standards of behavioural restraint; or

2. that the offence for which the offender has been convicted is a serious personal injury offence . . . and the offender, by his or her conduct in any sexual matter including that involved in the commission of the offence for which he or she has been convicted, has shown a failure to control his or her sexual impulses and a likelihood of causing injury, pain or other evil to other persons through failure in the future to control his or her sexual impulses.

7. Howard Zehr (2002).

8

Applications in Native American Indian Tribal Communities

Julie C. Abril

Various models of restorative justice are derivatives from cultures such as the Australian Aborigines, Canadian Aboriginals, New Zealand Maoris, and various other indigenous cultures (see, e.g., Van Ness and Strong, 1997; Johnstone, 2003). Some models reference those once thought to be used by Native American Indians and those currently used by Alaskan Natives. In this chapter, I discuss how the Southern Ute Indians, whose home is located in southwestern Colorado, use both contemporary and traditional methods to restore justice after victimization and conflict in their twenty-first century tribal community.

My purpose in this chapter is to examine some of the contemporary and traditional practices used by the Southern Ute Indians (hereafter Indians) to respond to social deviance and conflict among their members and to restore a sense of justice to the community. This is important to do because relationships in the community are often strained when there does not exist a feeling of justice at the end of conflict or victimization. I also report on repercussions to tribal informal social control when nontribal methods of justice were introduced. Finally, I discuss some of the strategies offered by the tribal members to respond to social deviance; criminality, in particular elder abuse and deviant youth behavior; and social conflict (e.g., intratribal and interpersonal conflict). It is important to consider youth behavior and elder abuse, because both types of deviance may be considered harbingers of future community illness. In addition, when communities are able to survive and thrive after such victimization, much can be learned from their experience. Lessons learned may be transferred to other indigenous groups who have experienced similar victimizations as well as to those outside the pan-Indian community.

Keywords: Native American Indian, culture, identity, cultural conflict, social control, victimization

In this chapter, restorative justice is conceptualized as how the collective cultural and ethnic identity helps to guide communal responses to victimization and conflict. The collective identity helps to protect victims and take action against offenders, because the offending behavior is not part of the collective cultural and spiritual identity of the Ute people. This definition is somewhat different from standardized definitions of restorative justice found in the literature and in this text. The focus of the Ute people is not on restoring the community back to where it was before the offense but rather to fortify it against future similar problems. Reliance on the cultural and spiritual practices and values of the Ute people helps them to better prepare for the future well-being of the tribe. In the paradigm of the Utes, it is foretold that conflict and victimization would occur among the people. The Utes respond to conflict and violence not as a foretold evil but as a sign that reinforcement of their culture and spiritual identity must continue for the tribe to prosper into the future. Without a shared collective cultural and ethnic identity, it would be impossible for the Ute community to become resilient to the negative residual effects of conflict and victimization. A shared identity helps repair damages to the community and restore dignity and pride where conflict and crime once occurred, because it reinforces group belonging and social solidarity among the people.

Survey and interview data were collected during the Southern Ute Indian Community Safety Survey (SUICSS) to understand how a modern Native American Indian tribal community effectively responds to community conflict and victimization. The community, for example, offers solutions for righting harms caused by its own members. Building on traditional mechanisms of informal social control and modern tertiary agents (such as the police and the courts), the tribe may be able to overcome damage caused by various types of victimization. Elder abuse, deviant youth behavior, and conflict between tribal members are the types of behaviors the tribal community seeks to control. Social control is important to restoring justice because it impedes repetitive negative behaviors and helps return social situations to preoffense conditions while providing a lesson on what to protect against in the future. Most important, weak informal social control eats away at the community psyche and lessens the community's ability to be efficacious in the future. The Utes can serve as a good example of how reliance on their collective cultural and spiritual identity aids in building their community within a constructive framework that protects it from future offenses.

Who Are the Southern Ute Indians?

The Southern Ute Indian tribe is a federally recognized American Indian tribe that holds a "nation-to-nation" relationship with the US government. Because the Southern Ute tribe is considered by the federal government to be a semisovereign nation, similar to other nations, this tribe has the authority to develop and use laws and punishments that are often similar to yet different from those of other nations in an effort to respond to lower-level crimes and conflicts. Moreover, the tribe is keenly interested in and makes great strides to restore justice to the victims after crime, social deviance, and interpersonal conflicts so that social cohesion among the members is not further compromised. Such justice is important for this tribal community so that it may continue to prosper beyond the twenty-first century. Prior to contact with European Americans, there did not exist a "Southern Ute Indian Tribe"; there were only Ute people who spoke seven different dialects of the Ute language. Because designation as the "Southern" Ute is a relic of former federal policies to control and assimilate the Indians, I refer here to these Indians as Ute people or Utes, in an effort to help restore their former collective identity. This practice may be viewed as helping to restore an identity viciously disregarded and to respond to this historic communal injustice.

Methodology

Data for this report came from 312 completed surveys from Indians and eighty-five personal interviews with Utes.[1] The Tribal Code (book of laws) was used to determine tribally approved punishments and their perceived value to the community; as Durkheim (1933) suggested, codified laws would be a reflection of those values held most dear to a society. Unique culture-specific aspects of the Ute community were uncovered regarding how the tribe attempts to restore justice in their own community (Abril, 2005).

Cultural and Other Definitions

Some other terms used in this chapter have definitions that may differ considerably from those used in mainstream society. Tribal youth, for example, are traditionally defined as anyone younger than the community elders. This differs from the mainstream definition of youth as those under the age of eighteen in that usually individuals in their mid-to-late forties are often considered by the tribal community members to be youth. That is, anyone who is not an elder is a youth.

Primary victimization involves the actual victim of a crime, or parties directly in conflict with each other. Secondary victimization involves the effects of the primary victimization on the loved ones of the victim of a crime or a conflict. Tertiary victimization involves the effects of the victimization on the entire community. For example, although one may not be the primary or secondary victim, simply knowing that the criminal event or conflict occurred in the community may have devastating effects on the entire tribe. The events of September 11, 2001, and its national and global effects are an example of tertiary victimization where all people were affected.

Primary social control occurs when people regulate their own behavior because they have been taught to do so. Secondary social control occurs when people regulate their own behavior because they fear adverse responses from others. Tertiary social control involves the use or threat of formal institutions such as the courts and the police. When these types of social control fail in the tribal community, alternative or traditional methods of social control are used. Such alternatives include the use of "Bad Medicine" or "Good Medicine," which are forms of sorcery or magic, as well as other traditional methods such as dancing and singing.

The Bear Dance, for example, was used in the Ute culture as a means for divorce, as it allowed women to choose another mate for sexual variation and other concerns without significant internal strife. When the Euro-American culture clashed with the indigenous peoples of North America, non-Indians wanted formal social control mechanisms that mimicked their own, such as codified laws, punishments, and civil legal proceedings. These mechanisms undermined traditional methods of social control. When tertiary mechanisms of social control—for example, the police—attempted to control tribal members' behaviors, they failed because they were not accepted by the indigenous community. Over time, the community has introduced strategies to rekindle older methods of justice restoration as a means to end some deviance and conflict and the subsequent tertiary victimization of the community. Because the central focus of justice restoration in the tribal community is on prevention of future violations, the offenders are held accountable for their actions.

Justice in Indian Country

Euro-American Culture and
Formal Methods of Social Control and Justice

As a result of Ex Parte Crow Dog (1883), criminal jurisdiction over major crimes was taken from tribes and delivered to the federal government. Crow Dog was an Indian who had been found guilty of murdering another tribal member. When federal officials discovered the perceived lax punishment administered to Crow Dog (he was accused of murder and required by the tribe to compensate the victim's family with blankets and other items), they approached the US Supreme Court with the matter. To solidify the federal position over tribes, Congress enacted the Indian Country Crimes Act of 1834 (18 U.S.C.A. § 1152) thus depriving tribes of jurisdiction over many criminal matters and extending the laws of the United States to Indian reservations. Following this act, the Major Crimes Act of 1885 (18 U.S.C.A. § 1153) enunciated specific crimes committed by one Indian toward another to be prosecuted by federal officials and punishments to be carried out by the same. Such crimes covered by the original version of the Major Crimes Act included murder. The Assimilative

Crimes Act of 1898 (18 U.S.C.A. § 13) made all other behaviors occurring on reservations crimes if they would be considered crimes in any other part of the United States. This had the effect of limiting tribal sovereignty and debilitating traditional tribal justice systems—a source of extreme conflict.

Failure of Tertiary Mechanisms of Social Control Instituted by Outsiders

When tertiary mechanisms of social control—for example, the police—attempt to control behavior, they often will fail if they are not accepted by the indigenous community. The tribal community engages in a negotiation of power between community members and the formal justice system. One such negotiation relates to having the police respond to spiritual matters because the tribal community demands that the police "do their job." Most Indians in this community felt the police were responsible for responding to community problems. An example of this was given by a female in the study. When asked on what matters she would call the police, she responded, "If something weird or evil is going on. I mean, Skin Walkers, they're all over the place! And they [the police] can't do anything about them!" [Question: What's a Skin Walker?] "It's a shape shifter [an Indian spirit]. Those poor little people [the spirits of the Skin Walkers] have to be like this. They can't face you in broad daylight. [When the Skin Walkers are around] I tell my daughter to go get the police. . . . [Skin Walkers are] the old Spanish people who used to be alive." This suggests that at least some tribal members believe the police should respond to cultural matters. Other subjects confirmed that they expect the police to be involved in such cultural matters. Several reported that the Southern Ute Police Department often helps with the Walk of the Warriors ceremony and other cultural events and that this is satisfactory, becauses "the police will just be there talking to tribal members," many reported. This simple action aids in solidifying social cohesion and enforces community values regarding preventive crime and conflict policies. It also illustrates how established institutions are incorporated into the restoration and prevention processes.

Rekindling Traditional Methods of Social Control and Justice

The community has introduced strategies to rekindle older methods as a means to end some deviance. Participation in cultural and spiritual ceremonies such as the Sun Dance, the Bear Dance, the Walk of the Warriors, and the sweat lodge are often used to reunite members of the tribal community who have been in conflict. This also functions as a mechanism to restore social solidarity and community cohesion, thus leading to a stronger collective cultural and ethnic identity and decreasing the opportunities for further deviance and conflict.

Modern Methods of Justice Restoration

Tribal Police

The tribal police often adjudicate conflicts between parties while the officer is working in the field. In matters of public disturbances, such as loud parties and leaving empty beer cans on neighboring yards, the police often communicate to the parties the deleterious nature of the situation. They often arrive at a somewhat agreeable solution to the conflict using legal measures such as arrests or citations, but usually giving only a warning to the offender. Sometimes this may include an apology to the victim from the offender. Apologies are considered to be one of the fastest and most effective means of restoring justice. Other conciliatory or mediation methods are also used in these field situations.

Tribal Court

In matters of crime, the court often balances the community demands for justice with the local standards. This may include requiring the offender to pay for losses or damages to property. The court also mediates family matters such as those related to child custody, estate distribution, and others. Because the Ute are a matrilineal society, these family conflicts are often resolved according to tribal custom, which suggests that all property go to the female party, as dictated through ceremonies such as the Bear Dance. However, in matters of child custody or child neglect, the best interests of the child dictate how a conflict or criminal matter (e.g., neglect) will be resolved, regardless of the gender of the parent.

The Tribal Code permits the court to use testimony from persons knowledgeable about Ute culture and traditions in settling matters where such knowledge is needed. The community prefers the court to employ traditional elements of dispute resolution, especially those that pertain to cultural affairs and conflicts. It should be noted that in cases of conflict relating to cultural affairs, the Tribal Council may involve itself. In the balance of this chapter, I describe how the victim and the community are central to the justice process. I also discuss how the first priority of the community is to protect the victim and punish the offender.

Hybrid of Contemporary and Traditional Responses to Crime and Conflict

Traditional Cultural Practices That Once Defended the Ute from Internal Strife

Traditional cultural practices once defended the Ute from internal strife. The Bear Dance, for example, was used in some Indian cultures as a means for divorce, as noted earlier. Today, the Bear Dance is more of a social event and less of a mating ritual. The tribal court now responds to requests for divorce.

The most severe punishment imposed on a tribal member would have been banishment. Death sentences have not been imposed in the history of the tribe. When I spoke to a tribal official, she told me why capital punishment was never used and why banishment was the most severe sanction. She told me that anyone could be strong enough to survive a whipping (lashing) or other type of physical punishment (except capital punishment) but that banishment involved harm to one's pride. Pride is intimately related to one's family and social standing within this warrior-based society. If one's pride had been harmed by ridicule or banishment, then the harm resulting from such could be irrevocable during that person's lifetime. Moreover, this harm can be transmitted from one generation to the next. We can see evidence of this today, as some entire families have derogatory reputations that are the result of transgressions by members who lived many generations ago.[2] Condemnation of entire families because of transgressions of generations past may or may not be restricted to these Indians, but it certainly separates the way the Ute perceive the world from the way non-Indians do.

Violent Victimization in Indian Country

Rhetoric surrounding Indian Country often includes the notion that much violence occurs within reservation communities. Domestic violence, fighting while intoxicated, and other types of combat were found to occur on the Ute reservation. Although reports of violent victimization were significant, the actual prevalence was not dissimilar to that found in non-Indian communities. As violence does occur here and is sometimes taken to extreme levels, the tribe takes steps to prevent it and restore order and give the victim a sense of justice while punishing the offender.

Tribal Responses to Violent Victimization

Victims. Victims of violence are provided the services of the crime victim services unit within the tribal police department. The services are similar to those found in non-Indian communities. Victims of crime are also encouraged to participate in cultural and spiritual activities in an effort to restore their spirit, which is likely to have been harmed by the violence. As is the case with violent victimization in other communities, substance abuse may have played a role in the event. If this is the situation, the victim is also offered substance abuse treatment to prevent further incidents. Informal counseling while engaging in cultural practices such as pottery making, basket weaving, and beading is a common form of social comfort offered to female victims. Victims of crime are also given the opportunity to participate in the legal proceedings against the offender. Other studies have shown this to have somewhat of a healing or justice effect on the psychological well-being of the victims and their families.

Offenders. Violent offenders are usually incarcerated and, depending on the severity of the offense, face trial in either the tribal court or the federal court, or both. Being that substance abuse in this community is associated with violent offending, offenders are often court-ordered to attend the drug and alcohol treatment program called Peaceful Spirits. Because it is widely believed in the tribal community that those who engage in violent behavior are more distant from the cultural values, a culturally based rehabilitative program was instituted in the tribal jail. However, other research has shown that those most involved with the Indian culture and with a strong Indian identity are often victimized more because of that (Abril, 2007). Thus, it is unclear if these culturally based rehabilitation programs are beneficial to an offender. However, the community and the offenders themselves believe them to be beneficial and, in the end, the perception that they are helpful in permanently ending the violence and conflict is what matters most.

Elder Abuse in Indian Country

Carson (1995), in his review of the literature on elder abuse in Indian Country, deduced several factors that might put elders at risk for abuse and might protect them from such. He cited a study by Wolf and Pillemar (1989, p. 18) that describes the types of abuse that elders suffer, such as physical violence, psychological abuse, material abuse, misappropriation of personal items, active neglect, and passive neglect. Sexual abuse is often cited by researchers as a form of abuse that is directed toward elders (Steinmetz, 1990). Evidence of sexual or physical abuse of elders was not found in this study. There were no other differences found in the study of this Indian group.

Carson (1995, p. 29) reported that certain risk factors exist. These include poverty, changes in kinship systems, acculturation stress, and other factors that include financial dependency, poor health, the negative effects of technology, changes in values, a lack of interest in the elderly by the young, and the fact that many young people are leading the tribe as opposed to the elders. Protective factors included efforts to teach children to respect their elders; a culture based on mutual dependence and respect; strong extended families; deep tribal cultural customs; optimism and contentment derived from a "cosmic identity" or a deep sense of spirituality; and ritualistic and religious practices. Many of these protective factors were located in this community. Finally, my studies of violations of Indian cultural values by Indians found that Indians view the disrespect of elders as a very serious matter (Abril, 2004, 2005, 2008, 2009). This value may be responsible for the limited nature of the types of abuse uncovered in Carson's study, which were predominantly financial abuse and neglect.

Tribal Responses to Elder Abuse

Victims. Victims of elder abuse are cared for with great sensitivity and concern by the tribe. Many subjects reported that it is the elders who hold the future of the tribe because they have the knowledge of the past. Therefore, the elders are expected to be treated with great deference. Using court-appointed conservatorships and placing elders in the tribally run nursing home to be cared for are among the methods employed to bring feelings of justice to victims, as well as to protect them from future harm. Also, the Council of Elders visits with the abused elders to keep them informed on tribal matters.

Offenders. Because it is widely believed and the data show that much of the financial abuse stems from the offender's substance abuse problems, additional steps in addressing the offender are used. Restitution, participation in Peaceful Spirits, jail, prison, and temporary restraining orders are often used. In extreme cases, the Tribal Council will enforce the Removal and Exclusion Act to permanently remove the offender from the reservation community—the modern form of banishment.

Tribal Youth Behavior in the Community

Community members reported that graffiti, gang wannabes (not real gang members), petty theft, loud music and parties, garbage thrown about on neighboring lawns, and young people victimizing or terrorizing each other (with loud music and "glares") are common youthful behaviors that negatively affect the tribal community. It has been reported that those who are not into the stereotypical "drinkin' and druggin'" scene are often targeted by youth for victimization (Abril, 2007). One mother reported that her son is often "picked on and bullied" in school because he chooses to wear his hair long. Males who wear their hair long have a unique attachment to their culture, and the practice has spiritual significance.

Tribal Responses to Youth Behavior

Victims. Placements in tribal foster homes and care facilities are used as a last resort to help victims of youth behavior. Tribal officials work with both the victims and the offenders to come to a conciliation regarding the original cause of the conflict. There are recognized tribal officials charged with this responsibility.

Offenders. The police department and court juvenile officers work together to end the offending behavior and to prevent future offenses. Helping to get the youth back on the "right path" is viewed as critical by the tribe and its identity. When these efforts do not work, the usual methods of the criminal justice system are employed. Also, meetings with the Council of Elders and/or the Tribal Council may be used if it is perceived to be beneficial to both the victim and the offender. Most Utes stated that they would do something to stop elder abuse if they saw it. One man reported that he used a Ute dialect (*witawac*) as a form of reproach for tribal youth he witnessed disrespecting the tribal elders. He reported, "I would ask them, who's your parents? Do you understand? I'd tell them in Ute. That means really dirty. I'd disrespect them [the youth]. Or, who are your parents? [in Ute language]." [Question: How would you say that in Ute?] "Meguit whatuwakata." "Yeah, that's what it means. I can speak real good Ute because that's how I grew up." Not only does this example illustrate that individual community members will take action to stop crime and conflict, but the larger data suggest that the entire tribal community would do the same.

Violations of Indian Cultural Values by Indians

Elder abuse and tribal youth deviance include financial fraud, neglect, and physical, emotional, and sexual abuse. Again, no sexual abuse was uncovered during this study and no specific individual victims were identified. However, there were other behaviors discovered during this study that reflect both the development of elder abuse and youth deviance and their extent within the tribal community. Offenses such as one's personal use of tribal resources when they are not available to everyone is one example. Many Utes reported that the chairman used the tribe's attorney for his DUI arrest when others are not allowed to do so. Nonparticipation in ceremonies, not knowing the Ute language and culture, not holding doors for the elders, and cursing at the elders—all these types of youth behavior are important to immediately address because the future well-being of the tribe depends on the restoration and maintenance of their core cultural values, which are pivotal to the communal collective cultural and spiritual identity of the tribe. In this regard, the entire community is the victim. In these instances, the responses to restore justice come from the community itself.

Tribal Responses to Violations of Indian Cultural Values

Victims. When the community is the victim, such as when Indian cultural values are violated, it causes conflict within the community. When the former chairman of the tribe used the tribe's legal resources for his benefit, the community used its power to remove him from office. This was done not because he had been arrested and was caught driving drunk. It was because he used something that belonged to the entire tribe. This was seen not just as unfair but as the theft of tribal resources. Data from the study indicate the theft of tribal resources is a serious matter to the members. When the community acted together to address this offensive behavior, they exerted their social solidarity and, in doing so, reinforced the values and identity of the tribe.

Offenders. Removal from office via ballot measure (voting out), enforcement of the Removal and Exclusion Act, meetings with tribal elders, cultural training in school, and language proficiency requirements are all part of an ongoing effort to restore justice to the communal psyche after violations of Ute Indian cultural values have occurred. Again, the focus is on restoring a sense of justice to the community.

Settling Conflict Between Tribal Members

Internal conflicts between tribal members (e.g., child custody, divorce, damage to personal property) are common issues addressed by the tribal court. Although the tribe is a matrilineal society, issues of marital asset distribution have changed somewhat from the past. Traditionally, all marital assets belonged to the wife. Contemporary approaches used in the tribal court mimic those used in non-Indian courts; the only exception to this are conflicts over cultural or spiritual items. These items stay with the original owner. Court judges are diligent about having the conflict amicably resolved so that the identity of the community is not fractured. Otherwise, the outcome could make the community more prone to fissures that could bring about its eventual destruction. From this perspective, it is critically important to resolve the conflict quickly.

Tribal Responses to Internal Conflict

Victims' "Good Medicine." Along with the usual court adjudication processes, traditional methods of healing are common in this Indian group. Traditional healers are called medicine people (*eiyweepee*). It is common for tribal members to use the services of medicine people for physical, psychological, and spiritual ailments. Comments from interviewees reveal that there is a belief in the power of the Spirit World to affect the lives of the living both in a positive and healing way and in a negative and harmful way. These comments are important because they show a strong attachment to spiritual beliefs, which are part of the core of this Indian group's values and identity. Shared beliefs serve to reinforce the collective identity of members of the tribe. Illustrative comments include the following:

> I've gone to Eiyweepee (he is a Medicine Man) meetings and those sort of things. He'll get together with others and he'll ask the Spirits to come and heal that person. He does some ceremonies . . . it makes you feel good.

> You wouldn't go to a Medicine Man if you had a cold. You'd go for different things. Sometimes people feel there are outside forces trying to do something to them or their family . . . like Evil Spirits. Or, people are trying to use things against them to harm them. I've seen them use a Medicine Man for that.
>
> If I'm real ill or someone in our family passes on for no reason, we go to see if somebody is trying to do this or that . . . witchcraft.
>
> [Question: Does that go on a lot, witchcraft?] Yes.

Finally, many people reported that when they do use the services of a medicine person, they usually leave the reservation and meet with others on different reservations. The use of medicine people is a distinct area of difference between Indians and non-Indians. Using medicine people has long been a common practice of this group and is a part of the cultural and spiritual practices that contribute to the collective identity of the Ute. Non-Indians may not have access to this form of healing and thus may not have incorporated it into their non-Indian identities and methods of restoring justice.

Offenders. Along with repair, replacement, or compensation for damages or theft, there are some members who turn to ancient methods to restore justice. Witchcraft, or "Bad Medicine" as it is often called by members of this group, is practiced by some Indians. These practitioners are often viewed as outsiders by the majority. When asked if the practice of witchcraft was common on this reservation, one woman replied carefully, "Yes, they use it a lot. I can't talk about it." Many people felt that witchcraft is being used to bring about ailments to people. A number of subjects reported to me that they had been stricken with maladies as a result of witchcraft being used against them. Comments by interview subjects reveal that witchcraft is a method by which one may attack another. Other subjects reported to me that they had themselves used a form of witchcraft or knew of others who had used it against them. Another subject laughed at the use of witchcraft and the label of "witch" that had been applied to her by other tribal members. These comments are important to this study because they further illustrate a shared belief system in this type of informal social control. Shared beliefs are important to reinforcing a collective identity that will prevent future conflict and violence. The following comments were common and are illustrative of the types of misery inflicted on offenders by witchcraft:

> I had a pain in my chest. I told my dad and he talked to a Medicine Man. My dad took me down there to see him. He helped me with my pain. I also had something wrong with my vehicle. I always felt there was gonna be a really bad accident with my vehicle. I think jealousy was the cause of the badness. After I went to see the Medicine Man there was a calm . . . a calm feeling after that. He was a—Medicine Man.
>
> Sometimes people feel like there are outside forces trying to do something to them or their family . . . like Evil Spirits. Or, people who are trying to use things against them to harm them. I've seen them use a Medicine Man for

that. . . . At that time in my life there was Evil Spirits and stuff, there was evil brought upon me . . . through mishaps. [Question: How would someone bring evil upon you?] If they had contact with a cloth or a string of [your] hair. It was a blessing [to see a Medicine Man] because you could see what they were doing . . . how they were getting a hold of me.

Other subjects reported that either they were witches or knew of people who are considered to be witches. One tribal elder reported to me her experiences with a former sitting Tribal Council during an election period: "The Election Board said I had 'witched the Election Board.'. . . They [the board members] started calling me and said I had 'witched' the board. . . . So, then I became a Witch to them."

This subject went on to tell me that her reputation as a local witch was documented in an international newspaper in South Korea:

I have a friend, a Korean woman, who said, "Let's go to Korea." On our way home they were passing this Korean newspaper around, and they said they knew about it, what went on with me [at home on the reservation with the Election Board]. I said I can't read Korean but one of the men could and he did. He said, "You're not a local witch anymore, you're an International witch!" [Subject laughs at the memory.]

The Indian belief in the power of witchcraft and sorcery may be different from non-Indian beliefs, yet it reinforces the Ute collective identity and social solidarity, as well as works as a means of informal social control. Whether good or bad medicine is used, it indicates that the community feels that traditional methods of justice restoration be used.

Cultural Violence and Victimization by Non-Indians

Encroachments on tribal sovereignty, such as a recent pact between the tribe and the State of Colorado to release tribal criminal history records to the state in exchange for what the general membership perceived to be minuscule returns, conflict with tribal society. Acculturation via globalization (e.g., the Internet, satellite TV, cellular phones) forces the tribe to respond. They do so with much focus on traditional social solidarity-building practices.

Tribal Responses to Cultural Violence and Victimization: External Conflict

Cultural victims. The tribe encourages members to participate in their cultural and spiritual practices. This helps reinforce social solidarity and a collective identity. Additional efforts to reinforce culture and identity in children involve special school programs for Utes only in the elementary school. Indeed, the tribe has built a school based on the Montessori philosophy that includes having the elders tell tribal stories and a requirement that children become proficient in one of the Ute dialects. As I spoke with a woman about her involvement in Ute cultural practices, she reported that she teaches a dialect, which she demonstrated for me. She said, "Yes, I teach Ute culture, the language. I'll say hello to you, '*Micu.*' '*Agadana*' means 'How are you?' These are all cultural values that I teach." When tribal members are immersed in the dialect and practices of their tribe, identity with the tribe is strengthened. Among the Ute people, a strong identity somewhat shields the group from the cultural victimization that results from external conflict.

Cultural offenders. The tribe uses its sovereignty status to fend off perceived attacks on its culture by federal laws and decisions made by the US Supreme Court and presidential proclamation. But these are not the only cultural offenses suffered by the tribe. When non-Indians come to the reservation and make comments about Indians based on stereotypes of what an Indian "should be," take items from the reservation, and exhibit other such behaviors, they are violating the Tribal Code and the community itself. People engaging in such disruptive behaviors are subject to being removed and permanently excluded from the reservation via tribal legislation.

Restoring Justice to the Community

Facing encroachments on tribal sovereignty and acculturation via globalization, Utes must rely on cultural and spiritual activities to solidify collective efficacy and on activities to restore justice to the tribe from within the tribe. For this society to become and continue to be efficacious, it must emphasize social cohesion, informal social control, social organization, and a unified identity as Ute Indians and as members of the larger pan-Indian community. This can be accomplished by banding together not just with one another but also with the larger pan-Indian society. As I have illustrated in this chapter, the concept of restorative justice in this tribal community is largely based on preventive measures and a hybrid of contemporary and traditional responses. The Ute people are not attempting to restore the community to the past (as far as that is possible) but rather to prepare it for the future. In the words of one woman, "We Utes are taught to survive; to adapt."

Discussion

Tribal communities have been able to survive this long despite repeated attacks from outside and within because they are resilient. The collective force inherent to resiliency acts as a rubber band around the community. The rubber band pulls the community back together when social forces pull it apart, as when the community is victimized. What is required for tribal community resiliency?

1. Ownership of social, human, spiritual, and cultural capital
2. Three levels of social control (primary, secondary, and tertiary)
3. A unified identity among its members (ethnic, cultural, and spiritual)
4. Social cohesion among members (e.g., shared values and perceptions of acceptable behavior)

Restoring Justice and Community Resiliency

Community resiliency is the ability of a community to prosocially respond to various levels of victimization while maintaining both its cultural identity and social structure. Rutter (1987) defines resilience as the "the observation that some individuals, in spite of adverse circumstances or stress, do not develop negative outcomes but overcome life's hazards" (as cited in Ahmed et al., 2004, p. 388). Masten and Coatworth (1998) identified three types of outcomes from resilience: positive outcomes, despite high-risk environments; competent functioning, in the face of acute or chronic life stresses; and recovery from trauma. Ahmed et al. (2004) extend these conceptions of resilience from the individual to the community level. This study of three South African communities identifies several dimensions required for community resiliency: physical security, community cohesion, community structures and leadership, social supports, access to knowledge, and community hope.

Physical security is required for members of the community to be able to move freely and participate in the life of the community. Cohesion is necessary because if the community members do not "get along," they are less likely to respond cohesively to deviance (Sampson, Raudenbush, and Earls, 1997). Community structures and leadership are critical in times of stress and turmoil. Solid social structures and good leadership are often what community members seek out in times of crisis. Social supports such as relatives and pseudo–extended family members are often what individuals who have experienced trauma seek out in an effort to return to normalcy after victimization. Community members often come together to seek social support and a return to the condition previous to the trauma. Without access to knowledge of resources and capital, communities may needlessly suffer. Finally, without hope, a community is likely to retain a victim's mentality, which could become a self-fulfilling prophesy. In this chapter, I have discussed how and why the victim and the community are central to the justice processes. Restoring justice to the victim and the community and holding the offenders responsible for their actions will aid in the preservation of this tribal group.

Conclusion

This study found that social deviance, criminal behaviors, and conflict should not be perceived as unavoidable. Affirmative actions taken by both tribal and federal authorities may be required to prevent the more extreme cases of elder abuse and youth crime. Protective factors such as communal ethnic, cultural, and spiritual identity may be able to insulate the tribal community from the negative effects of past assimilationist policies, economic disparities, and the inevitable intrusion on tribal life of an advancing technological world that has brought about the Internet, satellite TV, and other invasive technologies. Community action in both group and individual efforts may be critical in responding to and preventing the types of social deviance and conflict described earlier while controlling for technological advances in society that may have effects on future tribal life. Finally, it is important for the tribal community to define what is considered deviance and conflict so that it can respond appropriately. More important, however, is that the tribal community be free to develop its own solutions to these matters and to restore justice as soon as possible.

Notes

1. For a complete discussion of the methodologies used in this study, see Abril (2005).
2. Personal interviews, 2003.

9

Mediation: The Case of Bulgaria

Dobrinka Chankova

Restorative justice, one of the most attractive modern policies in criminal justice worldwide, is gaining more and more supporters in Bulgaria (Chankova, 1996, 2002; Chinova and Ivanova, 2005; Panev, 2008; Salkova, 2008; Trendafilova, 2001). Considered to be a new and more humane paradigm of criminal justice, it is based on the idea of promoting recovery of the victim and the offender, repairing damage, and restoring balance in society. This new approach to crime enjoys wide support among not only academics and practitioners but also society at large, because it is focused on the victim and is geared toward the future and not the past.

Restorative justice works through several different models. The most widely used is victim-offender mediation (VOM), but other successfully implemented models include family (group) conferencing, sentencing circles, and restorative conferencing. At the moment, attention in Bulgaria is focused on introducing mediation in criminal matters, although restorative practices are also being implemented in other areas such as schools. This contributes to establishing a restorative culture and climate in line with modern trends and, to some extent, in contrast to traditional repressive penal policies for dealing with crimes.

Mediation in criminal matters is an established practice in most states in Europe, in North America, and in Australia, although in most countries it is far from universally available. The results in comparative terms are positive. A number of international acts recommend introducing mediation in criminal matters in the legal order, the most important of which are the European Union

Keywords: restorative justice, victim-offender mediation, Bulgaria, policy developments, survey findings

Council's framework decision of March 15, 2001, on the standing of victims in criminal proceedings (which is binding for Bulgaria as a member state of the European Union); the Council of Europe's recommendation (No. R[99] 19) on mediation in penal matters; the Council of Europe's 2007 guidelines for a better implementation of the existing recommendation concerning penal mediation; and a series of resolutions adopted by the United Nations, of which Bulgaria is a member state.

The Bulgarian Mediation Act was adopted in 2004 (promulgated in State Gazette No. 110/2004, amended in State Gazette No. 86/2006). It introduced mediation as an alternative method for the resolution of family, civil, administrative, and other disputes between natural and/or legal persons. A much-praised achievement of the law is Article 3, Paragraph 2, which provides for mediation in criminal matters as envisaged in the Criminal Procedure Code. Bulgaria belongs to the continental system of law; hence, for mediation to be implemented, a detailed legislative regulation is necessary. Despite an explicit requirement in the law to that end, the new Criminal Procedure Code of 2005 did not provide for any cases where mediation could be applied and left this issue to subsequent amendments.

At the same time, a number of government acts adopted in the last few years reiterate the need of particular measures in this area. The updated Strategy for the Reform of the Bulgarian Judiciary (2001) prioritizes establishing a comprehensive system for alternative dispute resolution. The National Concept for Reforming the Criminal Justice System (2004) also envisages new alternative procedures, including mediation.

In 2006, the Bulgarian government adopted the National Strategy for the Support and Compensation of Crime Victims. Section 13 of the strategy's guiding principles affirms that victims may use mediation in relation to criminal proceedings. Section 2 of the immediate objectives of the strategy refers to possible legislative amendments to "ensure the possibility that victims take part in mediation in the course of criminal proceedings," which constitutes a clear government policy in this area.

The Bulgarian penal procedure law distinguishes various deviations from the established general proceedings for investigating and punishing crimes. There is a trend of gradually rejecting traditional proceedings that comes close to the position that classical criminal proceedings should be the exception rather than the rule. At the same time, the Bulgarian substantive criminal law and other modern legal systems, which are attempting to reduce the use of the criminal justice system as much as possible, provide for a series of alternative measures. At the intersection of these two trends is victim-offender mediation.

Led by such concerns, experts and nongovernmental organizations (NGOs) working in the area of mediation have undertaken numerous initiatives aimed at persuading the government and the parliament that a legislative initiative to this end is necessary. Their theoretical analyses have been backed up by several polls conducted in 2005–2007 by South-West University ("Neofit Rilski") in

Blagoevgrad and the Institute for Conflict Resolution in Sofia. The polls covered the following samples of persons: criminal justice officials such as judges, prosecutors, investigating magistrates, police investigators, and lawyers; offenders; victims of crime; and civil society at large.

The polls were conducted by written inquiries and interviews in Sofia, Blagoevgrad, Plovdiv, Varna, and Sliven and the respective court districts. Some 100 persons from each sample group, both male and female, aged nineteen to sixty-five and with educational backgrounds from secondary school to university, took part in the polls.

The survey aimed to assess the need to introduce mediation in criminal matters in Bulgaria; estimate the preparedness of offenders and victims of crime to take part in mediation in criminal matters; and provide data to serve as a starting point for new analyses and legislative proposals.

The results of the surveys were published (Chankova, 2006; Chankova and Staninska, in press; Chankova, Georgieva, and Bakalov, 2008). The more important results are summarized in the sections that follow.

General Knowledge of Victim-Offender Mediation

The majority of each sample group that took part in the survey are acquainted, at least to some extent, with VOM. In fact, all the law enforcement authorities in the survey have some knowledge of mediation. Mediation is popular among 78 percent of the offenders and among 81 percent of the crime victims in the survey (Figures 9.1 and 9.2). To a large extent, the general public is also aware of mediation in criminal matters.

Figure 9.1 Offender Awareness of Mediation

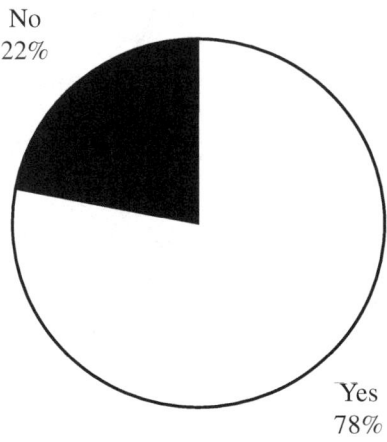

No
22%

Yes
78%

Figure 9.2 Victim Awareness of Mediation

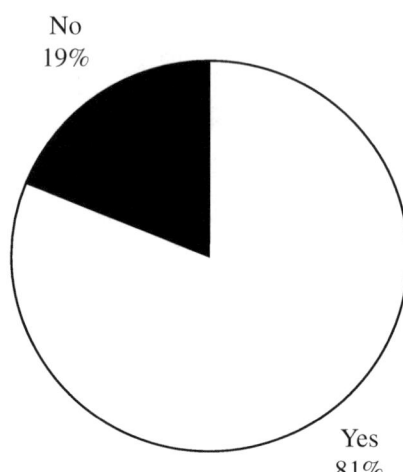

Question: *For which crimes is mediation appropriate?*

The law enforcement authorities give the following replies (Figures 9.3–9.6).

Naturally, legal professionals demonstrate a diversified approach and a good level of systematization of different crimes. Nonprofessionals seem to mix different criteria, but the data are nevertheless a good indicator.

Offenders consider crimes against property as the ones most apt for mediation; this is the case for some 55 percent of those questioned (Figure 9.7). A high percentage, 35 percent, believe that mediation is generally appropriate, regardless of the nature and seriousness of the crime. Although theory and practice in different countries come to support this view, it is not universally endorsed. Many of those surveyed exclude murder as a crime to which mediation may be applied. Some 11 percent think that mediation is adequate in relation to less serious crimes, but without specifying which ones. Let us assume that they refer to crimes punishable by up to five years imprisonment or less severe punishment. Seven percent think that mediation is an appropriate option in case of crimes against individuals, also without being specific, and 6 percent welcome mediation for negligent crimes and, especially, traffic accidents, whereas the rest could not specify any particular crimes. However, the survey indicates that offenders can be considered as interested in applying mediation to the widest possible scope of crimes.

Figure 9.3 Law Enforcement Authorities' Opinion
Concerning Appropriate Types of Crime for Mediation

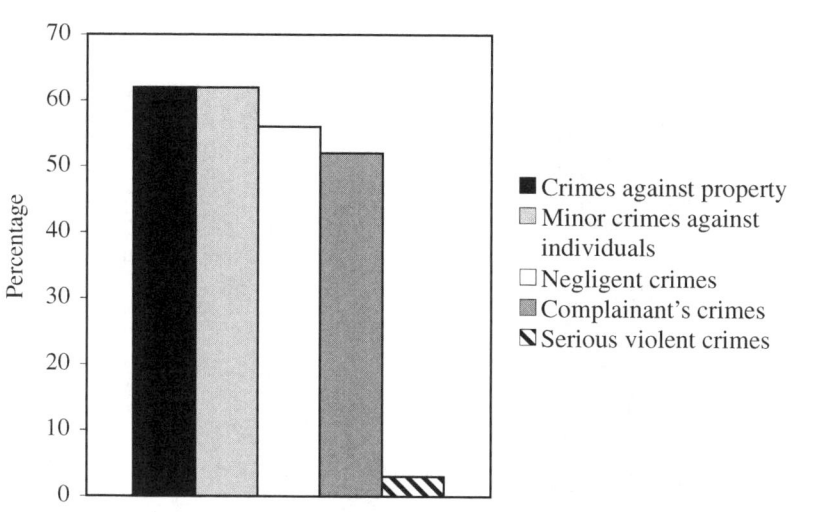

Figure 9.4 Law Enforcement Authorities' Opinion
Concerning Appropriate Offenders for Mediation

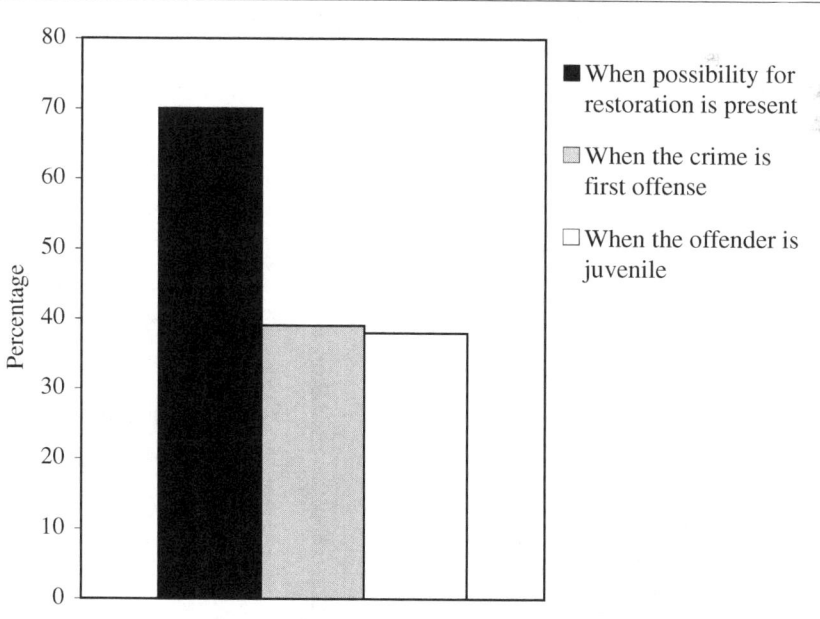

**Figure 9.5 Law Enforcement Authorities' Opinion
Concerning Appropriate Victims for Mediation**

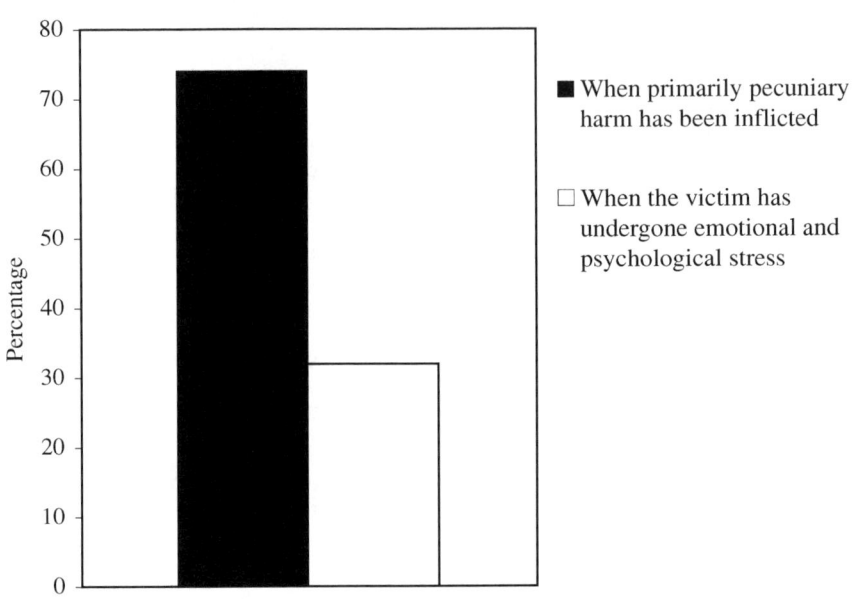

**Figure 9.6 Law Enforcement Authorities' Opinion Concerning Appropriate
Victim-Offender Relationships for Mediation**

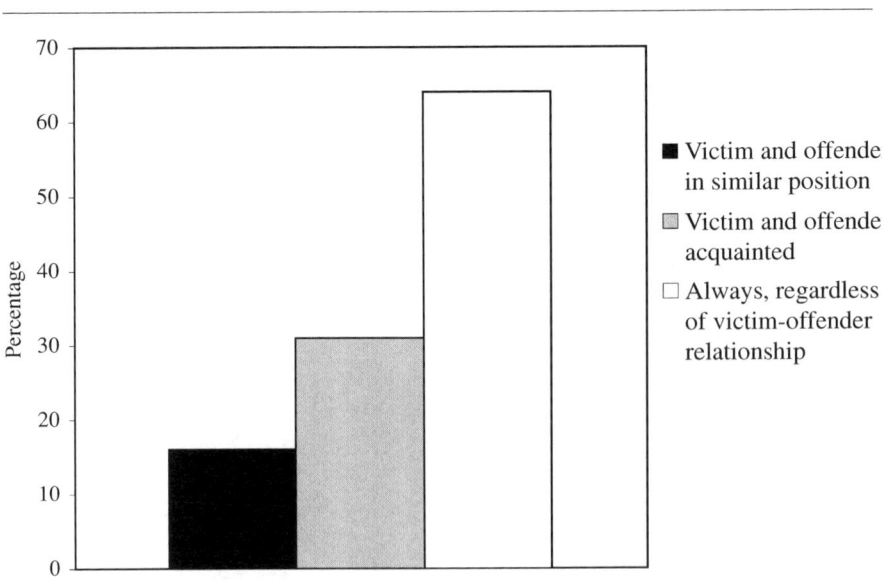

Figure 9.7 Crimes That Offenders Consider Optimal for Mediation

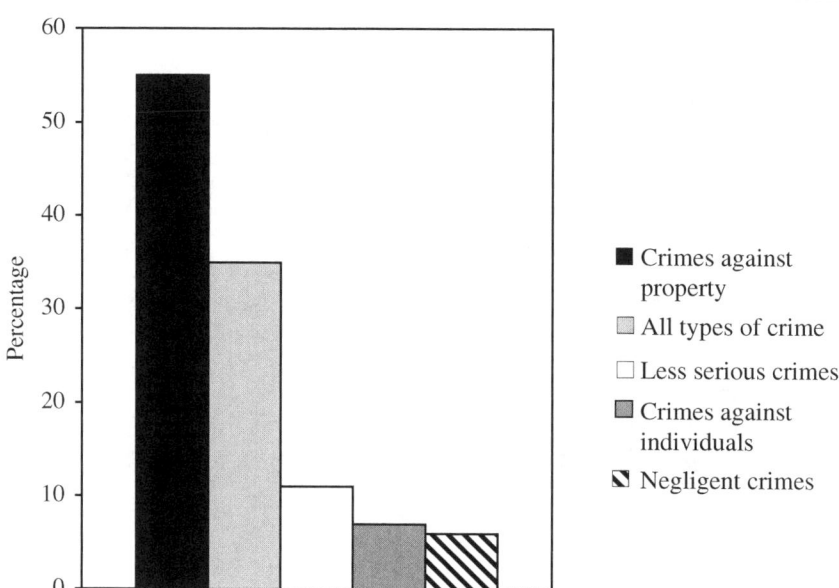

Victims of crime most often refer to crimes against property as the ones most apt for mediation; this is the case for 32 percent of the respondents (Figure 9.8).

Twenty-seven percent believe that mediation is applicable to less serious crimes against individuals. For 14 percent, the most suitable crimes for mediation are the complainant's offenses (i.e., those which are prosecuted only if the injured party makes a complaint), and for 10 percent, they are negligent crimes. For three percent, mediation can also be applied in cases of domestic violence, without specific details. Only one respondent refers to crimes committed by minors, and another one refers to almost all types of crimes. This largely reflects views found elsewhere.

Representatives of the general public in the survey also support mediation in relation to crimes against property and some less serious crimes against individuals but exclude it in relation to more serious crimes.

Question: *When do you think mediation will be introduced into the Bulgarian criminal justice system?*

Law enforcement authorities largely believe that the time for mediation has come; 57 percent of the respondents believe that Bulgarian society is ready for

Figure 9.8 Crimes That Victims Consider Optimal for Mediation

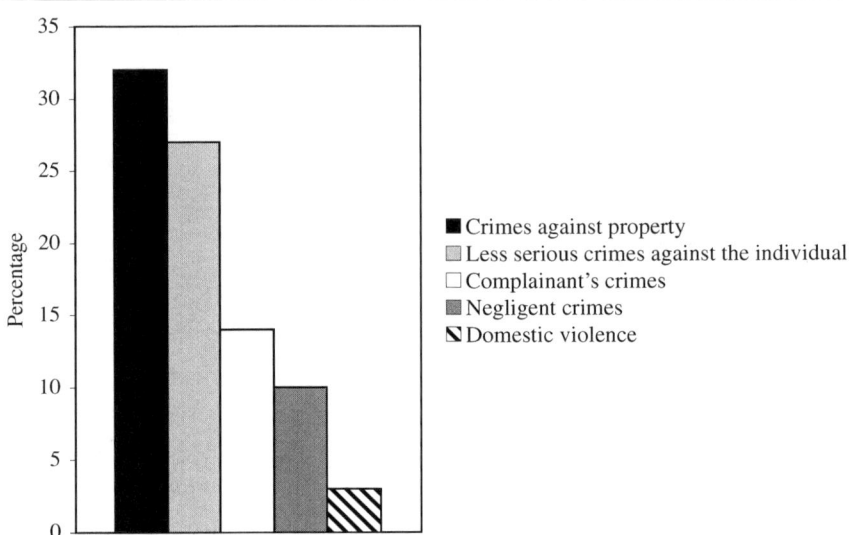

this and that mediation can be introduced immediately (Figure 9.9). To this group of optimists, one should add those 10 percent who think that mediation will be applicable within one to two years. This period is usually considered necessary for drafting and adopting the required legislation and establishing the existing European standards in Bulgaria.

At the same time, some 26 percent think that five years are needed before civil society and public opinion are mature enough to accomplish the necessary preparations, including conducting an awareness campaign, testing the procedures, adopting legislative regulation, and ensuring that the necessary human, financial, and technical resources are available. Six percent even believe that another ten years are needed.

For 54 percent of the offenders, the immediate introduction of mediation is the only alternative, whereas 6 percent believe that another couple of years are necessary for preparatory work (Figure 9.10). At the same time, 24 percent think that five more years will be needed to put the proper conditions for mediation in place. One of those asked believes that we, being a full member of the European Union, are far too late, and two respondents think we will never be ready to introduce mediation. The rest of the respondents provided no replies.

For 47 percent of the crime victims, introducing mediation immediately is appropriate, and 12 percent think that a couple of years are necessary for awareness and preparatory work (Figure 9.11). For 25 percent, the required preparatory phase is five years, and for 16 percent, it is ten years. This seems to be the more pessimistic group, although it too is supportive of mediation.

**Figure 9.9 Law Enforcement Authorities' Opinion
on the Time Frame to Implement Mediation**

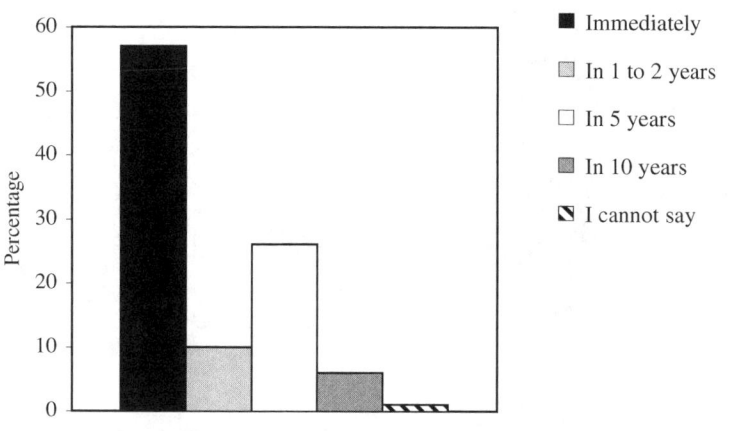

**Figure 9.10 Offenders' Opinion on the Time Frame
to Implement Mediation**

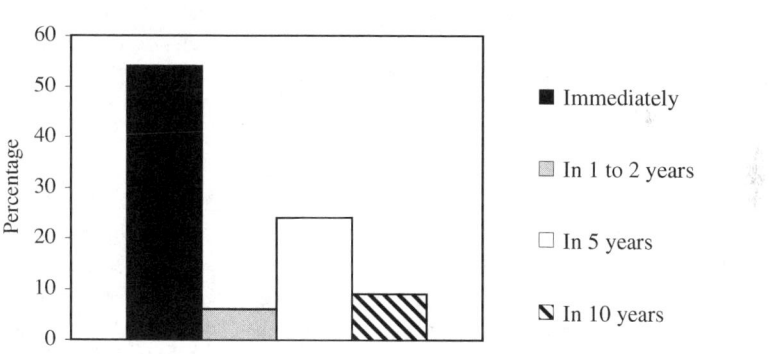

Only 14 percent of the general public are pessimists about the near future of mediation in criminal matters in Bulgaria, whereas 12 percent are moderate skeptics and 74 percent are positive about the good prospects for mediation in the country.

Integrating Restortative Justice Models

All these inquiries unambiguously demonstrate sufficient knowledge among the general public and a good level of preparedness among the law enforcement

Figure 9.11 Victims' Opinion on the Time Frame to Implement Mediation

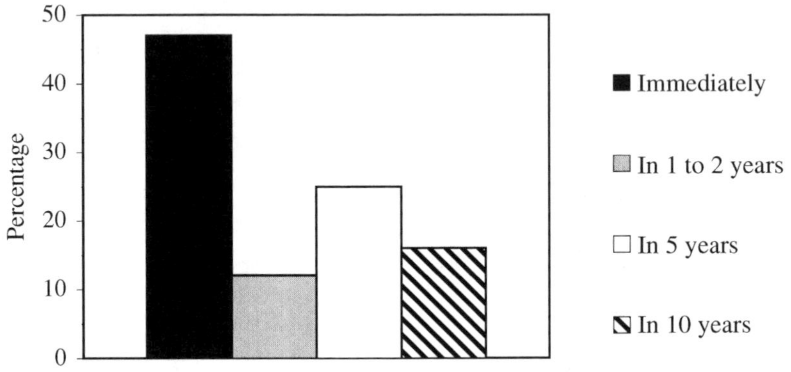

authorities in relation to mediation in criminal matters. This restorative justice model, although uncharacteristic of the continental law system and the Bulgarian general mentality, is nevertheless well known and trusted by the general public and legal professionals. The early years of establishing the idea of VOM met some resistance on the part of the lawyers' association, in particular, and that was well understandable. That body was not interested in having more and more cases diverted from traditional legal practices, as this would jeopardize its historically acknowledged monopoly on conflict resolution. This period can safely be assumed to be over, as more and more legal practitioners admit the advantages of mediation for the parties to the conflict, as well as the career advantages and advantages in more general public terms.

The awareness and readiness to experiment with new ideas that have been demonstrated gave a substantial impetus to the efforts to introduce mediation in criminal matters. The role of the National Association of Mediators (NAM), which endorsed this as a priority in the last two years, must be mentioned in this respect. A roundtable, "Perspectives for Mediation in Criminal Matters," was held in December 2007. Officials of the Ministry of Justice, judges, prosecutors, investigating magistrates, academics, and NGO experts took part. A Concept for the Legislative Regulation of Mediation in Criminal Matters was endorsed. Training in this particular type of mediation started as well. A task force of academics, representatives of the judiciary and the executive branch, NGOs, and others was formed with the NAM at the beginning of 2008 to work out drafts amending and supplementing the Criminal Procedure Code and the Criminal Code, taking into account the results of the conducted polls and available expertise, with a view to introducing mediation in criminal matters. These drafts were discussed and given wholehearted support during the Bulgarian-German conference on mediation held in May 2008, again with the involvement of representatives from the government, the judiciary, and academic circles. The decisive step of adopting those drafts and delivering on commitments already made is what remains to be done now.

It is a common belief that mediation cannot, and does not attempt to, replace traditional criminal justice but rather aims at complementing it sensibly. One cannot possibly believe that all deficiencies of justice administration will be offset by introducing mediation. However, mediation incorporated in the criminal justice system as an integral element can indeed bring better results— namely, satisfactory compensation for the victims of crime, faster procedures, a reduction in procedural formalism, and reduced use of imprisonment.

In the meantime, while the parliament and the cabinet alike are being convinced that introducing mediation in criminal matters as an instrument of restorative justice is only a matter of when, not if, a number of NGOs have started and successfully implemented the training of mediators, judges, prosecutors, and other professionals in the field. Apart from the National Association of Mediators, the Institute for Conflict Resolution in Sofia, the Union of Bulgarian Jurists, the "Help!" Foundation, and others work intensively in this area.

In September 2009, an international project, "Tools in Network: An e-net Approach to Sharing Mediation Competencies," in the framework of the European Union's "Leonardo Da Vinci" program, ended. The project was coordinated by the Juvenile Justice Department of the Italian Ministry of Justice, and the partners were Center for Research in Social Affairs (CRAS) Onlus and the Psychoanalytic Institute for Social Research—NGOs from Italy; the Christian Youth Village Foundation (CJD) in Germany; the Foundation International O'Belen in Spain; the Institute of Conflict Resolution in Sofia, Bulgaria; the Association for Probation and Mediation in Justice in the Czech Republic; and the Association "Riga City Mission" in Latvia. This project addressed the need for a further exchange of experience gained in different countries as well as elevated debate of common qualifications and competencies for penal mediators.

In March 2009, a new European experimental project on penal mediation began. It is coordinated by the French NGO Citoyens et Justice and involves the French Ministry of Justice, the Juvenile Justice Department of the Italian Ministry of Justice, the Bulgarian National Association of Mediators, and the General Direction of Justice of the Province of Rioja in Spain.

The academics, on their part, contribute likewise: special courses in alternative dispute resolution, restorative justice, and mediation in criminal matters were introduced at the New Bulgarian University and South-West University ("Neofit Rilski"), as well as at the Institute for Postgraduate Studies of the University for World and National Economy.

Before becoming an accepted part of the traditional criminal justice system, restorative approaches are already being established in other areas—for example, in schools. In the capital of Sofia, as well as in other cities throughout the country such as Plovdiv, Pazardzhik, and Rousse, a number of pilot projects, again at the nongovernmental level, were successfully implemented to experiment with restorative justice practices in the school environment; these are currently being replicated. Restorative practices are more frequently applied in prisons and in cases of disputes among members of the same neighborhood.

Let us hope that restorative justice will progress until it is a recognized institution in Bulgaria.

Note

I am most grateful to Martin Wright, a senior research fellow at the Faculty of Health and Life Sciences of De Montfort University in Leicester, UK, for his comments on the draft of this chapter.

10

Restorative Justice and the Death Penalty

Howard Zehr

"So how does restorative justice apply in death penalty cases?" Every so often someone would ask that question—the kind of puzzler, perhaps, that religious leaders used to pose to try to stump Jesus. "Of course, the death penalty and restorative justice are incompatible," I might respond, but where does one go from there? Then I was drawn into a case that brought these together in a way that I had never foreseen.

During the months leading up to the trial of Timothy McVeigh, accused of the 1995 bombing of the Alfred P. Murrah Federal Building in Oklahoma City, I received a call from the defense attorneys handling the sentencing phase of the trial. They were overwhelmed by the magnitude of the crime and the sense of isolation they felt from the larger community. Moreover, they were concerned that the trial would further victimize survivors and would deepen wounds in the community. They wanted help.

Tammy Krause, then a graduate student in our program, and I were eventually appointed by the trial judge to help these attorneys work with victims. We, along with several homicide survivors, provided training for the defense team on victim experiences and needs. In addition, we set up a neutral hotline for survivors who might want contact with the defense, and Tammy identified and worked with survivors opposed to the death penalty who were feeling isolated because of their position. A year after the trial, we facilitated a powerful circle process that brought together some of the survivors who testified at the trial and several of the penalty-phase attorneys. Overall, our work—and especially Tammy's—made a difference in the lives of some people and did affect the way

Keywords: restorative justice, victim outreach, victim assistance, death penalty trials, capital trials, death penalty defense, defense-initiated victim outreach (DIVO)

133

the defense treated survivor witnesses during the trial. But the work we did in this case was limited, partly because we had so little time and partly because we were finding our way in uncharted territory.

When the trial was over, we thought we were done, but the attorneys—and especially longtime death penalty defense attorney Richard Burr—began to say that there was something in our work that would change the paradigm for death penalty defense in the United States. Tammy and I were not sure what that meant, but Dick convinced Tammy—who clearly had real gifts for this work— to pioneer in this field, focusing on the federal death penalty. Two prestigious awards to Tammy made this possible: a Soros Fellowship and, following that, an Ashoka Fellowship. Dick and I, along with others, served as a reference or oversight board for the work during this period and, until a few years ago, the central clearinghouse and training center, JustBridges, was housed in the Center for Justice and Peacebuilding at Eastern Mennonite University, where I teach. A new field of work, defense-initiated victim outreach (DIVO), has emerged.

In the past ten years, interest within the capital defense community has become intense, and numerous people have been trained and are working on both federal and state death penalty cases. Tammy and her colleague, Mickell Branham, have provided leadership for this work from a base in the federal defender system. In addition, under the leadership of Pam Leonard (another graduate of our program) and Elizabeth Beck of Georgia State University's School of Social Work, a state-based pilot project is operating throughout Georgia. Entitled the Georgia Council for Restorative Justice, it is providing training, consultation, and mentoring, as well as case referrals and monitoring. Although the primary focus is on Georgia, the project also serves as a resource for victim outreach workers from the Southeast and other areas. The Circle of Peers, which serves as its advisory body, includes a number of people from outside Georgia, including practitioners and the father of a man who died in the September 11 attacks.

In December 2004, DIVO was recognized by the Defender Services Committee of the US Judicial Conference—the committee of judges who oversee all federal indigent defense—as a legitimate component of capital defense. The 2003 American Bar Association Guidelines for the Appointment and Performance of Defense Counsel also recognized victim outreach as not only a legitimate but also a necessary defense function (American Bar Association, 2003).[1]

For some survivors and defense attorneys then, DIVO actually is changing the nature of death penalty cases.

DIVO as Restorative Justice

DIVO is not full restorative justice. It rarely involves a direct encounter between victim and offender, for example, and it does not work with the offender/defendant side of the equation in any depth (though it does aim to reframe somewhat the role of defense attorneys in relation to both survivors and defendants). It is, however, founded on two key restorative justice elements: the importance of victim/survivor needs and choices and, to a lesser extent, the principle of encouraging offender accountability.

To expand this further, the following restorative justice principles and assumptions are most relevant to DIVO:

1. Justice must address the harms to and the resulting needs of victims.
2. Those who offend have an obligation to those they have harmed.
3. Victims (and offenders) should be involved as much as possible in outcomes.
4. Collaborative outcomes are preferred over imposed outcomes.
5. As much as possible, processes should be tailored to the needs, cultures, and genders of the people involved.
6. Justice should be respectful to all, balancing concerns for victims and for offenders.

Why DIVO?

Victims/survivors have many needs, but there is a cluster of common needs that I have elsewhere termed *judicial* or justice needs—needs that can and should be addressed by a justice process.[2] When those needs are addressed, survivors may be more successful in transcending their trauma; conversely, when their needs are not met, they are more apt to get stuck. These needs include measures to ensure the safety of their loved ones and others; information about the offender, the offense, and the justice process; opportunities to express their feelings and tell their stories to significant people; experiences of empowerment and involvement; a sense of vindication that can come from the appropriate assignment of responsibility for the wrong; and measures that bring a sense of a balance between the offense and the response.[3]

Yet, as anyone who has experienced the criminal justice system knows, the process is not usually a friendly one for victims and rarely meets these needs. The high stakes and highly adversarial nature of death penalty trials, as well as the drawn-out nature of the appeals process, makes this especially so in these cases. Family members of victims often feel sidelined and even retraumatized. Sometimes they feel neglected even by prosecutors; several survivors have told me that the prosecutor in their case refused to talk with them because the state, not the survivors, was technically the victim. Meanwhile, defense attorneys often see themselves as zealous advocates for their clients, regardless of their guilt or innocence, with little or no responsibility for the health or needs of victims/survivors. The result is not only unmet needs but also new layers of trauma.

In this context, DIVO seeks to offer a way for victims to define and meet some of their justice-related needs, especially those connected to the defendant and the defense, and a way to reduce some of the trauma involved in capital cases. It also encourages defense attorneys to help their clients take appropriate responsibility, because survivors often ask for this. Finally, it encourages defense attorneys to reframe their responsibilities to include victims and the larger community; it asks them to think of themselves as both advocates and healers or peacemakers. To do this, victim outreach specialists help sensitize defense attorneys to the needs and experiences of victims and keep them aware of these perspectives throughout the case.

What Is DIVO?

DIVO uses trained victim outreach specialists (VOSs) who are asked into the case by the defense, serving as a link or a bridge between survivors and the defense. A VOS has a relationship with the defense team as an expert, providing expertise the defense team needs but not becoming a defense advocate. If survivors choose to work with the VOS, the task of the VOS is to help survivors identify what they need from the justice process and from the defense, then to serve as a liaison between the victims and the defense to help the victims meet their needs. In a sense, the VOS becomes an advocate on behalf of the surviving family members to the defense team, offering new options. The VOS's role also complements that of the victim advocate provided by the state, often with links to the prosecution. Their task is not to assist the attorney and his or her client in avoiding the death penalty.

These judicial needs might include information about the crime or the case—information that only the defense and the defendant often have—or an opportunity to convey their feelings and wishes to the defense. They may include a desire for information about why a lawyer would defend someone like the defendant or information about the "what" and "why" of various hearings or other legal proceedings. Survivors may have concerns about the nature of the testimony and cross-examination that they wish to communicate to the defense. In some cases, they may wish to convey to both the defense and the prosecution their desires for the outcome of the case. In a few cases, including high-profile cases such as the Yosemite murders in 1999, those desires have become the basis for a plea agreement that avoided the death penalty by meeting the needs of survivors for admission, safety, information, restitution, and so on. In the trial of Moussaoui (charged with being part of the planning for the September 11 attacks), VOSs played an important role in inserting victim perspectives into the process. One unusual result was that some survivors chose to serve as defense witnesses for the victim impact testimony, including in their testimony stories of their healing, rather than focusing exclusively on their loss, as the prosecution often has victim witnesses do.[4]

To get a feel for what DIVO involves, consider the following imaginary scenario. It is imaginary because a trained VOS would never overwhelm a survivor with all this information in an opening monologue or even an initial letter. But it does give a sense of what is involved in the VOS task:

Hello. My name is Martha Fullerston. I have been asked by the defense team to make myself available to you in case I can be of any help. It's totally up to you whether you want to have anything to do with me, but I would like to explain why I am here so you can make your choice.

First, though, let me say how sorry I am for your loss. I have tried to comprehend what it must be like, but I am sure that unless it would happen to me, I'll never fully understand. No one should have to go through a loss like this, and the legal process often makes it worse. I have been asked to see whether there is anything that can be done to help.

As you know, the defense team's job is to avoid the death penalty for their client, but that's not why I am here. If you choose to have me work with you, I'm here to try to ease some of the difficulties of the legal process for you and to offer the possibility of more information and more choices than you would otherwise have. My job is to help out with any needs that you may have that the defense team or the defendant might be able to address. The defense knows that this may not help their case. However, they are aware how difficult all this must be and are concerned that they not make it more difficult for you.

For example, you may have questions about the legal procedures or about what the defense team is doing. If you are going to testify, you may have concerns about how you will be treated by the defense. You may have questions about what happened or other questions that have to do with the crime or what has happened since. I don't necessarily have immediate answers to those questions—I'm not on the defense team and I have never met their client—but I can try to get answers from the defense team to the extent that they are able to provide them. In other words, if you have questions, I will try to find answers. The attorneys in this case have agreed to share everything they can without jeopardizing their legal duty to their client.

You may favor the death penalty or you may be against it. Either way, I am available if you wish to use me. I am a bridge to the defense that you can use as you wish.

I am not here to take the place of any victim assistance that you may be getting through the prosecutor's office or a victim/witness program. They provide an important link to the prosecution and to support services that may be valuable to you. Rather, I am here to provide a missing link in the criminal justice system, a connection to the defense side. The prosecutor knows that I am contacting you, and I am happy to have your victim/witness support person meet with us initially if that would be helpful to you.

Again, although I was asked in by the defense team, I am not part of the defense team. I am a victim outreach specialist and have been specially trained for this work. The work requires that I be guided by a set of strict principles of practice. These principles emphasize that you, not the defendant, are my priority. I am happy to share these guidelines with you.

You can choose what you want to tell me and what you do not want to. If you feel that I am showing a bias toward the defense or trying to change your views on the death penalty, I encourage you to let me know. The training I have received and the principles under which I work require that I resist such biases or ulterior purposes.

This work is relatively new but has been going on for some years and is now recognized by a growing number of federal and state courts and by the American Bar Association. We have found that the service is often helpful to family members of those who have been murdered. If you would like to talk with another family member survivor with whom we have worked in the past, I will try to arrange that.

Let me give you some examples of things family members have asked for in the past.

1. Information about the dates and purposes of various hearings.
2. Information about what happened.
3. A chance to convey their concerns about possible cross-examination as witnesses.
4. An opportunity to have their wishes and needs be known to the defense and/or be part of a plea agreement if one is negotiated.
5. A chance to talk directly with the defense attorneys about these things.

If you don't wish to relate to me in an ongoing way, you are still free to contact me at any point in the process if you have questions or would like to convey something to the defense team. Do you have any questions? I'm happy to check back with you in a few days after you have had a chance to think this through. Here is my contact information. (Zehr and Leonard, 2006)[5]

A further understanding of the VOS role can be gained from the overview of DIVO that accompanies the *Principles of Practice* that have been adopted as a grounding for the work:[6]

1. Defense-initiated victim outreach seeks to address the needs of victims and their families throughout the legal process by providing a link between survivors and the defense, especially in capital cases.

2. Defense attorneys who represent the accused in criminal cases increasingly are recognizing the potential of the adversarial process to further traumatize victims/survivors.

3. In an attempt to ameliorate this source of trauma and to help meet victim needs, defense attorneys seek the assistance of trained victim outreach specialists to bridge the gap that usually exists between victims and the defense team.

4. Victim outreach specialists provide an opportunity for victims to have access to the defense team. This allows victims to interact with both prosecution and defense teams in order to address their questions, concerns, and needs.

5. The mission of a defense-initiated VOS, then, is to help victims/survivors identify and meet those needs that can be addressed through direct or indirect contact with the defense team.

6. The VOS works on behalf of victims at the request of the defense team, serving as an advocate for victims' interests and concerns.

7. As appropriate, the VOS encourages collaborative processes and outcomes that are mutually beneficial to all parties.

8. The VOS is considered an expert consultant, not a "core member" of the defense team. The VOS must maintain the trust of and be accountable to the defense team while focusing on victims' needs and concerns.

9. It is essential that the VOS be appropriately trained in victim trauma and how to work with victims; in the processes of capital cases; in the specific tasks, responsibilities, and limits of the VOS role; and in the basic principles of restorative justice on which this work is based.

The Future of DIVO

More than ten years of experience have shown that defense-initiated victim outreach has great potential to improve the experience of victims/survivors and offers benefits to defense attorneys as well. In the best-case scenarios, case outcomes are determined collaboratively in a way that meets victims' needs while providing an alternative to the death penalty for defendants. Even when the latter does not happen, victims can have a more positive experience and attorneys can find more satisfaction in their roles.

But as is true for all interventions, including restorative ones, there are risks as well. Indeed, DIVO is probably more risky than most restorative justice interventions because of its susceptibility to misuse. If the VOS is not properly trained and/or is not guided by clear principles, the work could easily hurt survivors as well as defense cases. Indeed, in at least one case of which we are aware, a person misrepresented himself as a victim outreach specialist when he was clearly working for the defense's agenda. Fortunately, we were able to work with the survivor and undo the harm, but we might not always be so fortunate. Less obvious than misrepresentation are the subtle biases that can enter in. For example, many people who have worked with the defense as mitigation specialists or in other capacities have developed a real interest in this work and have significant gifts as well. Years of offender orientation, however, results in subtle biases that must be identified in training and monitored through mentoring and other accountability structures.

Because of these dangers, those involved in this work express strong caution against engaging anyone in the work who does not have this specific training. Nevertheless, the popularity of the work combined with a shortage of trained VOSs has caused some attorneys to utilize people in this role who have not been trained. Those guiding this work strongly urge that no one without this specific training and mentoring engage in this work and that attorneys do not draw on people who have not been so trained.[7]

Will DIVO transform the death penalty defense to the extent Dick Burr and others initially believed? There are encouraging signs in the volume of requests for information, training, and victim outreach specialists as well as the number of death penalty cases that are using a VOS; indeed, most high-profile cases in the United States today probably have a trained VOS engaged. We envision a day when victim outreach specialists will be as normal a part of a death penalty case as are mitigation specialists. But only time will reveal the full implications of the work.

As I draft this chapter, a number of developments present specific challenges. There is currently no central clearinghouse for referral, screening, training, and consultation in this work. Since the end of funding for JustBridges, these functions have been provided somewhat ad hoc by Tammy Krause and Mickell Branham from their positions in the federal defender system and by Pam Leonard and Elizabeth Beck at the Georgia Council for Restorative Justice. Tammy is now leaving direct service to begin a doctoral program. Although she will remain connected to the work, her absence will accentuate the challenges of pursuing this work without a central, national organization.

In this context, the Defender Services Committee of the federal defenders system is now being asked to consider legitimizing this work as a national project sanctioned by the committee. If that happens, we can expect the profile of this work to increase dramatically—with all the potential benefits and risks that implies. At a minimum, it will force this newly emerging field to struggle further with issues such as credentialing procedures and the search for a clear organizational home.

All of this represents an area of application that those of us involved in the early days of restorative justice never imagined. It is a reminder of three fundamental values that I believe must underlie true restorative justice: respect for everyone involved, even those who appear to be "enemies"; humility about the limits of what any of us can know; and, finally, the importance of approaching this work—and all of life—with a spirit of awe or wonder. Who knows what uncharted territory lies ahead?

Appendix 10.A Principles of DIVO Practice

1. Victim-survivors should be provided as much information about the crime, the case and the process as possible, in non-technical language, without compromising due process for defendants.
2. Victim-survivors should be assisted in identifying and, to the extent possible, obtaining what they need through the justice process.
3. Victim-survivors should be provided as many options as possible for their involvement.
4. All possible precautions should be taken to avoid or reduce additional trauma to victim-survivors through testimony, cross-examination or other parts of the process.
5. If they wish, victim-survivors should be provided contact, directly or indirectly, with defense attorneys in order to address the above principles.
6. The confidentiality of the information provided to the VOS must be maintained consistent with the victim-survivor's wishes.

7. Victim Outreach Specialists must maintain the confidence of the defense team and do nothing to undermine their work.

8. Because their primary focus is on the victim-survivors and their needs, a VOS should not be an immediate member of the defense team, should not be involved with any other aspect of the case (such as mitigation, advising) and, unless so requested by the victim, should not have contact with or direct knowledge of the defendant or his/her family.

9. Involvement with DIVO is fully voluntary on the part of victim-survivors and should be available to them regardless of their stand on the death penalty. Once a relationship is established, the VOS should remain available to the victim-survivors throughout the legal proceedings and for a reasonable time beyond.

10. To guard against misuse and unintended consequences, DIVO practice should be regularly evaluated and victim-survivors and/or victim advocates should be on DIVO oversight committees.

Source: The Circle of Peers of the Georgia Council for Restorative Justice 2006. Available at http://www.gcrj.org/Site/DIVO.html (accessed July 21, 2009).

Notes

1. Refer to Commentaries to Guidelines 10.7, 10.9.1, and 10.11.

2. For an excellent answer to the question of "why DIVO?" see Burr (2006). See also Leonard (2006).

3. See, for example, Zehr (2001) and Beck, Britto, and Andrews (2007).

4. Supreme Court precedent prevents victim witnesses from giving their opinion on the nature of the sentence they think should be imposed on the offender. They can testify only about the life of the deceased person and the consequences for the witness and victim family members of the death of the victim.

5. The *Defense-Initiated Victim Outreach Training Notebook* is available only in conjunction with the training. Used by permission.

6. This is an adapted form of the preamble taken from Zehr and Leonard (2006).

7. For information about training, contact Pam Leonard (pleonard@gsu.edu) or Mickell Branham (Mickell_Branham@fd.org).

PART 2

Bringing Restorative Justice to the Broader World

11

Restorative Politics

Arthur Wint

It is probable that for some the idea of "restorative politics" is far-fetched, given the reality that they see and read about daily. Politics may be the art of the possible,[1] but attaining restorative justice in politics seems to be the impossible.

Given the evidence, who can blame these cynics, really? We constantly hear of wars and rumors of war, and it would appear that the prophet was correct when he lamented about those who cry "peace, peace when there is no peace."[2] Furthermore, the efforts of peacemakers appear to be short-lived or simply futile.

How many peace accords have been entered into in the Middle East since Dr. Ralph Bunche won the Nobel Peace Prize in 1950 for negotiating peace between Egypt and Israel? What restorative practices ensued in Vietnam following the awarding of the same prize to Dr. Henry Kissinger and his Vietnamese counterpart, Le Duc Tho, in 1973? From Camp David to Annapolis, hope has sprung eternal that peace, justice, and restoration will occur, yet former president Jimmy Carter was moved to label the relationship between Israel and the Palestinian community as "apartheid" (Carter, 2006, p. 189). Yes, peace, peace, when there is no peace!

However, notwithstanding all the doubts, despite the cynicism, there remain glimmers of hope. From Europe to Asia, peacemakers have been striving to help justice roll down like a river and righteousness like an ever flowing stream.[3] Two of these points of light stand out in my mind: the accord reached with the Irish Republican Army (IRA) in Ireland and the step taken by the South Korean president to reach out to North Korea amid the rattling of sabers regarding the war on terrorism and the "axis of evil."

Keywords: Afrikaner, ANC, AWB, forgiveness, IRA, kaffir, restorative justice, Sharpville, Sinn Fein, Truth and Reconciliation Commission

145

An Olive Tree in Northern Ireland

An amazing event occurred in April 1998: parties to the ongoing conflict in Northern Ireland signed a landmark agreement, which has come to be known as the Good Friday Agreement, in the quest for a lasting peace.

Five years later, an American scholar living in Northern Ireland stated that "restorative justice is flourishing" in Northern Ireland (Schrag, 2003). In July 2005, the IRA announced that all its clandestine units would end their armed campaign. Part of the proclamation stated:

> We are conscious that many people suffered in the conflict. There is a compelling imperative on all sides to build a just and lasting peace. The issue of the defence of nationalist and republican communities has been raised with us. There is a responsibility on society to ensure that there is no reoccurrence of the programs of 1969 and the early 1970's. (IRA, 2005)

Subsequently, in March 2007, the hard-liners in the bitter conflict, Gerry Adams of Sinn Fein and Ian Paisley of the Democratic Unionist Party, did another amazing thing: they came together and agreed to share power. This is an amazing glimmer of hope in a scorched and bitter struggle.

Reaching Out in Korea

The world held its collective breath as President Roh Moo-hyun of South Korea took that fateful step and crossed the line drawn in the sand of international politics. The Bush administration of the United States was skeptical. Would the head of part of the "axis of evil," Kim Jong Il, rebuff President Roh? Would Roh be caught in a swirl of international manipulation and intrigue? Would the Bush administration's insistence on full denuclearization in North Korea before any talks on formally ending the Korean War stymie this latest peace effort? Roh's intent was to take this step without requiring reciprocation. It was an opportunity to "put an end to the existing armistice mechanism and build a lasting peace mechanism" (Leaders, 2007).

There was no sudden change of heart on the part of the North Korean dictator. However, the signing of a joint declaration on South-North relations and the agreement to pursue four-way peace talks provided a glimmer of hope that would not have occurred but for the willingness on the part of Roh to take that necessary step with outstretched hands. These efforts on the part of the heads of state provide us with some hope that equity and justice will be restored as agents of society commit to being constructive, seek out ways to restore equity, and explore covenants for future behavior.

Perhaps the polestar of unlikely restorative justice in politics is the Government of National Unity in South Africa.

South Africa: Beacon of Restorative Justice

In his inaugural address, President Nelson Mandela called for his newly re-formed nation to "enter into a covenant that we shall build the society in which all South Africans, both black and white, will be able to walk tall, without any fear in their hearts, assured of their inalienable right to human dignity—a rainbow nation at peace with itself and the world" (Mandela, 1994; the full text of Nelson Mandela's inaugural address is found in Appendix 11.A).

This native son, who suffered at the hands of a government steeped in racism, refused to "turn the tables" when the forces for equality and justice prevailed. Instead, he called for South Africans to

> act together as a united people, for national reconciliation, for nation building, for the birth of a new world.
> Let there be justice for all.
> Let there be peace for all.
> Let there be work, bread, water and salt for all.
> Let each know that for each the body, the mind and the soul have been freed to fulfill themselves. (Mandela, 1994)

From a retributive lens, this is totally counterintuitive! Clearly, the intuitive expectation for a society crawling out of the abyss of apartheid was that the tables would be turned and that retribution would hold sway. The evidence close at hand certainly seemed to confirm this lowered expectation.

The dire circumstances of Zimbabwe under the presidency of Robert Mugabe clearly set up an expectation that under black South African rule, white South Africans would suffer retribution for atrocities engaged in over the brutal history of apartheid. In Zimbabwe, white Africans had their farms seized and handed over to black Africans who were not farmers, with the end result that much productive land went fallow. The former breadbasket of the region disintegrated into a desperate, poverty-stricken caricature of itself, plagued by racial conflict and white flight.

That, too, was the expectation of many South Africans who doubted that black African rule of South Africa would be anything better than what had occurred in Zimbabwe. Indeed, Prime Minister Margaret Thatcher of England is attributed with stating in 1987 that anyone who thought that blacks could run the government of South Africa was "living in Cloud Cuckooland" (Boynton, 1997). Yet, just a few years later, on Sunday, April 24, 1994, Nelson Mandela and the African National Congress (ANC) took over the helm of the government in South Africa, to the consternation of the *bittereinders* of the Afrikaner Weerstandsbeweging (AWB).

Who could blame the AWB for their consternation? Given the history of their forbearers' treatment of "natives," it is no wonder that they expected the *kaffirs* to engage in the practice of "turnabout is fair play." From the massacre of black miners in 1922, to the benchmark atrocity of the Sharpville Massacre in 1960, to the imprisonment of Nelson Mandela on Robben Island in 1964 and the death of activist Steve Biko in 1977, the many manifestations of the white community's racial fears and hatred were pervasive. The entire society was steeped in a culture of oppression and dominance (Krikler, 2005), coupled with the expectation that if the tables were turned, black South Africans would be doing the same thing to white South Africans.

The "Rand Revolt" of 1922

Steeped in the DNA of Afrikaners are events such as the New Primrose Gold Mine massacre of black miners by white miners who were striking for better conditions and wages in the gold mines of the South African Witwatersrand (the Rand), and who took out their fury on the black miners who were charged with the responsibility to "guard" the mine that fateful day. Although the black miners were armed only with sticks, spears, and pick axes, the white miners circulated rumors that the blacks not only were illegally armed with firearms but also had fired on striking miners.

The result was a call to arms that brought white South Africans from the region to the black compound at the mine where they commenced to open fire on the blacks, picking them off as they scurried about to secure hiding places from the hail of bullets coming into the compound. In addition, wounded blacks were bludgeoned to death. This was "justified" as a response to the rumors that "Africans were attacking white people . . . murdering innocents and rising in rebellion" (Krikler, 2005, p. 4). The fear of a Black Peril resulted in the death of many innocent, unarmed black miners. Fear of blacks informed the behavior in the 1920s and informed the apprehension about the prospect of blacks running the country in the 1990s.

Afrikaners are aware of their history as it relates to the Primrose Mine massacre and other atrocities, as well as the exercise of raw power and oppression used to enforce apartheid. Another of these atrocities was the killing of unarmed protesters at Sharpville on April 21, 1960.

The Sharpville Massacre of 1960

According to Philip Frankel (2001, Foreword), the massacre at Sharpville was "a seminal event in the dark history of the apartheid era, which had far reaching effects." Among those effects was the banning of the ANC and the Pan-African Congress (PAC), as well as a turn away from passive resistance to armed struggle on the part of the ANC. As Nelson Mandela and the leadership of the ANC declared in the *Manifesto of Umkhonto* on December 16, 1961, "The time comes in the life of any nation when there remain only two choices—submit or fight. That time has now come to South Africa. We shall not submit and we have no choice but to hit back by all means in our power in defense of our people, our future, and our freedom" (quoted in Asmal, Chidester, and James, 2003, p. 33).

The passive resistance at the police station in Sharpville and the deadly exercise of raw white power that responded to it changed the nature of the relationship of the struggle for freedom. The ANC went underground, moving on to acts of sabotage as the next level of struggle against apartheid. The government tightened its oppressive tactics. Fear, hate, and oppression bred more hate and more resistance. This massacre served as a defining event, focusing on the entrenchment of the culture of apartheid and the determination of Africans to resist it.

Under the leadership of the charismatic Robert Sobukwe, the PAC—a spinoff of younger, more Afrocentric activists—determined to highlight the evil of apartheid by staging a "stay-out" and refusing to use passes. They focused their attention on Sharpville. Sobukwe and a few of the leaders tried unsuccessfully to get arrested by turning in their passes at a police station a few miles from Sharpville. They were more successful in keeping black workers from boarding buses to take them to their various job sites. As a result, a swelling crowd descended on the police station at Sharpville, raising the fear of attack on the nearby white residential area. In addition, as with the Primrose Mine massacre, rumors were spread that many in the crowd were armed and prepared to use these firearms against the police (Frankel, 2001).

As the tension grew and attempts to get the leaders to disperse the growing crowd failed, a nervous stray shot by a young police recruit triggered the responding firepower of the police:

> The result was a huge discharge of well over 1,000 rounds—at least a quarter of the potential fire-power of the police—first into the face of the crowd, and then into their fleeing rear—all within the course of less that a single frozen minute. . . . It was, as apartheid's critics allege, a largely gratuitous act of violence inextricably connected with the whole system of racial violence in South Africa. (Frankel, 2001, p. 116)

Fear. Oppression. The exercise of raw power—deadly power. These were the instruments of a system that spanned more than 350 years. It is no wonder that fear of retribution ranked high among those who were afraid of what would occur in "Cloud Cuckooland" under black rule. What would hold sway—the spirit of retribution or the spirit of forgiveness?

No Future Without Forgiveness

> The world had expected that the most ghastly blood bath would overwhelm South Africa. It had not happened. Then the world thought that, after a democratically

> elected government was in place, those who for so long had been denied their rights, whose dignity had been trodden underfoot, callously and without compunction, would go on the rampage, unleashing an orgy of revenge and retribution that would devastate their common motherland. Instead there was this remarkable Truth and Reconciliation Commission to which people told their heartrending stories, victims expressing their willingness to forgive and perpetrators telling their stories of sordid atrocities while also asking for forgiveness from those they had wronged so grievously. (Tutu, 1999, pp. 260–261)

The deluge of reprisals did not occur. The massive exercise in retribution did not happen. Instead, under the leadership of Nelson Mandela, opportunity for forgiveness and reconciliation was provided on a vast national scale. This unlikely exercise of restorative justice in politics remains the polestar, guiding the way for other states in conflict to emulate. Indeed, states in conflict can look to Mandela's example as proof that out of the bile of hate and oppression can come forth a season of hope, reconciliation, and forgiveness.

This is not a pie-in-the-sky exercise. It was (is) an exercise to liberate both the oppressor and the oppressed (Graybill, 2002). Forgiveness deals with the past candidly and realistically. It opens the door to healing and a future. It is a pragmatic realization that forgiving liberates. It opens the windows of a dark and dreary place to the light and freshness of hope and true freedom, not only for the present actors but also for generations yet to come (Tutu, 1999). This is what the Truth and Reconciliation Commission helped to carve out for the National Unity Government and the "rainbow nation" of the new South Africa—a place where wrongs were recognized, offenders and victims got to tell their stories, equities were restored to the extent possible, and agreements were made as to future behavior.

As James Gibson (2004, p. 332) concluded after an analysis of the process and results of the Truth and Reconciliation Commission, "reconciliation seems to have made inroads into a sizable portion of the South African population." On December 16, 1995, Nelson Mandela declared:

> Reconciliation means working together to correct the legacy of past injustice. It means making a success of our plans for reconstruction and development. Therefore, on this 16 December, National Day of Reconciliation, my appeal to you, fellow citizens, is: Let us join hands and build a truly South African nation. (quoted in Asmal, Chidester, and James, 2003, p. 138)

This result was unexpected. It clearly serves as an example of reconciliation in an unlikely political environment. It is tangible evidence of the power of an unwavering commitment to be constructive. Indeed, it is the crowning measure of a man and the nation that chose to follow his example of forgiveness, reconciliation, and hope.

Summary

To behave restoratively takes effort. It is not the intuitive thing to do. It is not unusual for a wronged people to seek retribution. Unfortunately, that is the norm. It is even more unlikely for nations to engage in restorative practices with their enemies—to put aside the exercise of the retribution of the state and instead to commit to being constructive—to endeavor to restore the broken equities and reconcile the broken relationships and heal the grievous wrongs.

President Roh Moo-hyun of South Korea reached out restoratively when he stepped over the line to engage North Korea's President Kim. Two former bitter enemies, Gerry Adams and Ian Paisley, did the unlikely thing not only in setting aside decades of hate and violence but also in their amazing agreement to share power in Northern Ireland. Nelson Mandela, Desmond Tutu, and the "rainbow nation" did the unlikely thing in opening up a hate-ravaged nation to the healing power of restorative justice. Still, acting restoratively remains a challenge. It is far more likely that people and nations—thus politics—will be viewed through a retributive lens. The hope, however, lies in these glimmers of light that shine as examples for us to follow. Will we have the will or the courage to engage each other in restorative practices? Can nations rise above retribution and vengeance to restoration and hope? This hope remains, along with the realization that, as stated by Nelson Mandela, "the long walk continues" (quoted in Asmal, Chidester, and James, 2003).

Appendix 11.A
Nelson Mandela's Inaugural Address, May 10, 1994

Your Majesties, Your Highnesses, Distinguished Guests, Comrades and Friends:

Today, all of us do, by our presence here, and by our celebrations in other parts of our country and the world, confer glory and hope to newborn liberty.

Out of the experience of an extraordinary human disaster that lasted too long, must be born a society of which all humanity will be proud.

Our daily deeds as ordinary South Africans must produce an actual South African reality that will reinforce humanity's belief in justice, strengthen its confidence in the nobility of the human soul and sustain all our hopes for a glorious life for all.

All this we owe both to ourselves and to the peoples of the world who are so well represented here today.

To my compatriots, I have no hesitation in saying that each one of us is as intimately attached to the soil of this beautiful country as are the famous jacaranda trees of Pretoria and the mimosa trees of the bushveld.

Each time one of us touches the soil of this land, we feel a sense of personal renewal. The national mood changes as the seasons change.

We are moved by a sense of joy and exhilaration when the grass turns green and the flowers bloom.

That spiritual and physical oneness we all share with this common homeland explains the depth of the pain we all carried in our hearts as we saw our country tear itself apart in a terrible conflict, and as we saw it spurned, outlawed and isolated by the peoples of the world, precisely because it has become the universal base of the pernicious ideology and practice of racism and racial oppression.

We, the people of South Africa, feel fulfilled that humanity has taken us back into its bosom, that we, who were outlaws not so long ago, have today been given the rare privilege to be host to the nations of the world on our own soil.

We thank all our distinguished international guests for having come to take possession with the people of our country of what is, after all, a common victory for justice, for peace, for human dignity.

We trust that you will continue to stand by us as we tackle the challenges of building peace, prosperity, non-sexism, non-racialism and democracy.

We deeply appreciate the role that the masses of our people and their political mass—democratic, religious, women, youth, business, traditional and other leaders—have played to bring about this conclusion. Not least among them is my Second Deputy President, the Honorable F.W. de Klerk.

We would also like to pay tribute to our security forces, in all their ranks, for the distinguished role they have played in securing our first democratic elections and the transition to democracy, from blood-thirsty forces which still refuse to see the light.

The time for the healing of the wounds has come.

The moment to bridge the chasms that divide us has come.

The time to build is upon us.

We have, at last, achieved our political emancipation. We pledge ourselves to liberate all our people from the continuing bondage of poverty, deprivation, suffering, gender and other discrimination.

We succeeded to take our last steps to freedom in conditions of relative peace. We commit ourselves to the construction of a complete, just and lasting peace.

We have triumphed in the effort to implant hope in the breasts of the millions of our people. We enter into a covenant that we shall build the society in which all South Africans, both black and white, will be able to walk tall, without any fear in their hearts, assured of their inalienable right to human dignity—a rainbow nation at peace with itself and the world.

As a token of its commitment to the renewal of our country, the new Interim Government of National Unity will, as a matter of urgency, address the issue of amnesty for various categories of our people who are currently serving terms of imprisonment.

We dedicate this day to all the heroes and heroines in this country and the rest of the world who sacrificed in many ways and surrendered their lives so that we could be free.

Their dreams have become reality. Freedom is their reward.

We are both humbled and elevated by the honor and privilege that you, the people of South Africa, have bestowed on us, as the first President of a united, democratic, non-racial and non-sexist South Africa, to lead our country out of the valley of darkness.

We understand it still that there is no easy road to freedom.

We know it well that none of us acting alone can achieve success.

We must therefore act together as a united people, for national reconciliation, for nation building, for the birth of a new world.

Let there be justice for all.

Let there be peace for all.

Let there be work, bread, water and salt for all.

Let each know that for each the body, the mind and the soul have been freed to fulfill themselves.

Never, never and never again shall it be that this beautiful land will again experience the oppression of one by another and suffer the indignity of being the skunk of the world.

Let freedom reign.

The sun shall never set on so glorious a human achievement!

God bless Africa!

Thank you.

Notes

1. Attributed to the late congressman Tip O'Neill, Speaker of the US House of Representatives.

2. Jeremiah 6:14.

3. Amos 5:24.

12

Solutions for Business Conflicts

Duane Ruth-Heffelbower

It can be tempting to dismiss restorative justice as something that belongs only in the criminal justice arena. That could not be further from the truth. Restorative justice finds its application any time one person does not feel respected by another, whether or not the other person knows it. It can also be the best approach to business regulation (Braithwaite, 2002).

Business regulators want to protect the public and the government treasury by effective rule making and enforcement. In many cases, the regulators and the regulated play a cat-and-mouse game to see how little compliance will be enough to avoid fines. John Braithwaite, an internationally recognized expert in both restorative justice and business regulation, assumes that compliance is the desired goal. He developed the idea of a regulator exit interview after a compliance review. Braithwaite says that "every business regulator knows that the best time to persuade a company to invest in a corporate compliance system is after something goes wrong and someone gets into trouble" (Braithwaite, 2002, p. 91).

The question to be asked in business situations is whether the goal is compliance or punishment. Restorative justice assumes that compliance is the focus. The restoration of relationships, be they personnel or regulatory, will almost always give the best result.

At a recent workshop I gave with another Western consultant, the officers of Pakistan's anticorruption team were hearing about restorative justice for the first time. These agents had the power to seize assets without warrant and to arrest and detain without trial. They were some of the country's most feared people.

Keywords: human resources, dismissal for cause, employee assistance, workplace discipline, workplace conflict

155

They were curious why they were being given a workshop on restorative justice. They were asked: "Is your goal to punish or to get the money back?" They all quickly agreed that getting the money back was the goal. "Are you more likely to get the money with the corrupt person's cooperation?" Again the answer was yes. We explained that restorative justice provides tools to do just that; once the issue of punishment is set aside, cooperation becomes more possible. The rest of the workshop saw eager questions about how this new idea works.

People working in fields not usually associated with criminal offenses have begun to realize that restorative justice has something to offer them. Sociologist Declan Roche writes that

> restorative justice proponents tend to focus their attention on criminal justice initiatives in a small number of developed countries, but restorative processes (which encourage citizens to negotiate among themselves, rather than rely on professionals to adjudicate), and restorative values (which emphasize the importance of repairing and preventing harm), can be found across a wide range of regulatory fields. Teachers, social workers, corporate regulators, civil mediators, members of truth commissions, diplomats, and peacekeepers all, at least some of the time, practice a variety of restorative justice. (Roche, 2006, p. 217)

The officers of a business asked me, in my role as a consultant, what to do about feuding employees. People who had to work together as a team were refusing to speak to each other, passing messages through intermediaries. These were valuable long-term employees who had been with the company when it was a tenth the size it now was. Their leadership was seen as being critical to the continued success of the business, but the feud was driving newer employees away, increasing training expenses, and affecting productivity. The officers had no idea what to do, so they brought me in as a specialist to consult.

My talks with employees made it obvious that the problem could not be cured by the standard "play nice or be fired" demand, because these two key employees could easily find new employment and take customers with them. It also became obvious to me that the problem between them was perceived disrespect. One of the wonders of respect is that it does not matter whether disrespect is intended. The perception is what matters. If the disrespect is intended, the problem is much larger, but that is not the usual situation. Only outside intervention had much chance of success in healing this rift. Internal intervention had already failed.

The term *restorative justice* may be off-putting in a business context. Yes, the aggrieved persons feel that they have experienced injustice, but we do not usually speak of hurt feelings in a business context as justice issues unless the maltreatment falls into the discrimination or hostile work environment definitions. This way of thinking has been one of the reasons for businesses to be slow in applying restorative justice principles in the workplace. Fortunately, consultants do not need to explain the theoretical basis for their recommendations.

Working in Indonesia as part of a local university-based peace center, I found that the term *injustice* was meaningless. Indonesia has never had a functioning justice system available to ordinary citizens, so any search for justice is done through demonstrations if the government has created the problem; village elders if it is a village dispute among peers; personal vendettas if there is no village group able to handle the problem; or mob violence against the malefactor where there is no other trusted method for approaching the problem. It was not uncommon for a motorcycle thief to be beaten and then burned to death in the street.

The idea of injustice became clear to people when it was replaced with the term *luka hati,* or "wound to the heart." That is probably the best description of the concept for English speakers too, because it removes any legal connotations.

The term *restorative justice* refers to the need for an aggrieved person or group and the person or persons who are the source of the feelings of injustice to use restorative practices to work through the problem in a way that improves relationships and builds trust. My focus here is on identifying these processes, and it may be more helpful for the reader to think of "restorative practices" rather than "restorative justice" to remove any vestige of adversarial legalism from the equation. For better or worse, industrialized societies have adversarial systems of law that do not promote restorative practices and tend toward adversarial practices.

Many times, hurt feelings do not seem serious to those whose behavior has caused them. What supervisors do not realize is that it does not take many of these small slices of disrespect to add up to a major problem, particularly when there is a difference in level between the offender and the offended. The ancient torture method called "death by a thousand cuts" comes to mind. Disrespect that is reported to superiors and ignored can build up resentment quickly in a workplace setting. The impressive jury verdicts awarded to employees whose supervisors did nothing to stop repeated disrespect are enough reason in themselves for businesses to adopt restorative practices.

In a recent consultation for a medium-sized organization with three levels, the leader of the bottom-level group asked the leader of the second tier whether those in the second tier respected his group. That was a bit of a shock to the leader of the second-tier group. As the two teased out the problem, it became apparent that third-tier people simply did not have the nerve to confront second-tier people about their perceptions of disrespect, so those feelings festered and led to low morale.

Businesses wanting to be proactive in heading off this type of problem need to develop systems that use restorative processes to manage the inevitable feelings of disrespect that arise in every organization. Another important dynamic is that when one person feels disrespected, all the employees similarly situated have a tendency to share the feeling and to fear that their turns will come. Lack of information about the issue breeds additional insecurity. Insecurity at one level in the organization can easily breed insecurity at other levels and always affects productivity.

The Center for Peacemaking and Conflict Studies (CPACS) of Fresno Pacific University helped the university develop a restorative personnel system for managing problems with employees. It is modeled to some extent on the system previously developed and fully implemented for student disputes and discipline issues, which resulted, in its first two years of operation, in all student disputes and discipline issues being resolved in constructive, cooperative ways, mostly through mediation. The relevant implementing passage from the Faculty Handbook is attached as an appendix.

The plan has yet to be applied to administrators and staff, but those applications are in process. The CPACS operates a university mediation center that accepts all disputes, and its professional staff members have intervened in or facilitated resolution of all manner of disputes within the university and the greater community.

Stated simply, the problem sought to be addressed by this new system is that feelings of disrespect are harbored and grow if there is no well-accepted mechanism for handling them, or if some people seem to be exempted from the process. This lack of a system results in both passive and active aggressive behavior by employees seeking to reduce the resultant anxiety, as well as low morale. Neither result is conducive to organizational productivity.

For more than twenty years, the principals of the CPACS have provided consulting to businesses whose employees are having difficulties with others on their same level or with those above them. Over the years, it has become obvious that every situation encountered stems in large part from perceived disrespect. Each situation is different, but all have many things in common. The two large categories are problems between people on the same level and problems between people on different levels. Power differences and peer issues are handled quite differently, but there are substantial similarities.

One of the larger similarities among all of the businesses that have sought the services of the CPACS is the lack of a well-accepted mechanism for handling internal disputes. In all cases, this lack of a system for conflict resolution resulted in an explosive situation waiting for a spark to ignite it. The CPACS has been consulted both pre-spark and post-spark. The difference in outcome has been dramatic. In those businesses that called for outside intervention before the explosion, the loss of key employees was rare. In those that waited until after the explosion, the best employees were gone before the interveners arrived. The best employees can easily find a better work situation.

These businesses are not unique in their failure to establish an internal dispute resolution system. The majority of businesses have no such system, or if they have a system it does not have broad support. The US Postal Service provides an excellent example of what can happen when a business establishes such a system. "Going postal" entered the American lexicon in the 1990s when there was a relatively constant barrage of news stories about Postal Service employees showing up at work with a firearm and shooting their coworkers. Between 1986 and 1997, there were about twenty such incidents with forty people killed.[1]

The Postal Service responded by creating a complete internal dispute resolution system called REDRESS (Resolve Employment Dispute, Reach Equitable Solutions). One no longer hears of a postal worker going berserk. The system reports more than 90 percent satisfaction from users (US Postal Service, 2007).

To establish an overall workplace conflict intervention template, it is helpful to review the world of victim-offender dialogue. This peculiar technique emerged in the 1970s in the United States and Canada, developed independently in New Zealand, and spread from those places all over the world for use in criminal cases. The concept is simple: When you have offended someone, it is appropriate to acknowledge the offense, agree together how to make things right between you, and reach agreements about the future. Statistics that I developed from the Victim Offender Reconciliation Program of the Central Valley, Inc., in Fresno, California, show that 99.5 percent of all cases where victims and offenders meet result in an agreement.

This pattern was created through victim-offender reconciliation programs, not the least of which was the one in Fresno County, where this basic three-movement process was originally codified after a decade of experience by Ron Claassen (Claassen, 2002). Not surprisingly, this pattern has an indigenous analog in all human societies so far studied, in the sacred texts of all world religions based on texts, and in all world religions not relying on texts. That alone is an extraordinary amalgam of human agreement on basic life principles. (Those who believe they have an aberrant society are invited to fund research on that society, which I would gladly undertake.)

Not all societies prefer to handle these three movements directly. Most of the world's people would be appalled at the idea of a victim and an offender sitting down together to work through the problem. That particular methodology is preferred only by those who trace their culture to northern Europe. Most people expect to work through the three movements indirectly, making use of third parties chosen for their wisdom or position.

The use of indirect means to achieve victim-offender dialogue has been effective in the United States but is rare and normally occasioned either by a person from another culture's being part of the process or one of the parties refusing to cooperate with a direct approach. Outside North America and northern Europe, the direct approach is rare. The indirect method is not to be confused with evaluative mediation, where the parties do not meet together and the mediator shuttles back and forth. That method is used by unbiased technical experts, whereas the indirect approach as described here is done by wise people knowledgeable about the situation and biased toward the mores of the community. Although the direct approach is more efficient in general, it may not be in a particular case.

Both direct and indirect approaches need to accomplish the same three movements: acknowledge injustices, restore equity, and clarify future intentions. The problems that ensue when these three movements are not done are vividly portrayed in the situation comedy *The Office* (Daniels and McDougall, 2006). The boss, armed with a conflict resolution manual, attempts to clear up years of written worker complaints about other workers that the human resources department had handled by filing them neatly. As the process goes less and less well, the boss begins imposing solutions in the guise of mediating the disputes.

For those of us in the conflict intervention business, the television show is both hilarious and painful to watch as it caricatures every bad workplace conflict resolution practice. The redeeming value in the piece, besides the obvious bad example, is that it shows how difficult it is for insiders to intervene in workplace conflict. In this particular case, the boss has already decided which employees are worth listening to, making the situation less than safe for the other workers. Neither does it work for someone with the power to hire and fire to try mediating worker disputes. The problem is exacerbated in this example by the human resources department's violating the employees' trust by showing their complaints to the boss. Once internal trust is lost, an outsider is necessary.

Restorative justice has a place in business. Most interpersonal problems in business are based on perceived disrespect. The need to create a system for handling these problems is intense. Successful businesses develop a plan, whereas others fold. In this age of multimillion-dollar employee lawsuits, no business can afford to be without a conflict resolution system.

The system is not difficult to create, assuming one can hire a trained and experienced director for the program. That is where the problem rears its ugly head. The truth is that there are only a handful of such persons in North America, and they all have jobs. Most universities have created an academic program in conflict resolution designed to train such people, some with online programs, but coupling books with practice is rare, for the simple reason that few universities have ongoing conflict resolution programs with caseloads that provide practical experience to students. There are many people with training in mediation and other conflict resolution techniques, but few who have practice.

Conflict resolution in business settings requires knowledge of the culture—something anyone in business can easily get—and requires experience in handling the sorts of disputes that arise in a business setting—something difficult to get. Few universities provide such training, but recognition of the market is growing. Fresno Pacific University is unique in its practice-based training, but other institutions are following its example. Soon, hiring the appropriate human resources director will not be so difficult.

Appendix 12.A Excerpt from the Fresno Pacific University Faculty Handbook: Termination for Cause

(This section of the handbook was approved by the faculty in May 2007 and by the Board of Trustees on March 8, 2008.)

2. Procedures: Questions of Character and Dismissal for Cause

   a. When the president and the provost become aware of matters which raise the issue of character that could lead to dismissal for cause, reasonable cooperative efforts will be made under the direction of the provost to deal with the causes of concern and, if possible, to remedy them by agreements made with the faculty member.

   b. If the procedure outlined above is unsuccessful, the provost shall involve the Center for Peacemaking and Conflict Studies (CPACS) or other professional services in resolving the matter.

   c. If managed by the CPACS and under its rules, participants of the mediation session will include the affected faculty member, a member from the CPACS who will lead the process, a faculty member chosen by the affected faculty member, and an administrator or faculty member chosen by the provost. When agreed by all parties, it is assumed that agreements made and kept will rebuild trust and restore the faculty member's relationship with the university. The key elements in this process will be a mutual commitment to be constructive, the acknowledging of harm, the restoration of equity through actions which make things as right as possible, and clarity regarding future intentions.

   d. Where the faculty member is unwilling or unable to participate in a cooperative process as described above, or where the cooperative process fails to achieve mutually acceptable results, the president and/or the provost will solicit a resignation.

   e. If the faculty member does not resign, the president may give written notice of termination including the effective date of dismissal, a statement of cause, terms and notification of the right to appeal.

   f. The faculty member shall be given an opportunity to respond in writing or to request a hearing before the Faculty Personnel Committee. Failure to request a hearing or to respond in writing within the time specified in the notice of termination shall be deemed an acceptance of the termination and the president shall so notify the Board of Trustees.

   g. If a hearing is requested, the Faculty Personnel Committee shall be convened as soon as possible, and in any case, within ten working days of the request. Those members of the Faculty Personnel Committee appearing at a duly noticed hearing constitute a quorum. The faculty member and the Faculty Personnel Committee shall be notified of the date, time and place of the hearing. The faculty member shall be allowed, either personally or through a representative of the faculty member's choosing, other than an attorney, to present documentary evidence, to introduce witnesses and to refute evidence. The case for dismissal shall be presented by the president or the president's chosen representative.

   h. The Faculty Personnel Committee shall consider the charges set forth in the notice of termination together with the written statement or the evidence and arguments presented at the hearing, and on the basis of the total evidence, shall make a recommendation to the president. The president, taking into account the recommendation of the Faculty Personnel Committee, shall confirm, modify or rescind the notice of termination and shall give written notification to the faculty member and the Faculty Personnel Committee within ten working days of the hearing.

Note

1. A description of the "going postal" phenomenon can be found at http://en.wikipedia.org/wiki/Going_postal (accessed December 9, 2007).

13

New Skills for Children and Schools

Marian Liebmann

It is often assumed that restorative justice is a topic for adults and possibly wayward teenagers in the criminal justice system, but not for children, as they would be too young to understand the concepts. However, there is much work that has shown how restorative approaches can be used with children of all ages, even as young as two or three years old. Restorative approaches actually make more sense to children and fit in with their developing ideas about fairness and justice.

This chapter provides an overview of the different processes that involve a restorative approach in playgroups, primary schools, and secondary schools. Case studies of these processes are included.

Brief History of Work with Children in the United Kingdom

Conflict resolution work in schools was started in the United Kingdom in 1981 by the Kingston Friends Workshop Group. The emphasis was on teaching conflict resolution in schools to help students with their relationships with others and foster a peaceful and constructive atmosphere in schools. Several schools developed this into training children and young people to be peer mediators. The term *restorative justice* was not used at that time.

When restorative work with young offenders began to catch on, the term *restorative justice* began to be used for this. Although victim-offender mediation

Keywords: whole-school approach, conflict resolution, circle time, mediation, peer mediation, conferencing, restorative conferencing

had been practiced in the United Kingdom since 1983, it was not until the Thames Valley Police started using the restorative conferencing model with young offenders in the 1990s that the term *restorative justice* was used. In the United Kingdom, police undertake preventive work in schools, as young people who are excluded from school because of misbehavior often have little to do and are soon in trouble with the law. As part of this effort, the Thames Valley Police introduced the restorative conferencing techniques they had learned from Australian facilitators and referred to it as "restorative justice in schools."

These techniques have been broadened to include much more than sorting out difficulties and conflicts. Drawing on those who had been working in the field in schools for many years (Sue Bowers, Belinda Hopkins, and others), "restorative approaches in schools" has come to encompass an approach that seeks to prevent conflict, bullying, and destructive behavior by building good relationships throughout the school. The school is seen as a community in which everyone has a responsibility to help with this task.

A restorative approach in schools can be used not only in cases of clear-cut wrongdoing but also in cases of conflict between students, between staff and students, between staff and parents, and even between staff members themselves. Apart from the benefits for the participants, restorative approaches can help strengthen the school community and reduce the need to exclude children (Thorsborne and Vinegrad, 2002, 2004; Warren, 2004).[1]

It is not so widely known that considerable work has also been done with very young children at playgroups and nursery schools. This area is a crucial one because of the increasing anxiety concerning children and violence, and because it is an area of growth and hope. Conflict is inevitable, especially with children who are just learning to socialize; how it is handled is important. It is often easier for children to learn restorative approaches, as they do not have as much to "unlearn" as adults do. Restorative work with young children could provide the foundations to help transform relationships and the way we do things.

The key principles of using a restorative approach in a school or playgroup context include the following: (1) providing all those affected by a conflict or a problem the opportunity to air their experiences, their feelings, and their needs, and to feel heard; (2) involving everyone affected in finding a mutually acceptable way forward; and (3) ensuring that everyone involved becomes accountable for their possible contribution to the presenting incident (Thorsborne and Vinegrad, 2002, 2004).

Whole-School Approach

Although many schools adopt just one or two of the processes mentioned above, research has shown that these processes are far more effective if they are part of a "whole-school approach." It is rather undermining if a young person attends a conference in which he or she agrees to put things right and, despite this, is then excluded or punished as well, according to "school rules." It is clearly vital for a school to think out its whole policy so that all the processes fit together. This is expressed rather well in Belinda Hopkins's jigsaw diagram (see Figure 13.1).

The glue that holds the pieces of the jigsaw together is a common commitment to restorative values and principles. This means that staff, as well as students, are expected to demonstrate restorative values and model these approaches. It is sometimes hard for teachers and school management teams to relinquish traditional adherence to control and punishment techniques that have been used for generations.

Figure 13.1 Whole-School Approach and Constituent Processes

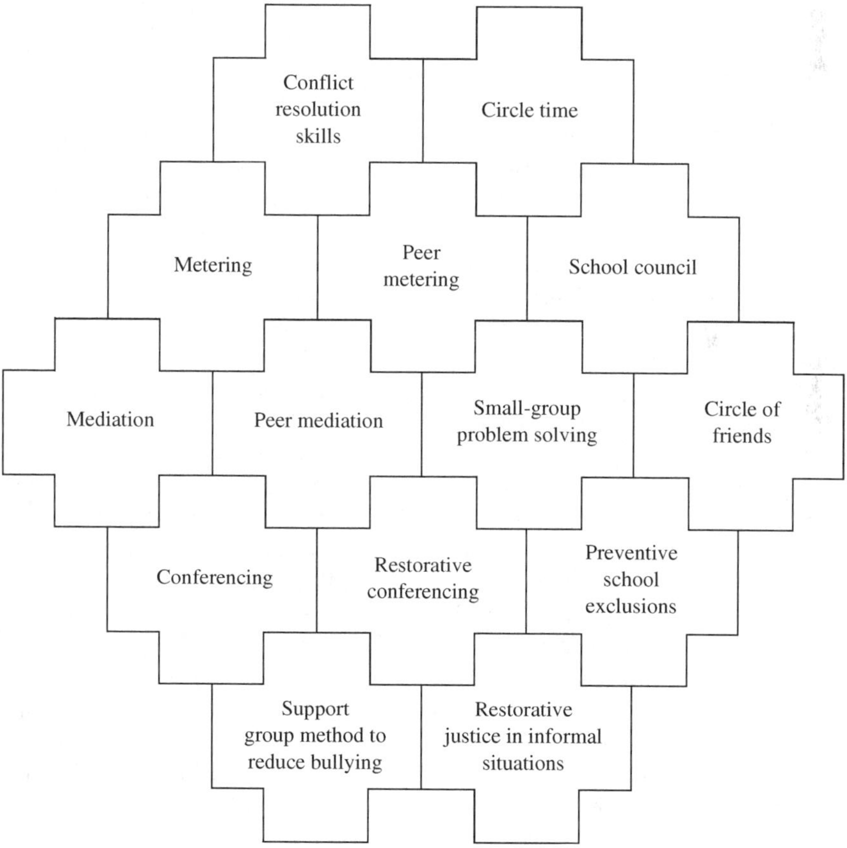

Source: Adapted from *Just Schools* (Hopkins, 2004) and http://www.transformingconflict.org, with permission.

Restorative Processes

Brenda Morrison (2005a, 2005b) describes three levels of activity needed in a school to achieve restorative justice: (1) a whole-school approach offering social and emotional education and conflict resolution skills so that members of the school community can resolve differences in a respectful, caring, and inclusive way; (2) methods for sorting out minor conflicts and problems; and (3) methods for dealing with serious conflicts, problems, and incidents.

Whole School

Conflict Resolution Skills

Many schools, especially primary schools, have introduced the teaching of conflict resolution skills—either in their own right or as a precursor to teaching peer mediation. Often a community mediation service or peace education project helps to initiate these lessons, at the same time training class teachers to be able to take them over. The lessons are designed to be fun and interesting, with games and interactive exercises that encourage children to reflect on their experiences and learn ways of resolving conflict.

One of the first British collections of activities was *Ways and Means* (Bowers and Wells, 1986), revised as *Ways and Means Today* (Rawlings, 1996), published by the Kingston Friends Workshop Group (now Kingston Friends Mediation). Part of their philosophy was to acknowledge that conflict occurs when communication has broken down—for example, when people do not listen to each other, when people feel bad about themselves, when people do not cooperate with each other, or when problems seem insoluble. Therefore, conflict resolution needs to rest on a base of values: affirmation, communication, cooperation, and problem solving.

All these are needed to resolve conflict. The exercises and games help children to affirm each other, acquire communication skills (especially listening), experience cooperation through games and tasks, learn problem-solving skills, and use all these in resolving conflicts between themselves.

A number of other projects, particularly by Quakers, followed suit. Many community mediation services and independent organizations have also developed school projects along these lines, teaching conflict resolution skills in schools, often leading on to peer mediation training. There are also drama projects run by a variety of organizations that teach these skills.

Most of the skills I have outlined here are now part of the national curriculum and can therefore be integrated into subjects such as English, social studies, PSHE (personal, social, and health education), religious education, and citizenship. Although establishing a timetable for such instruction is easier in a primary school, many secondary schools now include it as well.

Examples of conflict resolution activities include the following (Rawlings, 1996):

1. Active listening; for example, pairs talk about "something good that happened this week."
2. Listening for feelings behind what is being said.
3. Affirmation posters where children write good things about each other.
4. "Broken Squares" activity, where participants learn that parts of cardboard squares need to be given to others if the group is to complete all its squares.
5. Games such as "grandmother's keys," which are active and require group cooperation.
6. Story Circle, in which each child adds a sentence to a story, going round the circle; this involves listening and creativity.
7. Role plays where children can put themselves in others' shoes and learn empathy and how to explore different points of view.

For young children, the High/Scope approach was developed in the United States for preschool children in 1962, initially as part of the Head Start program. It includes several key elements: active learning, plan-do-review, choice of activities, and cooperative learning (Deloria and Weikart, 1970; Hohmann and Weikart, 1995).

Case study: Conflict resolution skills in a secondary school. Casey was often subjected to hurtful comments and pranks by other students in class. One of the ways she coped was by creating distractions and disruptions in the classroom. It became apparent that Casey was struggling with her work.

She was encouraged to join in a series of eight lunchtime sessions aimed at building self-esteem and dealing with the feelings that arise in conflict situations. She commented on the new ways she dealt with bullying behavior from her peers; for example, she talked to her close friends about her feelings and explained to those behaving unfairly how she liked to be treated, rather than withdrawing and bottling up her anger. She said this helped her move on from any incidents even if they still occurred. "I don't want to be angry, then go home and beat up my little brother! Talking to others has really helped me." As part of a team of ten classmates, Casey went on to train as a workshop leader and helped deliver conflict resolution skills sessions for younger students.

Small-Group Problem Solving

This process is used for general problems, such as children running when it is not safe, a noise problem, or a spate of name-calling. In the High/Scope approach (for nursery schools), adults call the children together in small groups to discuss the problem, at a time when the problem is not actually happening. They use the following strategies:

1. Provide props or snacks to help maintain children's attention.
2. Keep language concrete and specific.
3. Support participation.
4. Express confidence in the children and the process.
5. Focus on the problem, not the people.
6. Ask for and accept many ideas.
7. Balance the attention given to different children.
8. Be sensitive to the interest level (i.e., stop the discussion if interest wanes).
9. Summarize the ideas.
10. Decide a plan of action.

In small-group problem solving and in adult-child conflicts, adults often make use of "I-statements" to express their feelings, without accusing anyone—for example, "I feel worried about children running inside the room, because someone might get hurt" or "I feel sad about the book being torn."

Case study: Small-group problem solving in a playgroup (ages two to four). At one point, there were several children who were leaning back on their chairs, tipping them up. The playgroup leader said, "I'm really worried that the chairs will fall over and someone will get hurt." She asked the group to think of ways to solve the problem. One child suggested, "We could keep all the legs on the floor," and another one said, "Don't wobble the chairs." The playgroup leader fed these back to the group, and everyone agreed that they were good ideas. The playgroup leader commented that this worked much better than if adults imposed a "rule"; the children reminded each other of their ideas to stay safe, rather than talking about what they were not allowed to do.

Circle Time

Circles are a time-honored way of coming together to discuss, talk, and make decisions. In a circle, everyone can see everyone else and everyone is equal. But in traditional classrooms, desks, tables, computers, and other equipment often make this difficult. A tradition of teacher authority can also inhibit the idea of equality with students.

Many of the restorative processes are best taught in circles, and Circle Time has been introduced in many schools to provide an opportunity for children to share and build trust. It is easier to do this in primary schools, with their more flexible timetable, but some secondary schools also use it. Circle Time can include games, rounds, and discussions. Circle Time needs some simple ground rules to be successful:

1. Everything said in the room is confidential unless there is an agreement to take it outside the room (the exception to this is the disclosure of abuse or danger).
2. Everyone has the right to be heard and a duty to listen.
3. There are to be no put-downs.
4. Everyone has the right to pass.

Circle Time participants can also contribute to the rules, and everyone has a responsibility to see that those rules are kept. Often a "talking stick" or other object, such as an attractive shell or a smooth stone, is passed round, so that a person may speak only when holding the object (Hopkins, 2004; Rawlings, 1996).

Case Study: Circle Time to resolve thefts.   This case study shows how Circle Time can be used to deal with offenses if children are used to the format and have been using it previously for other things.

There had been ten or eleven thefts in a class of eight- and nine-year-olds, and the police had become involved. They got the children to sit in a big circle and asked them to talk about how they had been affected. The police knew that the children who had taken the things must be in the circle. They also asked what everyone could do to make things better, and suggestions were made—for example, that they should look after their things better and that they should tell their teacher when things were taken. Then a boy suggested putting a box out for the things to be returned, without identifying who had done it. By the next morning all the things were in the box. The restorative circle had clearly touched the child or children who had taken the things, and they decided to return them.

Mentoring

Mentoring is a one-on-one, nonjudgmental relationship in which an individual gives time to support and encourage another. There are many schemes in schools in the United Kingdom that involve adult volunteers as mentors to help children with particular needs—for instance, to help with reading or to help with children who have difficulties at home.

Peer Mentoring

Children and young people can also act as mentors to other children. The skills taught to trainee mentors include the role of a mentor; differences, values, and attitudes; communication skills; helping skills; ground rules; and techniques for starting the relationship.

Case study: Peer mentoring.   In one school, peer mentoring is used throughout the school. Year 7 and 8 (ages eleven to thirteen) students are encouraged to become "bus buddies" or "cyber buddies" to other school students. In years 11 to 13 (ages fifteen to eighteen), students can become one-on-one mentors and provide classroom support for younger classes. Peer mentors also manage after-school football (soccer) classes for younger students. The program has its own mentoring newsletter. The peer mentors' group visited Poland and the Auschwitz Museum to reflect on racism, prejudice, and asylum seekers, with a view to helping them with this aspect of their role as peer mentors (Mentoring + Befriending Foundation, 2005).

School Councils

School councils are democratically elected groups of students who represent their peers and enable students to become partners in their own education, making a positive contribution to the school environment and ethos. They give students a voice, improve communication in the school, reduce bullying and vandalism, reduce school exclusions, improve teacher-student relationships, provide education in citizenship, help schools develop into caring communities, and improve academic performance. Students feel valued as their views are acknowledged and acted on. School councils discuss issues that affect the whole school, such as meals, school improvements, and general behavior. The coordinating body, School Councils UK, has more than 10,000 member schools (School Councils UK, 2005).

Minor Conflicts

Mediation can be used for minor or major conflicts and incidents. In this section, we look at mediation to resolve minor conflicts.

Mediation

Mediation is a process in which an impartial mediator (or two comediators) helps two (or more) parties resolve a conflict. The parties, not the mediator(s), decide the terms of the agreement. Mediators first arrange separate meetings with the parties to assess the appropriateness of mediation and to prepare them for the meeting.

The joint meeting usually includes the following steps: (1) making an opening statement, introducing the participants, and laying down ground rules; (2) providing uninterrupted time in which each person tells his/her story; (3) providing an exchange period for questions; (4) building an agreement, if appropriate; (5) writing an agreement, if appropriate; and (6) closing the session and arranging follow-up. There are many ways in which a school can use mediation:

Teachers mediating between students. This can be difficult to achieve, as most teachers are more used to "arbitrating" (listening to both sides and then making a decision about what should happen). Mediation (helping both sides to come to their own decision) can be more time-consuming, and schools are usually busy places. But it can provide more lasting solutions and help to mend relationships.

Heads of year mediating between a teacher and a student.[2] This can be hard to achieve, as it can be difficult for teachers to have their judgment questioned in this way. But it can also lead to rewarding results.

Comediation teams of a teacher and a student mediating between a teacher and a student. This is a more balanced arrangement for mediation but requires a school that is committed to mediation and has trained staff and students.

Peer mediation. Students mediate each others' conflicts. They can often deal with conflicts that students do not feel able to bring to teachers.

Mediation for Young Children

The High/Scope approach uses a model involving six steps for adults to use with conflicts between young children of preschool age:

1. Approach calmly, stopping any hurtful actions.
2. Acknowledge children's feelings.
3. Gather information.
4. Restate the problem.
5. Ask for ideas for solutions and choose one together.
6. Be prepared to give follow-up support.

This is similar to the basic mediation model, but allowance is made for young children in considering the following factors (Evans, 2002):

Egocentrism. Young children view the world from the standpoint of their own feelings and needs, with little awareness of others' viewpoints. Conflicts are an opportunity to hear feelings and ideas that are different from their own.

Concrete thinking. Young children need to see the disputed object. The adult holds the disputed object while children talk and problem-solve, as otherwise the child holding the object has no incentive to discuss the problem.

Limited verbal skills. Young children need lots of time to be able to express themselves verbally.

Physical expressiveness. Young children may show their anger or frustration by hitting or grabbing. It is important to discourage these but not punish them—the aim is to help children learn to express their feelings appropriately and learn to problem-solve, so that they do not need to act out their distress.

Striving for independence. Sometimes this leads to conflict and needs to be channelled in a constructive direction.

"One-thing-at-a-time" thinking. Adults can help by restating the problem one bit at a time, until children feel their wants and needs have been fully understood.

Developing capacity for empathy. When adults acknowledge children's feelings, they help them become aware of others' needs and feelings, and this helps develop empathy.

Children's "misbehavior" is regarded not as naughtiness but as social mistakes. So hitting and punching are seen as behavior children use when they cannot explain what is wrong (Gartrell, 1994, 1995).

Case study: Restorative approaches and special educational needs. Jon (age 6), suffering from Asperger's syndrome, was excluded from school three times for aggressive behavior, despite having a Statement of Special Educational Needs and a full-time learning support assistant (LSA). The school saw punitive measures and exclusion as the only means to change children's behavior. Jon became more and more isolated, angry, and frustrated, and his behavior worsened.

Then a new teacher arrived, who was skilled in restorative methods, and read the needs behind Jon's behavior. When Jon upset another child, she got them to meet so that Jon heard how his behavior affected others. He was able to go some way to repairing the harm. He made friends with other children, and their parents changed from hostile to understanding of Jon's needs. Jon's teacher saw his strengths in music and involved him in singing and drama. Jon and his mother also painted a mural for the school as a way of saying thank you for the help to achieve improved relationships.

Peer Mediation

Peer mediation is a process in which children and young people act as mediators to help other children and young people sort out their conflicts, if asked to do so. Children as young as eight have proved they can be good mediators. Such schemes usually operate during breaks, when there are no formal structured activities happening. Often peer mediators work in pairs, with bibs or baseball caps indicating that they are on duty. The bibs or caps are labeled according to the scheme's chosen name for mediators—for example, Mighty Mediators, Conflict Busters, or Playground Peacemakers. They may resolve conflicts in the playground or may have a designated quiet area in the school that they can use. It is vital that there is good support and supervision of peer mediators from teachers who have been part of the training.

The training is often done by outside facilitators initially, who train the teachers to continue on their own. Often the training starts with lessons in conflict resolution, so that the children or young people get an idea of what it is all about. Then children volunteer to do further training if they want to be mediators. It is important to include some children or young people who may have reputations as "negative leaders," as they may lend "street cred" to the scheme; they are often good mediators and find the role gives them the status they need, in a more positive way.

The mediation process is similar to the basic model outlined but may be simpler for young children, who will take less time; a whole mediation may take only ten minutes. However, mediations involving teenagers may take longer than adult ones.

Here is a summary of the mediation process from a manual for secondary schools and colleges (Mediation UK, 1998):

Stage 1: Rules
- Make it feel safe.
- Agree ground rules for the session.

Stage 2: Problems
- What's the problem?
- Give both sides the chance to tell their story.
- Retell the problem for each side.
- Encourage both sides to hear the other person's needs and feelings.

Stage 3: Solutions
- Encourage them to find ways of solving the problem or new ways of looking at the situation.
- Make an agreement.

Case study: Peer mediation to address fighting and cussing. George and Jamie were both age twelve, in year 7, and got into a fight. It started when Jamie joined in with older boys "cussing" George and was pushed into punching him. George punched back. A teacher suggested mediation. The peer mediators helped the boys calm down and listen to each other.

George felt angry, and embarrassed, at being attacked for no reason and worried that it might happen again. Jamie felt scared of his parents' reactions if they found out, angry at being blamed for the whole episode, upset because he did not mean to hurt anyone, and worried in case he got a reputation as a troublemaker. They both apologized for punching each other and agreed to stay out of each other's way for a while; they also agreed not to spread rumors about what had been said in the mediation.

Circle of Friends

A Circle of Friends is a small group of friends who gather to support a child who needs help at any particular time, especially if the child's behavior seems to alienate other children. The formation of such a group provides friends who can comfort a child who feels unliked, and who can be trusted to alert the child to any behavior that seems to be leading the child into trouble.

Case study: Circle of Friends via the Cough Group. Raj had moved to a new school when he was nine and had experienced a few difficulties settling in, but he soon made friends. However, in year 6 (age ten), his last at primary school, he experienced renewed difficulties. Incidents escalated, such as name-calling, pushing, shoving, and harassment from other children. One day, Raj just blew up. He acquired a label of "being difficult" and became increasingly reluctant to go to school. Raj's mother, Jean, went to the school to ask for help.

Raj's teacher, Mr. P., spoke to the rest of the class (without Raj) and said that Raj needed a friendship circle. Lots of children put their hands up and Mr. P. chose a few. Then Mr. P. organized a meeting between himself, Raj, and the group of friends. He asked all the friends to say (1) why they wanted to be Raj's support person—what they found nice about him, (2) what Raj could do to be easier to be with, and (3) what signal Raj could use to ask for help.

As the group was called a Circle of Friends (COF), they decided to use a pun and call themselves the Cough Group. Their signal would be to cough, so they coughed if they thought Raj needed reminding of something, and they also summoned each other to their weekly meeting by coughing at each other. One thing that Raj did that seemed to annoy other children was walking in a deliberately silly way, so they coined the initialism MMSW, for Minimize the Ministry of Silly Walks.

Over the next half-term, things improved. Raj felt a bit surer of his friends because he had people on his side, and the group of friends eased his transfer to secondary school that autumn.

Serious Conflicts

In this section, we look at processes that can help with more serious conflicts and incidents of harm where parents and professionals may need to be involved; trained adults from the school or another agency undertake the facilitation.

Mediation

Mediation can be used to sort out serious conflicts as well as minor ones. It can also be used for incidents in schools where it is clear that one party has harmed another—that is, *victim-offender mediation,* although this term is not usually used in schools. It can be an opportunity for the persons responsible to apologize and explain why they acted as they did and an opportunity for the persons harmed to explain how they have been affected. There is often a conflict or misunderstanding lying behind the event, and this can be cleared up too—for instance, circulating rumors that lead to one student hitting another.

Case study: Mediation of an assault that had led to a broken jaw. Two eight-year-old girls, Crystal and Stacey, had been taunting each other in the playground for several weeks. This escalated to violent and aggressive behavior, culminating in an incident in which Stacey punched Crystal in her face, causing Crystal to fall down and break her jaw. The welfare officer at the school referred the case to the local mediation service.

The mediators visited Crystal and her mother, both very upset. Crystal was worried that Stacey might hit her again. Then the mediators visited Stacey and her grandmother (Stacey's mother had recently been killed in a car crash). It turned out that Crystal, who had severe attention deficit hyperactivity disorder (ADHD), had taunted Stacey about her mother's death and Stacey had lashed out in rage, not meaning it to go so far. Stacey had never been in trouble before her mother's death but was finding it difficult to cope.

They all met and aired their views. The headmistress was also concerned, because school staff were supervising the two girls separately during break times to ensure that they did not meet, and this took up a great deal of teacher time. The outcomes of the meeting were as follows:

1. Crystal and Stacey apologized to each other.
2. Both girls made promises of good behavior.
3. The two girls wanted to be allowed out in the playground together immediately (but the school asked them first to show that they could behave well to each other in class for three weeks).
4. The pastoral care teacher offered to see the girls any time they had any problems.
5. Counseling would be arranged for Stacey.

A review meeting was set for two months later, at which point all was progressing well.

Conferencing

Conferencing is the name often given to a larger group meeting that is convened to sort out a conflict. It can be used with any size group, from two people in dispute (when it is more usually referred to as mediation) to a whole class. Parents and other people can be involved if this is appropriate. With larger numbers, there is often a need for a more formal structure so that everyone can contribute in an orderly fashion. People sit in a circle so that everyone can see everyone else. Sometimes a talking piece (stone or other object) is used, as in Circle Time. Useful questions are as follows (Hopkins, 2004): What happened? Who has been affected and how? What has been the hardest thing for you? What can we all do to put things right? Conference facilitators may also need to decide on an appropriate order of speaking, and of dealing with issues, to help achieve clarity.

Case study: Conferencing to deal with bullying and fights. This case involved several girls and a complex, year-long history of friendship problems, taunting, name-calling, and bullying that eventually led to a fight between two girls, Helen and Katy, both fourteen. A year 11 (age fifteen) boy and a lunchtime supervisor split them up. A conference was suggested. Other girls had been involved in the problems during the previous year, and Helen and Katy wanted one of them, Nina, to be present at the conference. They were adamant that they did not want their parents there. Two conference facilitators were allocated— a volunteer and a teacher who knew them all well—and they prepared all the participants.

It took a while to get going, as the girls found it difficult to speak. After some "time out" and individual talks, they reconvened, reaffirmed the ground rules (especially trust and honesty), and this time the girls were able to talk about their feelings of jealousy, loneliness, regrets, and the need for each other's friendship. There were tears all round and an amazing transformation. An agreement was reached as follows:

1. Keep everything confidential.
2. No name-calling behind people's backs.
3. Don't make each other feel unwelcome.
4. Don't jump to conclusions—don't take gossip as truth, talk to each other directly.
5. Respect each other's friendship.

Another teacher happened to come by. She was amazed to see the three girls laughing and joking around together.

Restorative Conferencing

Restorative conferencing is the name often given to a conference that takes place after an incident of harm has occurred. It is important that the wrongdoer admits some responsibility, although there are often explanations to be made and sometimes conflicts to be resolved as well. Often parents attend (parents of both the person responsible and the person harmed), as do form tutors, year heads, and any other appropriate staff.[3]

Questions about the incident may need to be more focused than the ones used for general conferencing above; some examples follow (Hopkins, 2004):

1. Can you explain what happened?
2. What were you thinking at the time?
3. How were you feeling at the time?
4. What have been your thoughts since?
5. What are they now?
6. How are you feeling now?
7. Who else do you think has been affected by this?

Case study: Restorative conferencing relative to a cigarette lighter prank.
Just for a prank, Dean (age 14) used a cigarette lighter to brand two people.
This led to permanent scarring for one person. The school called the police.
The parents of the victims wanted the boy prosecuted. He had not been in trouble before, so the police suggested a restorative conference, if the school, the
victims, and their parents agreed. Everyone agreed, and the conference included
Dean and his mother, the two victims and their parents, and the conference facilitator. At the beginning of the conference, the victims' parents were very
angry about what had happened. Then Dean spoke about how horrified he had
been at the effect of what he had done and how sorry he was. The victims accepted his apology, and the conference ended with everyone shaking hands and
hugging each other. From this incident, Dean's mother and the parents of the
victims became friends. Dean never offended again. This process helped the
participants put the event behind them without criminalizing a young person
who made a mistake, albeit a serious one.

Preventing School Exclusions

Several schools use restorative conferences to prevent school exclusions (sus-
pensions or, if permanent, expulsions), or if exclusion is necessary, to help children reintegrate into school after exclusion.[4]

Case study: Restorative conference instead of exclusion for causing injury.
Four year 7 (age eleven) students had been running in a corridor. They came to
a sudden halt outside their classroom, and during the pushing and shoving, the
door to the classroom was flung open. Their teacher, Ms. Smith, who was standing on the other side of the door, was hit in the back by the door and knocked
across the room. She sustained minor injuries to her back and head and had to
go home as a result.

The deputy head of the school offered a restorative conference instead of
excluding the students. The students and Ms. Smith agreed to this. During the
conference, the four boys heard from Ms. Smith the extent of the harm they
had caused her, how she had to contact her partner to come and collect her from
the school, how upset and angry she felt about what had happened, and how let
down she felt by their behavior.

During the conference, the boys lowered their heads and spoke about how
bad they now felt, after hearing from Ms. Smith about the impact on her of their
behavior. They were able to take responsibility for their actions, and all four students offered apologies to Ms. Smith, which she accepted. The students agreed
to look at ways they could encourage other students not to run in the corridors.

After the conference, the students said that they were glad that they had
the opportunity to sit down with the teacher, even though they were scared at
first. They felt that their apology meant something to Ms. Smith and that they

would now no longer be embarrassed to go back into her class. Ms. Smith said that their apology felt sincere and she now believed they fully understood the harm they had caused her. She felt this would not have happened if the conference had not taken place.

Support Group Method to Reduce Bullying

The Support Group Method was originally called the No Blame Approach, but the name was changed to avoid the impression that bullies were let off, which was not the case. It was first used in the United Kingdom in 1991 and was developed by Barbara Maines (an educational psychologist) and George Robinson (a head teacher). It is a seven-step process used by a teacher or a facilitator when a child has complained about being bullied. This is a summary of the process (Robinson and Maines, 1997):

1. *Talk with the victim.* The aim is to concentrate on his or her feelings, not to gather facts or investigate. The facilitator then asks for the names of those doing the bullying and for some names of bystanders and friends.

2. *Convene a meeting.* The facilitator meets with the group of students mentioned by the victim, usually a group of six to eight. The victim is not present.

3. *Explain the problem.* The facilitator does not allocate any blame.

4. *Share responsibility.* The facilitator explains that no one is in trouble or going to be punished; rather, there is a joint responsibility to help the victim to be happy and safe.

5. *Ask for ideas.* The facilitator asks the group for ideas. Each member of the group is encouraged to make a commitment to help—for example, "I will ask him/her to sit by me in class."

6. *Leave it up to them.* The facilitator ends the meeting by passing over the responsibility to the group members and arranges to see them again about a week later.

7. *Meet with them again.* After about a week, the teacher discusses how things are going with each student separately, including the victim. It does not matter whether everyone kept to their intention as long as the bullying has stopped.

Case study: Support Group Method. Emma, age thirteen, was at the beginning of her second year at secondary school. She felt she was being laughed at and excluded by her group and spent all her lunchtimes in the school library. From being a confident, outgoing young person with many friends, Emma became more and more reclusive. In the end, she refused to go to school at all. At this point, her parents telephoned the teacher responsible for the Support Group Method at the school, and she arranged to meet them the next day.

Emma came with her parents but would not participate at first, until Mrs. S. skillfully drew her in. She then saw Emma on her own the next day and asked her to write down how she felt. Emma wrote that she felt she was "the odd one out" and "the one there was no room for." She said that sometimes she wished she were dead, as no one would miss her if she died. Emma gave Mrs. S. a list of the girls involved.

Mrs. S. then spoke to the girls concerned. They were shocked. "But Emma always seems so confident and she's good at everything. We had no idea she felt like that." They readily made suggestions to make sure they included Emma in their activities. Within a few weeks, Emma was back in the swim with her friends, enjoying a rich social life. It was a great relief to her parents.

Spread of Restorative Approaches

Many schools now use restorative approaches to inform their discipline policy and have found it has good results, confirmed by research (Bitel et al., 2005). A recent development is that several local authorities are embracing restorative approaches across all their schools and institutions. This is an exciting prospect.

In some schools, permanent exclusions have been reduced by 70 percent since 2003: "It's better to build bridges than walls," said one conference facilitator. In addition, a change in the schools' culture occurred: "It's not just about behaviour: it's a far more positive learning environment for the kids, a happier, more relaxed school, where the kids can engage with education more successfully" (Mirsky, 2006).

Conclusion

This chapter has provided an overview of the restorative processes being practiced in many schools and has demonstrated how they work in the school context. Schools that have adopted a whole-school approach are finding that the different processes work together well because they are all based on a restorative philosophy, and they have begun to make positive and lasting changes in the relationships that make up the school environment.

Restorative approaches can also be used in informal situations and with young children. The idea that very young children can learn restorative approaches to resolve conflicts is one that has great power; imagine a world in which all children have the opportunity to learn them as one of their first skills! This could significantly increase the world's resources to manage conflict and harm of all kinds.

Notes

This chapter draws on my book *Restorative Justice: How It Works,* published in 2007 by Jessica Kingsley Publishers. I would like to acknowledge all those who contributed case studies to that book and therefore to this chapter. They remain unidentified in order to maintain confidentiality.

1. Belinda Hopkins, director and lead trainer of Transforming Conflict, personal communication, 2006.

2. A head of year is a senior teacher responsible for a whole year group of several classes.

3. A form tutor is a teacher responsible for a class of students.

4. If students commit certain kinds of bad behavior, they may be excluded (suspended) from school, either temporarily (for a specified period) or permanently (expelled). In the case of temporary exclusions, meetings among the school, the student, and the student's parents or guardians usually take place before a student returns to school. In the case of permanent exclusions, students remain at home until they are found a place at another school, which can take several months.

14

Adolescent Bullying: The Whole-School Approach

Dennis Wong

Bullying is seen as repeated oppression, physical or mental, of a less powerful person by a more powerful person or group of persons. It occurs where there is an imbalance in power between people, and it is repeated or continued behavior (Olweus, 1993; Rigby, 1996; Smith and Sharp, 1994). There is considerable evidence that suggests that continued or severe bullying can contribute to immediate problems such as neurosis, sleeping difficulties, studying problems, truancy, and depression, as well as long-term problems such as chronic anxiety, low self-esteem, and dropping out of school. The worst outcome is that a severely bullied child takes his or her own life (Hugh-Jones and Smith, 1999; Olweus, 1993; Rigby, 1999; Whitney and Smith, 1993). School bullying has been identified as a major problem in many countries around the world (Carney and Merrell, 2001; Rigby, 1996; Smith et al., 1999).

In Hong Kong, there has been growing concern about bullying since a scrawny fourteen-year-old secondary school student, Luk, was tortured to death and burned as a result of group bullying in 1997 (Four offenders, 1999). Subsequently, more and more incidents of school violence were brought to the attention of the public. In 1999, a group of secondary students was reported for fighting each other outside the school, and a teenage girl was sexually harassed by a group of her classmates on the stairs of a housing project near the school (Stormy teenagers, 1999; Teen gangsters, 1999). In 2001, a grade 8 boy injured his classmate with a chopping knife during school recess after being verbally bullied for several months (Form 2 boy, 2001),[1] and a thirteen-year-old boy was eventually admitted to the hospital after being persistently bullied by five classmates for several months (Five bullies, 2001).

Keywords: school bullying, whole-school approach, conferencing, restorative practices

A more recent typical bullying incident happened in a secondary school and was eventually widely reported in the mass media in December 2003. The victim suffered serious attacks by his classmates on various occasions while some students secretly took video clips of the assaults and uploaded them on a website. The event immediately spread around the Internet. Afterward, the bullying issue was picked up by some media agencies. The police arrested most of the attackers the next day (Eleven secondary school students, 2003). In the end, eleven grade 11 students aged 16–19 were prosecuted and eventually placed on probation, or were sentenced to rehabilitation or detention centers. All these events caused alarm. It is important that school bullying is stopped within the schools to avoid a vicious cycle of school violence. What has emerged over the past few years is that not many schools in Hong Kong believe that they can do a great deal to stop bullying.

This chapter highlights the research literature and the findings of some local studies in Hong Kong related to school bullying. Using a vivid case of restorative conferencing and recent research findings on the effectiveness of a restorative whole-school program, I argue that a restorative justice approach is an effective strategy to prevent and stop bullying in schools.

Studies on the Prevalence of School Bullying in Hong Kong

In Hong Kong, there was no systematic study of the prevalence of bullying before 2000. It was not until mid-2000 that I, together with my colleagues, started to investigate the problem of bullying (Wong and Lo, 2002; Wong et al., 2002). In the first comprehensive research on teachers' and students' perceptions of bullying, 905 questionnaires were collected from teachers and social workers (Wong and Lo, 2002), as well as 3,297 questionnaires from students and 29 from secondary schools (Wong, 2003). I led another community-wide study of the prevalence of school bullying in primary schools in Hong Kong from 2000 to 2002 (Wong et al., 2002). In this study, 7,025 questionnaires were collected from forty-seven primary schools; results showed that more than half of the respondents were involved in bullying—as bystanders, bullies, or victims.

This local research on bullying found that 17.2 percent of the secondary sample and 24.2 percent of the primary sample admitted bullying other students at some time during the preceding six months. Similarly, 18.3 percent of the secondary sample and 31.7 percent of the primary sample reported that they had been the victims of physical bullying (Wong, 2003; Wong and Lo, 2002; Wong et al., 2002). The figures seem to reflect a high prevalence of physical violence compared with the results of studies conducted in the United States. Analysis of data from a representative sample of 15,686 students in grades 6–10 in public and private schools throughout the United States in 1998 indicates that 29.9 percent of the sample reported moderate or frequent involvement in bullying (including bystanders), either as a bully (13.0 percent), as one who was bullied (10.6 percent), or both (6.3 percent) (Tonja et al., 2001).

The studies have also identified risk factors and protective factors that contribute to the emergence and continuation of the bully-victim problem in Hong Kong. Results reveal that children's poor "psychosocial conditions" were related to their bully-victim problems. For example, when children were unhappy, emotionally unstable, and not satisfied with school performance, the likelihood that they were involved in bully-victim problems was higher. The relationship between peer victimization in schools and children's contact with violence, however, was inversely associated. Students who had more contacts with pro-violence gangs and peers were more likely to be involved in different types of bullying. To sum up, the studies have identified some risk factors that are conducive to bullying behavior, such as perceived strains at school, negative influence from peers, and poor psychosocial conditions. In contrast, protective factors, which have controlling effects on the problem, relate to the perception of school harmony and regulatory strategies adopted by the schools (Wong, 2003; Wong, 2004; Wong et al., 2002). It is important that school bullying is stopped within the schools or else it may create a vicious cycle of school violence.

A Restorative Justice Approach for Tackling School Bullying

It is now well established in the bullying prevention literature that the punitive approach—such as reprimanding bullies, calling parents to school, and suspending offenders—is ineffective. The punitive approach, which values establishing blame and individual accountability, not only cannot resolve conflicts but also makes the relationships between bullies and victims much worse. Worse still, when students encounter bullying, they often will not tell the truth in dealing with authorities and may take revenge afterward (Guadalupe and Bein, 2001; Morrison, 2002; O'Connell, Pepler, and Craig, 1999; Olweus, 1997).

One of the major reasons that the punitive approach is not the ultimate solution to school bullying is the interactive effect of various types of reinforcement among bullies, victims, and bystanders during bullying episodes. Thus, bullies are perhaps not the only ones to blame. Besides, revenge-taking behavior right after the punishment of bullies has always been observed (Cowie, 2000; O'Connell, Pepler, and Craig, 1999). It is apparent that to have a full understanding of the school bullying problem we may need to deconstruct the relationship between bullying and aggression. Fung, Wong, and Chak (2007, p. 6) argue that "proactive aggressors" are the true bullies, but often it is not easy to identify them. Whereas "reactive aggressors" are often identified by teachers and social workers as bullies, they are in fact originally victims. The ratio of reactive aggression as compared to proactive aggression is around 7 to 3. Their aggressive behaviors mainly develop from their past experiences of being bullied.

Their results echoed findings of a number of studies of children's aggression that found that children with aggression normally behave rationally and exercise self-control. On the contrary, reactive aggression is characterized by cognitive distortion, affective instability, and anger arousal (Fung and Tsang, 2007, p. 260). Fung and Tsang (2007, p. 261) further point out that children with reactively aggressive behavior are more likely to (1) selectively pay attention to hostile cues; (2) pursue a social goal that is likely to be damaging to relationships; (3) have normative beliefs and scripts supportive of aggression; and (4) generate more conflict-escalating solutions and interpersonal problems.

Unlike the punitive approach, the restorative justice approach aims to go through a dialogue-driven and participatory process to help all parties involved in the offending or victimization event to achieve a mutual understanding and future-focused outcomes (Marshall, 1995). Given the fact that children who exhibit aggressive behavior may continue a progressive developmental pattern toward severe aggression or violence, to stop the negative spiral effect of school bullying, restorative justice practice seems to be a well-balanced strategy that could involve the victim, the offender, and the stakeholders in the community in a search for solutions that promote repair, reconciliation, and reassurance (Wong, 2004; Zehr, 1990). Viewing restorative justice practices as a new paradigm for controlling crime (Bazemore and Umbreit, 1997; Johnstone, 2002), the restorative justice approach covers a wide spectrum of intervention tactics. Restorative justice practices range from informal restorative statements or impromptu conferences to formal victim-offender mediation meetings or family group conferences (Morrison, 2007; Van Ness, Morris, and Maxwell, 2003; Wachtel, 1997). To sum up, restorative justice practice not only focuses on working with the offenders but also comprises at least three main elements, including an emphasis on the offender's personal accountability, an inclusive decisionmaking process, and the goal of putting right the harm that is caused by an offense (Dignan and Marsh, 2001).

The Journey of Using Restorative Justice Practice to Tackle School Bullying

Few schools in Hong Kong before 2000 were aware of the use of restorative justice for tackling the problem of bullying. As part of our research, we worked with a group of teachers and a social worker to try out restorative justice practice in a secondary school in 2000 and 2001. The objectives of the project were to create a peaceful and happy learning culture among pupils, to decrease the number of bullying incidents, and to enhance pupils' intrapersonal as well as interpersonal skills. We first organized a series of activities for students and parents to raise their awareness of school bullying and to encourage their participation in the program. We also organized systematic lectures and workshops for social workers and teachers in the school in order to train them to use restorative justice methods for preventing and tackling bullying. If teachers know of bullying or suspect that it is occurring, they should deal with it in a systematic manner (Wong, 2004).

Apart from raising awareness and preparing teachers and parents, our team worked closely with the social worker to provide multilevel intervention—at the systemic, class, and individual levels. Apparently, the strategies used are somewhat similar to a trilevel approach, as suggested by Morrison (2007, p. 333). The trilevel, or three-tier, approach recommends making an intervention at the universal level (tier one), the targeted level (tier two), and the intensive level (tier three). Overall, we did try out restorative justice practices at different levels in schools as follows (see Wong and Lee, 2005):

Tier One: Universal Level

1. *Establish a set of long-term antibullying policies in school.* The basis for an effective approach is that all members of the school, including the school management committee, the principal, and the senior teachers involved in disciplinary and counseling matters, should formulate a common stance whereby school violence and bullying are dealt with positively. Without a clear and coherent mission for building a harmonious school, key members in the school may have different stances on disciplinary practices and thus do something that neutralizes each other's action.

2. *Set aside ninety minutes of class time each week to run peace education.* To teach students about restorative justice, a peace education curriculum should be provided to students in grades 7, 8, and 9 within the regular time of the formal curriculum. Overall, students will receive a total of twenty-one hours of peace education in each academic year during their junior secondary education years. The peace education curriculum consists of four key learning areas: self-understanding, emotional control, problem-solving skills, and interpersonal communication skills.

Tier Two: Targeted Level

1. *Promote a peaceful environment by using restorative justice practices.* Teaching students to restore relationships when they have conflicts is one of the important missions of education. If conflicts arise, we may appoint a social worker or a teacher to be a facilitator or mediator assisting both parties to resolve disputes and restore relationships. In the restorative process, it is hoped that bullies will understand how it feels to be a victim and realize what they did was wrong. Bystanders can be involved to enlighten both parties in understanding how problematic the conflict was. At the same time, victims can express their feelings during the conference and provide the chance for bullies to offer an apology and make compensation.

2. *Use a peer mediator.* Peer mediation programs are also useful restorative strategies. Teaching conflict resolution–peer mediation skills to "big brothers and sisters," such as class monitors, can help students build appropriate social responses and anger management approaches for use when they are faced with conflict situations. It can be a student-facilitated option to more traditional, punitive practices that rely on the adult to control student discipline problems. Schools should consider training a number of school harmony ambassadors or peer mediators to help teachers deal with minor bullying issues (Cowie, 2000; Sharp, 1996).

Tier Three: Intensive Level

1. *Assist victims in facing bullying assertively.* Although most of the victims tell their teachers and parents about the bullying, they do not tell them everything. Sometimes the victim feels that his or her own failings in resolving conflicts with classmates are partly or wholly to blame for what has happened. It is understandable that children often do not seek help. Because of the victim's passive personality, he or she never has the courage to face the bully directly. Teaching teenagers to be assertive is a crucial step to reduce bullying.

2. *Educate bullies who lack social skills.* Many first-time or "new" bullies mean no harm. They bully others because they do not know how to attract attention or control their emotions. These teenagers lack social skills and do not know how to communicate with others appropriately. We should organize workshops such as anger management, emotional control, and rational problem solving to train them not to seek attention through bullying acts.

3. *Shame in a reintegrative manner bullies who intend to do harm.* Effective discipline can help bullies realize what mistakes they have made and learn to improve themselves. The reintegrative shaming technique is one of the methods found useful in an Asian context (Braithwaite, 1989; Wong, 1999). For example, as Chinese people are often believed to be inner-directed and to be greatly concerned about shame, they may not be able to manage shame appropriately. Bearing in mind that shaming covers a broad spectrum of disapproving behaviors, ranging from those that are highly respectful of the bullies to those that are disrespectful (Braithwaite, Morrison, and Reinhart, 2003), shame management to help bullies or victims recover must be reintegrative but not stigmatizing in nature.

Use of Restorative Conferencing: A Case Illustration

Following is a good example of restorative justice practice that adopted a formal conferencing method to resolve school bullying in a secondary school. The incident started when a grade 10 secondary school student accidentally bumped into a grade 8 student's shoulder; it later turned into a brawl that caused several students to be seriously injured and three other students to be taken away by police.

The Incident

Anthony (grade 8) was the first participant who got hit on the shoulder while waiting outside the washroom for his friends. He was a new immigrant from mainland China and a member of a close group of other PRC immigrants in the same grade. Peter (grade 10) was the first participant who hit Anthony on the shoulder as he rushed through the hallway. He was friends with two well-known students, Calvin and Derek. Calvin and Derek (grade 10) were two popular students who were well respected by other students in the school.

As recess came to an end, Peter was rushing back to his classroom, when his shoulder was knocked by Anthony, who was just coming out of the washroom on the ground floor. Immediately, the two glared at each other and got into a verbal confrontation. "Hey! You ran into me. Why didn't you apologize?" Anthony asked. Peter countered, "How dare you hit my shoulder. You should apologize now!" Anthony was much shorter, scrawnier, and also two grades lower than Peter. He felt that he was being picked on, so he shouted desperately, "Brothers, come over here! Somebody wants trouble!" Immediately, seven grade 8 students jumped out from the washroom (some did not even finish putting on their trousers). All eight of them, including Anthony, surrounded Peter.

Anthony, the younger student, was being bullied at first, but the situation turned, and Peter, the older student, was surrounded by eight grade 8 boys who were apparently all new students who had immigrated from mainland China over the previous three years. They had always felt discriminated against by local students. This led them to have an implicit understanding of each other's situation. Therefore they developed a strong bond, and whenever one of them was being teased, the group would unite and defend that student unhesitatingly. Peter wanted to negotiate with the group but the eight grade 8 boys began to push Peter around (with both their hands and legs) and spoke in an intimidating way. Peter felt uneasy and thought he was being attacked. He blocked them, charged out of the crowd, and quickly ran back up to his grade 10 classroom.

In the classroom, two of his friends asked him what had happened. Peter claimed: "I just got ganged up on by that grade 8 group! They knew I was your friend but they treated me like dirt!" (Apparently, these two friends, Calvin and Derek, are very popular and well respected among the school's students.) Calvin and Derek decided to take revenge on Peter's behalf. All three rushed furiously to the grade 8 classroom. They also brought along three large boys to block the classroom door so that nobody could escape from the classroom.

Right away, Peter identified Anthony as well as two other boys who were involved in the earlier incident. The grade 10 boys began hitting the three grade 8 students, but the grade 8 students were all of a sudden unable to fight back.

Interestingly, they also believed that there might be more people standing behind the three large boys outside the classroom. They were only able to slightly block the attacks. However, this intensified the situation because the grade 10 boys thought the grade 8 students were fighting back. They each grabbed a chair and smashed the chairs over the grade 8 students. Anthony and two others were seriously injured.

When the teacher found out about this incident, she notified the school principal. The school principal then called the police. Unfortunately, the media were also alerted. The scene when the students were being delivered into the ambulance was captured and reported by many local newspapers. The principal was disappointed because the school had been complimented by the local school board just a year previously. She felt that her efforts were spoiled by this incident.

Three grade 10 boys were eventually taken to the police station. They were then bailed out by their parents the same day to await further investigation. Both parties of students did come back to school a day later. While the teachers were conducting a review of the event, they discovered that both parties had expressed their unresolved grievance and were afraid of revenge from the other party. Both parties had also indicated to teachers that they would call for external support (from gangsters) sooner or later for self-protection. The school principal feared that this might make things even more complicated and might also turn the original interpersonal conflict into a gang fight outside school; she then called me for help.

The Conferencing Process

Following the procedures of the script model of restorative conferencing (O'Connell, Wachtel, and Wachtel, 1999), the facilitators adopted the following conference protocols:

1. Have the offenders talk about what happened.
2. Address what they were thinking and who was affected.
3. Ask the victims and supporters to share their thoughts and feelings, and then ask the offenders' families and supporters to do so.
4. Then focus discussion on what needs to happen to make things right.

More than twenty persons attended the conference. Participants included Anthony and seven grade 8 classmates (altogether eight persons); Peter, Calvin, and Derek and three large boys from grade 10 (six persons); Anthony's class teacher and Peter's class teacher (two persons); the disciplinary master and the counseling master (two persons); the vice-principal and the principal (two persons); the school social worker; and the conferencing facilitators (a social worker and myself).

Having heard that Peter, Calvin, and Derek were on the verge of police prosecution, and that their parents were extremely angry with their behavior, in addition to seeing how depressed the school principal and teachers were, Anthony and some grade 8 boys showed great remorse about their retaliatory behavior outside the washroom. At the end of the conference, Peter profoundly apologized to Anthony and his friends for seriously hurting them. Peter took the initiative in shaking hands with Anthony. Interestingly enough, Anthony begged the school principal not to expel Peter, Calvin, and Derek from school. In the meantime, the teachers encouraged the students to work much harder in the future to rebuild the school image in the community. An agreement documenting that the two conflicting parties had agreed to restore relationships and promised to try their best to keep the school safe was eventually signed. A copy of this agreement was sent to the police station as a record. The police, after consulting the Department of Justice, agreed not to prosecute the three grade 10 boys but put them in the Police Superintendent Discretion Scheme. What could have been a tragic, ruined future for the grade 10 boys turned out to be a happy resolution for both parties.

Restorative conferencing is, in fact, one of the modern school discipline methods that can make both parties know what mistakes they have made and teach them to improve their behavior. During the conferencing process, students are often shamed in a reintegrative manner by various parties such as the victim, teachers, and parents without destroying their self-esteem (Braithwaite, 1989; Morrison, 2002). Conferencing is a delicate process critical to the outcome of restoration. To be a good mediator or facilitator, one has to be genuine and impartial, and speak less and listen more. Moreover, a facilitator has to be able to apply reframing techniques to facilitate understanding of the conflicting positions and the interests of the parties involved. Furthermore, a facilitator should know how to induce forgiveness and acceptance among the conflicting parties, with the goal of healing the offender, the victim, and the relevant parties.

Restorative Justice as a Healing Process

The event cited is certainly an incident caused by impulsive personalities, misunderstanding, or preconceived bias. Nevertheless, conflicts exist not just because of differences between parties, but because of the actions parties take in response to their differences. These moves and countermoves create and define the conflict, and they sustain it insofar as parties continue to make more moves and countermoves (Folger, Poole, and Stutman, 2005).

Although there are many ways of managing conflict in schools, such as punishing the offenders through demerits or suspension and calling parents to the school, the ultimate feelings of anger and hatred between the two parties might not be resolved. When hard feelings and anger are handled effectively, parties are able to move from a differentiated psychological condition to an integrated psychological condition. It is believed that as long as parties can avoid rigid and inflexible responses to differentiation, they have a good chance of navigating to an effective integration phase (Folger, Poole, and Statman, 2005). Thus, restorative conferencing with the help of a third-party facilitator is useful in moving the conflict from differentiation to integration.

In contrast with the zero-tolerance strategy, restorative justice practice is another means of minimizing the negative consequences of social control interventions and maximizing the opportunity for empowering proactive interventions (Kidd, 2006, p. 5). In affirming the stance of taking bullying seriously, restorative justice practice can be seen as a reintegrative shaming alternative (Braithwaite, 1989) to traditional school disciplinary practices, which could simultaneously educate bystanders, deter bullies, and empower victims. Most important, by going through a process whereby all parties with a stake in bullying come together to resolve collectively how to deal with the aftermath of the bullying event and its implications for the future, the school may develop a positive climate that makes students less vulnerable to proactive aggression as well as reactive aggression (Cowie, 2000). This kind of practice is definitely in line with modern social work practice, which emphasizes intervention by responding to any power imbalances between participants and their social and organizational context (Kidd, 2006).

Research Evidence of Restorative Justice Practices

Not many schools in Hong Kong are aware of the use of a whole-school restorative approach for preventing problems, despite the fact that there have been numerous discussions in this area around the world (Limper, 2000; Ortega and Lera, 2000; Roland, 2000; Salmivalli, 1999; Sharp, 1996). A survey on teachers' perceptions of school bullying in Hong Kong secondary schools showed that more than 80 percent of respondents opined that antibullying programs, including restorative justice practice, that are commonly adopted in other countries have never been organized in their schools (Wong and Lo, 2002). Surely, in many parts of the world, research literature has shown that some whole-school antibullying programs might create a culture to counter school violence and break the vicious cycle of bullying (Hopkins, 2004; Limper, 2000; Rigby, 1996; Roland, 2000; Smith, Schneider, and Smith, 2004; Thompson, Arora, and Sharp, 2002).

Guided by reliable intervention procedures and practical experience, our research team continued to investigate the effectiveness of the restorative approach in tackling bullying in Hong Kong. From 2004 to 2006, with the support of a grant from the Research Grants Council of the Government of Hong Kong, my associates and I conducted a two-year longitudinal study researching the effectiveness of the restorative whole-school approach in four government-aided schools with experimental and control conditions (Wong et al., 2007). The study, known as the RWsA program, consisted of a series of interventions and a range of research studies aimed at investigating the bullying conditions. An intervention team was set up to implement the program, while the research team focused on the scientific investigation of bullying conditions and related factors. Four schools participated in the study. The extent of participation in the program was negotiated with and agreed to by the schools. Therefore, the degree of implementation of the program was not entirely manipulated but assessed de facto by the research team. Based on qualitative and quantitative assessments, including field observation, documentary analysis, focus group interviews, and objective assessments, one school (School A) was assessed as having adopted full implementation of the RWsA, two schools were assessed as having partial implementation (Schools B and C), and one school did not implement the RWsA and so was used as the control group (School D).

Surveys were administered to collect students' ($N = 1,480$) ratings on bullying behaviors and other student behaviors. Three rounds of student surveys were conducted—before, during, and after the RWsA program. A total of 1,480 grade 7 to grade 9 students participated in the survey, in which 1,176 participants were successfully matched for within-subject analysis. Students' bullying behaviors, self-esteem, caring behavior, inappropriate assertiveness, lack of empathy, and ratings on quality of school life (sense of belonging and perception toward teachers) were measured (see Tables 14.1–14.4 in Appendix 14.A).

Comparing the results in Table 14.1 and Table 14.4, we can see contrasting findings between the fully experimental group (School A) and the control group (School D). Regarding prestudy/poststudy comparison (within-subject design), School A showed a significant decrease in bullying behavior ($p < .001$) and higher self-esteem ($p < .001$) after the study. No difference was found in other domains at .01 levels. This suggests that the RWsA program was significant in combating bullying behavior, as well as simultaneously enhancing students' self-esteem. Mixed results were found in partial implementation schools (School B and School C). No significant effects were found in self-esteem, lack of empathy, and harmony, whereas caring behavior and positive perception were significantly lower, and hurting others was significantly worse in both schools. Inconsistent results were found in bullying and sense of belonging. It was evident that without whole-school participation, the effects of an intervention program were markedly reduced. For the control group (School D), bullying was getting worse ($p < .01$), and all positive behaviors (except caring behavior) were significantly lowered in the poststudy measurement ($p < .001$). No significant pre-/postdifferences were found in self-esteem, lack of empathy, and hurting others. It was clear that without any RWsA implementation, the situation was deteriorating markedly over time.

Conclusion

The evaluation findings have shown a significant marked reduction of bullying behavior and lack of empathetic attitudes in the schools that adopted restorative justice practices fully as compared with those schools that did not. Bearing in mind that a heightened awareness of bullying and bullying behavior among students might have led to an elevation in levels of reporting (O'Moore and Minton, 2005; Smith and Sharp, 1994), the finding of the above longitudinal study definitely indicates some level of success of the RWsA. When we examined the actual implementation of the RWsA programs, we identified some elements that were highly related to the success of restorative justice practices in school. These include the following (Wong et al., 2007):

1. School management, in particular, the principal, having a firm stance in adopting the restorative justice approach in dealing with bullying
2. Collegiality among teachers and staff in school in building a harmonious school
3. Organizing restorative justice practice training for teachers
4. Involving parents in promoting school harmony
5. Providing a peace education and conflict resolution curriculum to students
6. Training students as peer mediators
7. Educating bystanders to take appropriate responsibility in stopping bullying

Results of this study also showed that any effective intervention strategy should involve students themselves and should adopt restorative practices in resolving the conflicts. By means of restorative practices, students are taught to adopt restorative problem-solving skills such as running a group or a restorative conference to help bullies understand the harm done to others, accept responsibility for their own actions, and make amends for harm caused. Restorative practices are increasingly being regarded as attractive options for dealing with bullying in schools. They focus on maintaining and strengthening social bonds to prevent pupils, either bullies or victims, from feeling isolated from or rejected by the school community (Braithwaite et al., 2003; Morrison, 2002).

To conclude, restorative justice practice gives bullies an opportunity to understand the consequences of their behavior for victims (O'Connell, Pepler, and Craig, 1999), enlightens bystanders to rethink the harmful effect of their noncommittal attitudes in the process of bullying (Cowie, 2000), and provides an opportunity for victims to regain self-worth, as well as to recover from the traumatic event through a process of apology and forgiveness (Braithwaite et al., 2003). Restorative justice practice is definitely a healing process that emphasizes interpersonal harmony. Interestingly, the emphasis on reintegrative shaming, forgiveness, and family responsibility for crime control through conferencing is a possible solution for delinquency in Chinese societies that value shame as part of their culture. Moreover, the protective factors that are crucial for preventing Chinese youngsters from engaging in criminal activities are positive shaming practices, forgiveness, brotherhood, and the logic of interdependency. Restorative justice is highly compatible with Chinese culture, which emphasizes collective values and the restoration of interpersonal harmony (Wong, 2001).

Appendix 14.A

Table 14.1 Comparisons of Scale Means Within School A

Variable	Pre-test			Post-test			Mean difference	t-value
	n	Mean	*SD*	n	Mean	*SD*		
Bullying[a]	353	1.40	.391	353	1.33	.327	−0.07	3.412**
Hurting others[b]	355	2.13	.823	355	2.14	.820	+0.01	−.105
Caring behavior[a]	349	2.47	.556	349	2.45	.555	−0.02	.741
Lack of empathy[b]	353	2.67	.929	353	2.54	.961	−0.13	2.353
Self-esteem[b]	352	3.99	.986	352	4.19	.900	+0.2	−4.006**
Harmonious school[b]	349	4.19	.870	349	4.27	.785	+0.08	−1.563
Sense of belonging[b]	356	3.92	.888	356	3.96	.842	+0.04	−.837
Positive perception[b]	345	4.39	.932	345	4.31	.931	−0.08	1.512

Notes: Because some of the students did not answer the questions, n may be less than the total number of students ($N = 363$).

a. 4-point scale: 1 = not at all, 2 = occasionally (once or twice), 3 = moderately (sometimes), 4 = frequently (once a week or more).

b. 6-point scale: 1 = definitely strongly disagrees, 2 = strongly disagrees, 3 = disagrees, 4 = agree, 5 = strongly agree, 6 = definitely strongly agree.

$*p < .01, **p < .001$

Table 14.2 Comparisons of Scale Means Within School B

Variable	Pre-test			Post-test			Mean difference	t-value
	n	Mean	*SD*	n	Mean	*SD*		
Bullying[a]	240	1.46	.430	240	1.47	.393	+0.01	−.604
Hurting others[b]	256	2.28	.855	256	2.51	.846	+0.23	−3.969**
Lack of empathy[b]	252	2.78	.926	252	2.91	.891	+0.13	−2.254
Caring behavior[a]	250	2.33	.606	250	2.20	.497	−0.13	3.524**
Self-esteem[b]	256	4.06	.857	256	4.04	.881	−0.02	.285
Harmonious school[b]	251	3.99	.774	251	3.96	.707	−0.03	.645
Sense of belonging[b]	252	3.82	.873	252	3.68	.756	−0.14	2.570
Positive perception[b]	238	4.27	.979	238	4.06	.793	−0.21	3.374**

Notes: Because some of the students did not answer the questions, n may be less than the total number of students ($N = 265$).

a. 4-point scale: 1 = not at all, 2 = occasionally (once or twice), 3 = moderately (sometimes), 4 = frequently (once a week or more).

b. 6-point scale: 1 = definitely strongly disagrees, 2 = strongly disagrees, 3 = disagrees, 4 = agree, 5 = strongly agree, 6 = definitely strongly agree.

$*p < .01, **p < .001$

Table 14.3 Comparisons of Scale Means Within School C

Variable	Pre-test			Post-test			Mean difference	t-value
	n	Mean	SD	n	Mean	SD		
Bullying[a]	310	1.44	.426	310	1.35	.370	−0.09	3.827**
Hurting others[b]	324	2.08	.919	324	2.25	.851	+0.17	−3.241**
Lack of empathy[b]	321	2.75	1.033	321	2.68	.903	−0.07	1.174
Caring behavior[a]	316	2.38	.575	316	2.26	.573	−0.12	3.304**
Self-esteem[b]	315	4.09	1.012	315	4.17	.857	+0.08	−1.518
Harmonious school[b]	320	3.99	.862	320	3.88	.842	−0.11	2.023
Sense of belonging[b]	323	3.91	.988	323	3.66	.857	−0.25	4.076**
Positive perception[b]	306	4.36	1.048	306	3.92	.998	−0.44	6.189**

Notes: Because some of the students did not answer the questions, *n* may be less than the total number of students (*N* = 334).

a. 4-point scale: 1 = not at all, 2 = occasionally (once or twice), 3 = moderately (sometimes), 4 = frequently (once a week or more).

b. 6-point scale: 1 = definitely strongly disagrees, 2 = strongly disagrees, 3 = disagrees, 4 = agree, 5 = strongly agree, 6 = definitely strongly agree.

$*p < .01, **p < .001$

Table 14.4 Comparisons of Scale Means Within School D

Variable	Pre-test			Post-test			Mean difference	t-value
	n	Mean	SD	n	Mean	SD		
Bullying[a]	186	1.48	.493	186	1.59	.541	+0.11	−2.558*
Hurting others[b]	204	2.34	1.030	204	2.43	1.049	+0.09	−1.094
Lack of empathy[b]	204	2.94	1.019	204	2.92	1.114	−0.02	.233
Caring behavior[a]	198	2.19	.608	198	2.33	.660	+0.14	−3.150*
Self-esteem[b]	200	4.00	.940	200	4.11	.850	+0.11	−1.504
Harmonious school[b]	198	3.77	.816	198	3.44	.831	−0.33	4.991**
Sense of belonging[b]	199	3.76	.875	199	3.37	.881	−0.39	5.106**
Positive perception[b]	189	4.07	1.082	189	3.66	1.056	−0.41	4.235**

Notes: Because some of the students did not answer the questions, *n* may be less than the total number of students (*N* = 214).

a. 4-point scale: 1 = not at all, 2 = occasionally (once or twice), 3 = moderately (sometimes), 4 = frequently (once a week or more).

b. 6-point scale: 1 = definitely strongly disagrees, 2 = strongly disagrees, 3 = disagrees, 4 = agree, 5 = strongly agree, 6 = definitely strongly agree.

$*p < .01, **p < .001$

Note

1. A form 2 boy is a student who is studying in the second year of a secondary school. There are seven forms in a secondary school in Hong Kong. Form 2 is equivalent to grade 8 in the United States.

15

Dispute Resolution in Higher Education

Ron Claassen and Zenebe Abebe

Dealing with college students' misconduct is as common for student affairs professionals as students going to classes. Most colleges and universities continue to resolve disputes the way they have done it for decades. At most institutions, it would not be surprising to find an elaborate system with various types of punishments and fines to be imposed, some of them quite stiff, for those who violate institutional rules and standards. Depending on the nature of the violation, some discipline may include fines, suspension, and even expulsion. The concern we want to address in this chapter is not so much about the kind of consequence, but about the process, which is typically combative, punitive, and not redemptive in nature, and how we have addressed this concern. This chapter describes the background and process that led to these changes and concludes with some of the results and observations regarding effectiveness.

Although the goals of our discipline policy at Fresno Pacific University (FPU) were clearly stated in redemptive and restorative terms, our process for responding to conflict, misbehavior, and violations was similar to the process previously mentioned. We asked, as do others using this process, three basic questions: Was a rule, standard, or policy violated? Who did it? And what should be their punishment? This paradigm was rarely, if ever, questioned.

In 1990, the Center for Peacemaking and Conflict Studies was established at FPU. Over the years, we became increasingly concerned about the structures that guide our institutional responses to misbehavior and conflict and the enormous force exerted by these unseen and generally unquestioned structures.

Keywords: higher education discipline, restorative justice, restorative discipline, conflict resolution in higher education, mediation in higher education, respect agreements, university/college conflict resolution, dispute resolution

What we noticed was that conflict resolution and mediation were generally seen as something that was appropriate and even effective in some selected cases but that the "real discipline system" continued to be based on the three questions mentioned. A primary goal of the center has been to encourage and assist institutions in reevaluating their goals, reconsidering their processes, and embedding conflict resolution and restorative justice into their structures.

At FPU, already in 1990, there were discussions about the possibility of utilizing mediation as part of the discipline structure and even trainings for student life leaders. For many years, occasional referrals were made to the center for mediation on selected cases that someone in the authority structure thought appropriate. Mediation/conflict resolution was seen as something in addition to the "real discipline system." The outcomes of these mediations were generally positive and seen as helping to achieve the stated goals in the discipline plan of redemption and restoration, but utilization continued to be occasional and an exception rather than the primary way of responding to conflict and misbehavior.

Zenebe Abebe became the new dean for the Division of Student Life at FPU in 2003. As part of his getting acquainted with FPU, he decided to review the student discipline policy. He asked the assistant dean to establish a committee that included students, faculty, and student life personnel to review the policy and make recommendations. Hearing about the policy review committee, Ron Claassen, director of the Center for Peacemaking and Conflict Studies, encouraged Zenebe to consider the possibility of incorporating restorative justice principles and processes in the student discipline policy. Ron, and later another Center staff member, were invited to be members of the committee.

In the first few meetings, the committee assumed that their task was to make adjustments to the current policy to improve it. After a few meetings of reviewing the current policy, Ron asked for, and was given, the opportunity to present the principles and practices of restorative justice along with an overview of the juvenile justice model that had been established in New Zealand. The rationale behind this presentation was the observation that most school (kindergarten through university) discipline policies operate a lot like a criminal justice system. Therefore, restorative justice principles and practices, which had developed within the context of the criminal justice system, must be equally relevant to student discipline policy. The presentation included the contrasting lenses of justice developed by Howard Zehr (1990); the fundamental principles of restorative justice developed by Claassen (1996a); the model and results from New Zealand (Children, Young Persons, and Their Families Act, 1989); and an overview of RJ City, a model in which a fictional jurisdiction works with all crime in the most restorative way possible.[1]

Zehr contrasts restorative justice with retributive justice in his groundbreaking book *Changing Lenses.* He compares two lenses for justice:

> *Retributive Justice.* Crime is a violation of the state, defined by lawbreaking and guilt. Justice determines blame and administers pain in a contest between the offender and the state directed by systemic rules.

> *Restorative Justice.* Crime is a violation of people and relationships. It creates obligations to make things right. Justice involves the victim, the offender, and the community in a search for solutions which promote repair, reconciliation, and reassurance. (Zehr, 1990, p. 181)

The FPU student discipline policy review committee could see that FPU goals were closely aligned with the restorative lens but that the FPU structure operated like the retributive lens.

According to Judge Fred McElrea of New Zealand, legislation was passed in 1989 that required that almost all juvenile cases, before being heard by a court, be given an opportunity to have a family group conference (FGC).[2] An FGC included the offender and several immediate and extended family members, if possible; the victim and several support people; some community and faith community representatives; at least one criminal justice official; and a facilitator, who led the FGC. The process in the FGC was to recognize what had happened, to decide on how to make things as right as possible, and to create agreements for a constructive future. If the FGC came to an agreement (which had to be unanimous), it was accepted by the court, and if the agreements were kept, that ended the case. By the end of five years, the number of cases needing to be decided by the court had been reduced by 75 percent, and the number of youth being incarcerated had been reduced by nearly 66 percent. The key to their huge success was their structural change.

Claassen suggested that the FPU could change the structure of its discipline program in a similar way. It could provide the opportunity for a community justice conference (a form of mediation including as many of those affected by the violation as possible) in all cases and, in doing so, align its goals and process.

The students on the committee immediately responded that they thought that this would be a good improvement and that students would be more likely to accept responsibility in this kind of system. The person from student life who had been responsible for determining guilt and for meting out punishments could see that this would substantially relieve that horrible weight from his shoulder and provide a redemptive option for those who were willing to accept responsibility. Everyone thought it was more consistent with our goals and yet everyone had serious doubts about it. By consensus, the committee decided to develop a restorative discipline policy.

Claassen and Abebe looked for university models and found many universities that had mediation programs. In the article "What They're Reading: The Power and Potential of Mediation," Michele A. Goldfarb (2004) writes that across the country hundreds of campuses are in the process of adopting mediation programs and integrating them into their student disciplinary and other grievance processes. It was clear that there is a movement introducing mediation to resolve conflict on college and university campuses. However, it was less clear if any college or universities had changed their discipline system to embed restorative justice and conflict resolution directly into their student discipline policy. A Wayne State University Web-based publication (Restorative justice city, 2004) states that while campus conflict resolution and mediation efforts are growing in popularity, they are still available on only about 12 to 15 percent of campuses nationwide. Of the college/university campuses we found that had implemented mediation programs, none had replaced their punitive student discipline system with a restorative one that made a mediation process the primary and central process while reserving the authority and coercive processes as their backup process. Rather, it seemed that most were offering mediation as an option parallel with their old system. And on many campuses, mediation was simply offered as a course and not as a process to deal with student conduct or with discipline.

In 2004, on the recommendation of the Discipline Policy Review Committee and with help from the Center for Peacemaking and Conflict Studies, the Division of Student Life decided to move from a one-person authority-based discipline process to a community-based mediation process as our primary process. In 2006, we developed a new student discipline policy we call *restorative discipline*. Because FPU is owned and operated by the Mennonite Brethren Churches, we developed a restorative discipline policy that is consistent with the Christian texts:

> You have heard that it was said, "An eye for an eye and a tooth for a tooth." But I say to you. . . . You have heard that it was said, "You shall love your neighbor and hate your enemy." But I say to you, Love [be constructive with] your enemy. (Matthew 5:38–48)

> If one of my followers sins against you, go and point out what was wrong. But do it in private, just between the two of you. If that person listens, you have won back a follower. But if that one refuses to listen, take along one or two others. (Matthew 18:15–16)

We called the policy restorative discipline to highlight the intended purpose. As stated in our handbook goals, we believed that this new process would enhance the academic purpose and atmosphere of the campus educationally, socially, spiritually, and developmentally. We were convinced that the process would encourage maturity while providing students with the opportunity to learn from their mistakes. It was designed to provide the opportunity for reconciliation of those who have been injured or estranged and to enable the restoration of an individual to his or her place in the community. We also believed that this process would encourage students to take responsibility by holding them accountable for their own actions, including making restitution for damages.

The Structure and Policy

The restorative discipline process is designed to provide students and other community members of the university with two main options (informal and formal) to consider when they are in conflict with each other. The informal option encourages students to go to each other directly to resolve issues and repair damages as much as possible. Depending on the personality and maturity of the persons involved, this may not be easy to do for some students. The informal option may also include a third person. All resident assistants and many student leaders are trained each year to provide informal mediation. Coaching and informal mediation are also available through the Center for Peacemaking and Conflict Studies. However, in the case of a violation, if an agreement is not reached and conflict is not resolved at this level, a violation report is filed that starts the formal discipline process.

The formal option contains up to three steps. The first step is to provide an opportunity for a community justice conference (CJC) for all cases. The CJC is convened by a graduate assistant who is employed, trained, and supervised by the Center for Peacemaking faculty. The convener or facilitator meets with all affected parties and invites them to participate. If the key people and adequate support or accountability persons decide to meet and if all in the conference mutually agree that the violation or injustice has been recognized and plans have been made to make things as right as possible (which must include restoring equity, future intentions, and a follow-up plan), and if at the follow-up meeting(s) all agree that the agreements have been kept, then a celebration ends the process. However, if the alleged offender thinks that he or she has been wrongly accused (refuses to accept responsibility) or if the convened group cannot come to agreement, then the case proceeds to the Student Judicial Board (SJB).

The second step of the formal process involves the SJB and, as mentioned, is utilized only when a case cannot be resolved cooperatively through a CJC. The SJB, which is made up of students, faculty, and staff, attempts to resolve the situation through a deliberative judicial process. The SJB's first task is deciding on responsibility. If judged responsible, the offender has another opportunity to enter a CJC or to have the SJB make that decision. The SJB is also guided by restorative justice principles and will decide on consequences that are respectful, that are intended to address the needs and obligations created by the offense, that restore individuals and relationships as much as possible, and that reintegrate the parties into their places in the community as much as possible.

The third and final formal step allows a student to appeal an SJB decision to the dean of students.

Implementation and Evaluation

The implementation process began by providing all university faculty, staff, and administration at least a one-hour introduction and training. Residence life staff, the director of safety, and those serving on the SJB received additional training. For example, all resident directors, the director of Resident Life and Housing, the assistant dean of Student Development Programs (who oversees

the discipline system), the dean of students, and the director of safety participated in the weeklong Basic Institute in Conflict and Management and Mediation. All resident assistants (undergraduate students) and many other student
leaders attend a one-unit conflict resolution class. The graduate assistant, who
is the case manager and often the mediator for the CJC process, is a graduate
student in the Peacemaking and Conflict Studies MA program.

There is a monthly meeting of a team (the dean of students and his staff
meet with faculty from the Center for Peacemaking and Conflict Studies and the
director of Campus Safety) to review how things are going and to discuss what
worked and what did not, what challenges lie ahead, and how the process might
be improved. Although we have the system in place, we see this as an ongoing
process to address issues that were not anticipated, to work out implementation
challenges, to discern where we can improve our system and learn from mistakes and successes we experience, and to monitor and evaluate case flow,
progress, and goals.

Results and Observations

The process is currently working pretty much as planned. One significant observation is that more conflicts and misbehaviors are being addressed at the informal level through direct discussion, student-led mediation, and resident
director–led mediation.

In the 2005–2006 school year, nineteen formal violation reports were filed,
which is the mechanism that initiates the formal option. Of those, eighteen were
resolved in the CJC process. Only one case proceeded to the Student Judicial
Board.

In the 2007–2008 school year, the number of discipline cases reached a
high of twenty-two. Five cases were sent to the CJC in the fall 2007 semester,
whereas seventeen were sent to the CJC in the spring 2008 semester. The majority of these cases resulted in an agreement. It was also during this school
year that the Center for Peacemaking worked alongside the Student Life Department on teaching restorative practices, as well as teaching the resident assistants
about respect agreements. Once the resident assistants learned how to create a
respect agreement, they helped lead this process within each of their living
areas.

During the following school year (2008–2009), five cases were sent to the
CJC for the entire year. There are a couple of reasons why we believe this occurred. One is that there were fewer residents living on campus. The other is that
the resident assistants and the Student Life staff were well trained in how to address and handle discipline cases. Therefore, many discipline issues that arose
were handled at an informal level, which is the ultimate goal of this process.

Following are observations from some of the staff who are central to the
implementation of the restorative discipline process:

My initial skepticism to restorative discipline was that I thought it was going to be soft and let people who had really done something wrong off the hook. What I have seen is that in most cases dealing with situations in a restorative way leads to greater ownership, accountability, and change as an offender. I now look forward to discipline situations knowing that there is great potential to come out with improved relationships and both victims and offenders who have grown. (Dave Obwald, resident director)

One of the most interesting things that I have noticed is that the more serious the case the better the outcome has been. When it is a more serious case, the student seems to be more willing to make things right. When it is not as serious, we have to deal with more apathy. They are more engaged when it is a serious violation. (Jason Ekk, graduate assistant and CJC case manager/mediator)

In a community that values group processing, to have one person wielding so much power just did not fit our culture, let alone the pressure of determining guilt and innocence and becoming the personification of campus discipline. Who wants to be known as "Judge Dread"? It was time for a change in how we operated our student discipline process. Adopting principles and concepts from the field of restorative justice has allowed us to create a new process that fits our community ethos of group decisionmaking and support. (Don Sparks, assistant dean of students)

Conclusion

One lesson for us has been that we now better recognize the power of structure and how important it is to be sure that the structure is consistent with the goals. We also now see that our students are capable of resolving many of their own conflicts and misbehaviors when given the opportunity, tools, and structures. We cannot expect more from students without providing these and modeling them ourselves.

Notes

This chapter is a revised version of "Restorative Discipline," *ACResolution* 6, no. 3 (Spring 2007). Reprinted with permission of the publisher.

1. The model and results of the New Zealand program are cited from the Restorative Justice Conference, Fresno Pacific University, October 1996, quoting Judge McElrea, who made a presentation. The RJ City program that was described can be found at http://www.rjcity.org/.

2. Notes from the Restorative Justice Conference, Fresno Pacific University, October 1996, quoting Judge McElrea, who made a presentation.

16

Restorative Discipline in Athletics

Dennis Janzen

Imagine the following scenario: You, the coach, are having the traditional team meeting at the beginning of the season. What normally happens in a meeting such as this is that you, the coach, present the team rules to the team. You may allow for a certain amount of team discussion regarding what kind of rules and standards the team will operate under for the season. You may also decide to simply announce what the expected rules for player behavior will be for the season. In any case, by the end of the meeting, all coaches and players know exactly what the team rules for the season are to be. Furthermore, you, the coach, or the team may also determine what the punishments will be for any violations of these rules. Typical rules may address such things as the use of alcohol or drugs, class attendance, diet and eating habits, dress codes in and outside a team activity, promptness to team activities including practice, and specific behaviors that may demonstrate respect for authority or teammates. You may scan the room and ask if everyone understands the team rules, at which time all team members will give the obligatory up-and-down head nod. On the surface, it would appear that all members of the team are in agreement with both the rules and the stated consequences for any violations that may occur. Everyone comes together at the end of the meeting, with all members of the team, coach included, putting their hands together in a circle that in our sports culture both symbolizes and suggests an agreement of team unity. Then you, the coach, or one of the team members, with a loud voice full of emotion, commands all in the circle that on the count of three everyone is to shout a chosen

Keywords: moral reasoning, violence, restorative discipline, athletics, sport, justice, psychology, character, citizenship, team, sportsmanship, rules, punishment, behavior, authority, community, social dynamics, agreement, retribution, consequence

word or a short phrase. This rousing team cheer serves to ceremoniously end the meeting and launch the promising new season to grand and anticipated heights of success.

Practices begin, everyone is motivated, and team unity is steadily strengthening. Players are working hard in practice, even encouraging each other despite the reality that they may also be in competition with teammates for playing time and a particular playing position. At this point, the stated and expected assumptions of commitment to teammates and the team goals override all other selfish ambitions or desires. To display or exhibit any selfish behavior would at the very least result in some degree of loss of respect from teammates and coaches. No one wants to risk such a sanction. Soon the team is playing games and doing well. Everyone appears happy and the team is improving. As the season moves along, certain players begin to emerge as team leaders either as a result of their play, their social interactions with teammates, or both. There is clearly an increasing level of social differentiation with respect to team roles and relationships. The evolution of the team dynamic appears to be progressing naturally and in a positive direction, with each team member accepting varied and emerging roles.

Suddenly, word gets out that one of the team leaders has violated a major team rule. What had appeared to everyone associated with the team to be a smooth, exciting, and promising season now appears to be in jeopardy. Everyone remembers from the season-opening team meeting what the team rules are and what the punishment is to be. In this case, the violation calls for dismissal from the team. Emotions and thoughts are ranging from anger to disappointment toward the offending teammate. Team agreements, pacts, and covenants have been violated. The thought of playing for a championship, the primary goal that forged everyone's commitment to each other and to the greater good of the team, now seems distant. The once promising season is now in definite peril because of the irresponsible and selfish behavior of a teammate. You, the coach, have little choice but to dismiss the player because that is what the team agreements call for. The relationships of teammates to this player have become strained and characterized by a high level of mistrust. The offending player begins to feel devalued and defensive in terms of his relationships and social position. People feel betrayed and the offending player knows it. The player feels genuinely bad about a poor decision that has cost him and his teammates something they had committed together to achieve. Everyone—the coach, the teammates, and the offending player—feels a strong level of powerlessness to heal or resolve the situation. What appears to be done is done. Action has been taken and the expectation is that there is no turning back. Everyone must "move forward." The offending player feels alienated, and no one really feels good about anything related to the situation. Everyone eventually moves on, and the players and coaches resume their efforts toward a good season. The offending player, in his new position as an outcast from the membership of the team he once valued and felt a valued part of, gradually fades away.

What are the lessons learned in this situation? That a rule is a rule and that respect for your teammates includes respect for the rules? That seems correct enough. In our athletic culture, respect for authority is seen as fundamental to a team's success. It is one of the major life lessons that our society hopes the participants learn in this type of environment. Are there other life lessons that emerge from the typical competitive athletic environment that seem to teach and educate people toward a better, more mature understanding of social growth, community function, and personal self-worth? The popular notion associated with involvement in our typical sports culture suggests that the aforementioned are a common and natural result of organized athletic activity. Yet, does the typical athletic social structure of accountability based on punitive consequences achieve the optimum results we want to believe come from the competitive athletic experience? Is the normal athletic model of accountability, discipline, justice, and authority the most effective model from an educational standpoint?

The purpose of this chapter is to examine the tenets of restorative discipline and justice relative to the social structures and traditions of our organized sports culture. On the surface, a model of restorative discipline and justice would appear largely incompatible with the traditional models of justice and discipline in our sports world. Yet, upon deeper examination, the restorative discipline and justice approach may actually be more effective in encouraging the growth and enhancement of a sense of personal accountability for one's actions and the maintenance and building of the cohesiveness of the group, team, or community.

Basic Tenets of Restorative Justice and Discipline

Fundamental to the effective functioning of any group, team, or community are the personal commitments to the values and agreements from each member to each other member of the respective group, team, or community. In essence, restorative discipline and justice is about building communities of care around struggling individuals while not condoning their harmful behavior. It is vital to understand that restorative justice and discipline are neither a relaxation of standards nor an absence of accountability. A few years ago, Bruce Brown—author of numerous books that focus on the development of character through the vehicle of athletic participation, the former chief spokesperson for the National Association of Intercollegiate Athletics Champions of Character Initiative, and the current director of ProActive Coaching—stated in a personal communication that "people will rise to the level of the standard, or fall to the level of tolerance." When an alleged violation suggests the need for a disciplinary response, restorative discipline and justice centers on an approach that focuses primarily on the development of agreements that can restore a sense of moral balance and "rightness" between the relationships of the offending member and the rest of the group or team members. Furthermore, restorative discipline and justice incorporates both a commitment to personal accountability for all members and compassion for the individual whose behavior has strayed outside the agreements of the group, team, or community.

When the group or team is formed, there is an overriding expectation to abide by the agreements, covenants, and formal regulations as determined by the community even though the member may not completely agree with all the standards. The hope is that compliance is seen by each member as a personal contribution to the greater good of the group, team, or community. Membership in the community is subject to the agreement to abide by the community standards and the member's willingness to function within these standards. Should a violation occur, the disciplinary response is one that provides both encouragement and accountability for the offender. It is an approach that seeks to illuminate boundaries that may help the offending member to better understand the reasons why he or she may not be in a right relationship with the standards that have been agreed upon and established by and for the members of the community, group, or team.

Jason Ekk, student discipline case manager and mediator for the Restorative Discipline Program at Fresno Pacific University and someone who has been involved in numerous restorative discipline cases, several of which have involved student-athletes, has said that he always felt that the process had a better chance for success for all parties when it involved a student-athlete because of the built-in community, the accountability structures inherent within a team culture, and the typically greater desire on the part of all parties—the offending student-athlete, teammates, and the coaching staff—to effectively deal with the issue and return to a level of relational synergy that characterizes most successful, highly functioning teams. An additional benefit that often happens is that the team can become even stronger internally because of the resultant recommitment to team goals by its members during the development of respect agreements, which are a vital part of the restorative discipline process.

The restorative discipline and justice approach seeks to use the occurrence of misbehavior in a way that can provide an educational opportunity that not only repairs the harm done to member relationships but also builds toward an understanding that fosters more socially responsible relationships and that takes others' perspectives into account. When violations occur, individuals are made to understand the degree of harm and the impact of their actions on their fellow members. They are reminded of, and assisted in recognizing, their social responsibilities toward the group. Persons who are involved in a violation are also shown how to make amends to those whom they have affected by their actions. It is hoped that the offending player will feel fully restored into good standing and acceptance into the community rather than continue to experience feelings of alienation and separation.

Common Notions of Justice in the Sports World

Like all basic social institutions, the world of organized sports has determined it will function by commonly agreed-upon rules and codes of moral, ethical, and legal behaviors. Furthermore, while all basic institutions and societies may have similar culturally universal standards for behavior, the degree and definition of comparative compliance for each is unique. The institution of athletics, while it represents a basic microcosm of the society in which it is embedded, also has within it different sports that carry their own unique codes of moral and ethical behaviors. The judgment of the "rightness" or "wrongness" of an individual's behaviors is largely determined on the basis of what has become acceptable behavior within a specific sport's culture. For example, take the game of ice hockey. Smith (1975) found that 96 percent of a player's teammates would approve of players fighting, even though it is against the rules of the game, if it helps the team to win. Contrast that with the "gentleman's" nature of golf and tennis where fighting is virtually unheard of and definitely viewed as unacceptable by both fans and players alike. In another example, if a person were to get into a fistfight on a street corner, that person most likely would get arrested, thrown in jail, and maybe even convicted for the crime of assault and battery. Yet, if a fight breaks out within the athletic context, most sports have much less severe penalties for such behavior. Certainly, jail time and an arrest record are not a part of these penalties. Our society normally views fighting in everyday life in a negative way. However, if a fight breaks out within the athletic context, some fans will delight in the brawl and, indeed, even elevate the stature of participants in terms of respect and esteem. How does one respond in terms of a definition of justice when the lines of inappropriate behavior can be somewhat blurred. What may have been seen originally as "wrong" by the team may soon become more difficult to judge in terms of its contextual "rightness" or "wrongness." Remembering that restorative discipline and justice still focuses on maintaining previously agreed-upon behavioral standards, the restorative model may actually be a more suitable disciplinary approach because it can better recognize and deal with the marginal behaviors that so commonly occur, especially if the lines of "right" and "wrong" begin to shift or blur.

Bredemeier (1993) suggests that sports may be a specific area that, structurally, tends to function differently from most mainstream "real-life" situations. Based on her research, Bredemeier and colleagues (Bredemeier and Shields, 1985, 1986; Coakley and Bredemeier, 1988) have proposed a theory of "game reasoning." The theory posits that "the unique context of sport elicits a transformation in moral reasoning such that egocentrism, typically the hallmark of immature morality, becomes a valued and acceptable principle for organizing the moral exchange." She goes on to say, "Sport may allow for the temporary suspension of the typical moral obligation to equally consider the interests of all parties, in favor of a more egocentric style of moral engagement as an enjoyable and non-serious moral deviation" (Bredemeier, 1993, p. 595). One of the bases for these assertions is that competition is by nature extremely ego-centric. Participants are taught that it is not appropriate to selflessly consider the needs, desires, or goals of their opponent. Second, the rules of a game (i.e., the sport's structure) tend to protect the participants from any negative sanctions that might otherwise develop from such an egocentric approach. Finally, the presence of coaches and game officials allow the participant an opportunity to temporarily transfer much of the normal moral responsibilities that may develop in other mainstream real-life settings (Bredemeier, 1993).

The Case for a Restorative Discipline and Justice Approach in Athletics

Why should a coach who has been relatively successful in terms of his or her win-loss record over the years change from a proven traditional model of coach-centered team rules, retributive justice, and punishment? It has been said that coaches tend to coach the way they were coached. The stereotypical coach is historically one who is clear in his or her expectations, who holds everyone to a high standard, and who the athletes know has their best interests at heart. We also expect that the typical coach is someone who will physically and mentally challenge the athletes beyond what they probably think they are capable of achieving. All of these are good things. However, the method of motivation and accountability under the stereotypical coach often involves the threat or the reality of punishment or a punitive response should players come up short in terms of expectations. An example of a shortcoming could be in the form of physical effort, mental focus or toughness, or attitudes toward team rules. The consequences are intentionally unpleasant, sometimes resulting in a deterioration of respect for the coaching staff by the players, especially when players do not fully understand or agree with the "why" of the consequence.

   All power in the team relationships, especially coach-player, is top-down. Respect for the coach often originates from a threat or the actual display of power or coercion by the coach over the players. Accountability and trust are typically demanded by the coach from the player. The coach's response is often some sort of conditional intention of reciprocating the agreement of accountability and trust to the player from the coach. In a sense, the coach is saying, "I will trust you only when you trust me." In organized athletics, it is not unheard of that the coach of a team demands a standard of honesty, integrity, and accountability within the team, yet is willing to violate these standards in order to gain a competitive advantage over opponents. The behavior can be easily excused or rationalized if it results in a win. The obvious inconsistency of personal ethics, morality, and social standards by the coach, who is the team's ultimate authority figure, can and should make the enforcement of standards within the team difficult if not impossible. Certainly, the normally powerful educational opportunities for the social modeling of desired life lessons are significantly diminished. Impressionable players who see that a highly valued standard or ethic, such as previously agreed-upon team rules that were initially presented to the team as the "uncompromising standard," is intentionally and successfully compromised by the coaching staff in the pursuit of a team victory may also decide that the lowering of a personal standard in the pursuit of a desired goal is acceptable. In essence, they may come to accept the well-known notion that the end justifies the means. In the final analysis, players will likely lose respect for their coaching staff. With this loss of respect, the likelihood of future discipline and behavioral issues by players would increase, and the educational and social opportunities for the student-athletes to grow and mature in their ability to function relationally would diminish.

A process of restorative discipline and justice along with a pervading atmosphere of trust from coaches through the student-athletes allows for greater development in the participants of the characteristics of respect, responsibility, and integrity. This foundation of trust within the team allows for student-athletes to learn socially from their mistakes. They become better teammates. They become more skilled at understanding how to repair relationships that are either strained or damaged. This type of trust atmosphere encourages student-athletes who have understood that their actions have damaged important teammate relationships, or the team in general, to take responsibility for their actions. They come to understand that they must work with their teammates to make things right with all those who have been socially injured. A final result is that offending members of a team will be made to feel that their teammates still value them and are more willing to accept them back into the social membership of the team, and yet they will still understand that they have the responsibility to correct the "wrong" for all involved.

Concerns with the
Restorative Discipline and Justice Model

Would a model of team involvement in the establishment of team rules and agreements/covenants, coupled with a model of restorative discipline and justice, be seen by the players as relinquishing too much perceived control of the coaches over their athletes? Some players simply expect their coach to exert absolute control over all aspects of the team. Anything less may be seen as a weakness of leadership by the coach. Could the restorative discipline and justice model cause the student-athletes to believe that they will not be held to a high level of accountability by the coach, and that if they violate a rule, they will actually have less respect for team standards, maybe even the coaching staff, because they perceive that they will always have an avenue to return to the team? Would employing the restorative discipline model then create a concern on the part of the coaching staff that they, in effect, have less control over their athletes than they might have under the traditional retributive justice—or punitive justice—model? A basic tenet of the restorative discipline and justice system is that the standards and the level of accountability that everyone must adhere to are not compromised. Restorative discipline and justice is not a model that should be perceived as "soft on crime" even though it is a more participatory model. While the restorative discipline and justice model focuses on the person who committed the "wrong," the process also seeks to maintain the feeling that the person is still someone who should be valued and that it is his or her actions that should be dealt with. Restorative discipline and justice works to reestablish a sense of social and moral balance between offending players and their teammates and coaches through the development of mutually arrived at "respect agreements." The intended result of a respect agreement is that all have agreed that once the agreement is satisfied, the social and moral balance between parties is restored and the "wrong" has been made "right." Along with this should come a recommitment by all involved to the core values that were originally established by the team. This entire process would typically serve to also reestablish the essential, yet genuine, feelings of trust among all parties.

The issue of perceived control by the coaching staff is an important one to understand in the competitive sports world. In a profession where the winning and losing so often become the most important standard for defining a coach's successes and failures, it seems only natural that coaches attempt to influence the competitive result in as many tangible ways as they can. This sense of feeling the need to control as many aspects of the team and players as possible is further influenced by the realization that there is still much that the coach has little or no control over. Coaches cannot really control whether a basketball team will have a great shooting night, or how a football may bounce off the turf, or whether a star player will remain healthy and not get injured during the course of a season. However, because the coaching profession in general believes that discipline is a necessary characteristic in the equation for athletic success, both in the sense of one's ability to remain mentally and physically on task and focused, and from the sense of consequence or punishment from undesirable behavior, it would seem logical that coaches would attempt to control the aspects of an athletic team and the players that they realize they do have some influence and control over. This need to feel as if they have a significant amount of control over the winning and losing can have a profound impact on both the player-coach relationships and the model of justice and discipline the coaching staff decides to utilize.

A Model of Restorative Discipline and Justice in Athletics

Restorative rather than punitive approaches to discipline deal more effectively with athlete misbehavior by encouraging athletes to take responsibility for their actions and find ways to "make things right" with those they have harmed. Restorative discipline empowers athletes to be accountable for their actions in an athletic environment that is caring and responsive. Restorative practices also create an environment where all members of the community are accountable for their actions, resolve conflicts, create positive relationships, and build an inclusive, respectful school culture. One of the best basic guidelines or rules that seems to encompass everything that a team or coaching staff may encounter can be summarized in the statement, "Don't let your teammates down." In essence, this statement actually covers every possible team or member behavior ranging from effort in practice or contests to violations of team or school rules, be they academic or athletic. Misbehavior is viewed more as a violation against human relationships rather than as a violation of a team rule. It is important to remember that the basic function of a set of rules is actually to create an environment of order and fairness relative to human relationships. The coach or the offended party must be sure to communicate in some way to the offender that it was the behavior that is the issue or problem and not the person him or herself. People are to be valued. Inappropriate behavior is not.

Part of the restorative model of discipline and justice is also based on the notion that the primary victim is the one most affected by the violation. There are usually secondary victims—teammates, coaches, the school, or the community—whose reputation might also be adversely affected.

Fundamental to a restorative discipline and justice model is the goal that recognizes that once a violation occurs, salient teachable moments for all team members become readily available. Just as the effective coach becomes skillful at either creating or recognizing teachable moments inside the practice environment, so should the skillful coach recognize or create teachable moments as a result of the conflicts or violations that inevitably will occur during the course of a long athletic season. All groups, including sports teams, inherently involve human social interaction. All groups possess certain common characteristics. Groups are dynamic, not static. In other words, they exhibit life, vitality, interaction, and activity among their members. Group dynamics always include varying degrees of harmony and conflict, effective communication, miscommunication, or the lack of communication. These social dynamics also include varying levels of commitment or lack of commitment toward either the group goals, processes to achieve these goals, or select members of the group. In essence, there is always a degree of conflict within the group dynamic.

Ron Claassen, program director for the Center for Peacemaking and Conflict Studies at Fresno Pacific University, and an internationally known expert in the field of conflict resolution and restorative discipline and justice, suggests that the notion of social and relational "conflict" is filled with dangers and opportunities. In fact, the Chinese symbol for *conflict* also makes reference to *crisis* and *crossroads,* hence implying danger and opportunity. Dangers include gossiping about other members of the group or team, putting down teammates or coaches, creating social distance from the group, and inflicting perceived or real hurt or injustices on teammates or coaches. Opportunities abound when a requisite agreement between the two parties to earnestly and genuinely work at reconciliation is put in place. Any level of personal selfishness or insincerity from either party will severely compromise the healing or restoration process. The beneficial results can include enhanced communication among members; building up of one another, particularly as it pertains to and encourages progress toward an agreed-upon group or team goal; a stronger sense of community or group cohesion; and, in case a hurt or an injustice occurs among members, repair and restoration. In summary, the group or team corporately and individually comes to feel a renewed sense of focus, recommitment, and drive toward the original team goal. In fact, the group or team may actually become an even stronger unit as a result of this crisis because of the level of greater interpersonal understanding that has now developed between team or group members.

Another important principle in the restorative discipline and justice process again focuses on the attitude of the two parties. The coach or the offended party must clearly (1) portray and possess an attitude toward the offending party that he or she values the offending individual as a person but disapproves of the behavior, (2) communicate that he or she is hopeful that respect agreements can be reached that will allow for the return of the offender to a full level of reacceptance within the social dynamics of the team, and (3) seek to establish a relational atmosphere that is seen by all as nonconfrontational and, in fact, is viewed by the offender as supportive and valuing. A confrontational approach typically serves only to create more walls that serve to limit rather than open and enhance the lines of communication. Obviously, without communication, the reconciliation and restoration of relationships simply cannot occur.

Everyone involved must also understand that at times the offending party may simply not be emotionally ready to enter into the process with a cooperative attitude. An effective model for restorative discipline and justice suggests that the invitation to enter into the corrective process should remain open to the offender. The invitation should remain as one that allows for voluntary involvement by the offender. Coercion and pressure should never be used, because the end result will likely not yield a respect agreement from the offender based on a genuine and repentant attitude of reconciliation toward the offended party. It should also be noted that on occasion, should the continued efforts to engage the offender and develop the essential respect agreements prove unsuccessful, a permanent separation of the offender from the team or group may be necessary.

Finally, after a successful respect agreement has been reached between the offender and the offended, appropriate accountability structures need to be put in place that will accomplish two things. The first is a perception on the part of the offender of support and the potential for full reinstatement into the social fabric of the group or team by his or her teammates. The second comes from the offended party. This involves approval and a clear understanding of the accountability structure that the offender has agreed to as well as a genuine commitment to the process of reacceptance back into the membership of the group or team. These understandings and agreements serve to form the building blocks for a reenergized sense of mutual trust that is so vital to the successful functioning of athletic teams.

Restorative Discipline and Justice in Action

Let us now refer back to the scenario that was described at the beginning of this chapter. Remember that in the previously described scenario, the members of the team engaged in common preseason activities and team-building rituals that often occur in our sports world. The virtues and benefits of being a contributing part of an evolving team remain one of the more engaging and enjoyable experiences in sports. The initial "coming together" process serves to create a strong, albeit untested, commitment to the identified group or team goals. The old sports slogan "TEAM . . . *T*ogether *E*veryone *A*chieves *M*ore" adeptly, yet naively, may best characterize the thinking of the team members' attitudes toward one another. Their perception of what the personal rewards may be if they commit to the group goals remains seemingly plausible. It should be noted, however, that in every group or team, there is what is known as a reciprocity of influence. In other words, we exert an influence on other people in the group and, in turn, they have an influence on us. How each team member feels and chooses to respond to this influence determines in a major way how the team or group will ultimately perform. Each team member will feel that some type of personally valued return must be received from the emotional and psychological investment that they make to the team and its goals. This psychologically based return may be something as simple as a feeling of membership or belonging along with the enhanced feeling of social prestige that comes from being identified by others as a part of this special team or group. The psychologically based return on investment may also require a particular amount of playing time, or a specific achievement or accomplishment such as a scoring average or some other performance-based measurement. The team leaders and coaches that team members ultimately choose to comply with or submit to are somewhat dependent on whether the individual team members perceive team leaders or coaches as able to provide them with the opportunity to receive this "acceptable benefit." Can the coach or team leader get me what I really want from this experience, especially if I'm going to invest so much personal time and effort toward the team goals? Furthermore, should I submit myself to the team goals for the benefit of the team if this act of personal submission would appear to not allow me to receive the social or psychological benefits that I feel I want from my commitment?

Remember that in the initial scenario, as the season progressed, everyone seemed to remain true to the agreed-upon commitments of the team. The trust level among the team members was building and the social dynamic appeared to be strengthening. All seemed well, and the spoken rewards of a possible championship that was to result as the product of each team member's commitment to the team goals seemed to be moving increasingly closer. People were buying into the leadership structure of the team, whether it came from a team member or a coach. Then suddenly, with no warning, a team leader and very important player violates a major team rule that carries the predetermined penalty of dismissal from the team. The coach, true to the team agreements, carries out the penalty and permanently removes the offending player from the team. The remaining team members are left to cope with their personal and corporately felt feelings of disappointment, anger, and frustration. The offending player logically feels these emotions projected onto him by his former teammates, which then results in an increased sense of alienation, social distance, and devaluation. The growing feelings of betrayal are serving to further drive everyone's feelings of social and psychological separation because of the growing sense of powerlessness to change or fix the situation. The traditional athletic model, used in this case, is based on a punitive response to a team offense. The use of this discipline model has done two things. One, it has limited both the coaching staff's and the teammates' options for a potentially constructive response to a lapse in judgment by the offending player. Remember that in this described scenario, everyone, including the player who committed the violation, had been a valued, contributing member to the positive team dynamic and had personally committed to the team goals. He had garnered the respect of his teammates, most likely because of a combination of playing ability and social strength within the team's relationship dynamic. The second thing that the use of the punitive response has done has been to eliminate the educational opportunities for the coach to demonstrate in a salient situation the social benefits of restorative discipline and justice on the processes of healing and restoring broken relationships. Our world and our success in it depend on our ability to constructively handle the conflict and stress that is an inevitable result of our many interpersonal relationships.

A possible scenario utilizing a restorative discipline and justice approach could have been developed for the following basic team rule, "Don't let your teammates down." This is an extremely powerful, yet simple, approach to establishing the parameters of team expectation and discipline. Let there be no mistake, I am neither advocating a relaxation of behavioral standards or expectations nor suggesting that there should not be significant consequences for violations of team standards. What I am suggesting is that with a basic team rule like this, in essence all situations are covered, and the coach—the final authority figure—is left with all possible options from which to respond should a team member commit a violation.

Fundamental, as emphasized earlier in this chapter, is the premise that standards must be established for any organization, group, or team to be successful in the pursuit of their agreed-upon goals. Remember also that it is ultimately the coach's responsibility to enforce the standard once it has been set. Meaningful educational opportunities for each member of the team emerge both when leadership and character training are intentionally emphasized and when violations of the team standards occur. Whether these agreed-upon team standards are in the explicit form of core covenants or are more inferred, the general yet powerful sweep that results from a simple, all-encompassing rule such as "Don't let your teammates down" creates a broad sense of program and interpersonal accountability. This powerful rule will often have the effect of causing a team member to think much more carefully about what effect possibly questionable behavior might have on teammates. In short, accountability levels are enhanced in a more positive way rather than in a punitive way. Team members find themselves increasingly thinking and caring more for their fellow teammates and the impact their personal actions may have on significant others such as teammates, coaches, schoolmates, community, or family. The foundations for a strong system of discipline that is based on valuing human relationships and hopefully restoring individuals back into a supportive and caring team environment, while at the same time providing offending players with a clear understanding of how their actions have hurt numerous people around them, frames the tenets of the restorative discipline and justice model. Team members must understand that the violation of team standards always results in some type of social or relational injury. Whenever team members become aware of program or team rule violations by fellow teammates, there will always be an initial erosion of trust for the offending teammates. In addition, all team members must begin to recognize that a violation is simply the result of behavior that suggests either irresponsibility or naivete to the needs and commitments of the community. As the coaching staff works to build the team culture into one in which its members learn to function within the framework of restorative discipline and justice, we would ask individual community members to take responsibility and ownership of the community environment. Ideally, should a minor offense take place, team leadership at the player level will have developed sufficient social maturity, as well as a familiarity and appreciation for the restorative process, such that they do not always need to bring in the coach when violations take place. By asking team members to confront their fellow teammates, each team member has a responsibility to do what is right not only for the team but also for the well-being of the offending teammate.

In the case of the teammate who under the first scenario was ultimately dismissed from the team, an approach that still focuses on people and relationships rather than simply on rules and regulations allows the offending player to better realize the full extent of the poor behavior. This particular athlete may even have had the opportunity to rejoin the team. Many people, under a punitive discipline system, never have the opportunity to fully realize how many people and relationships they have adversely affected. Learning from one's mistakes under a punitive system will typically occur with much less social support being available or extended to the offending person. This person must also be able to overcome the normal wash of emotion, anger, rationalizations, and alienation that usually comes with the realization that you have "let your teammates down." This may be especially true within the athletic environment simply because of the extended levels of relationships that can connect socially or psychologically to the team. Teaching people to understand the true impact of their decisions, especially when they affect relationships, and to then accept responsibility for their actions and mistakes, represents a major step toward social maturity.

Final Thoughts

The notion of utilizing a model of restorative discipline and justice in today's athletic world may seem somewhat idealistic. After all, in an industry in which results are broadcast, webcast, displayed globally on the World Wide Web, or written and scrutinized in the daily newspaper, coaches may feel as though they do not want to risk utilizing a discipline model that they may not entirely understand. Remember, particularly in our athletic world, "coaches tend to coach the way they were coached." Change in the coaching profession, particularly in terms of the understandings relative to the type of team culture that is associated with winning teams, is slow. Commitment, respect, and work ethic are still highly valued. Personal sacrifice, loyalty, and support for your teammates are also revered in our sports world. A model of restorative discipline and justice upon detailed examination represents a model that is both psychologically and socially more healthy for its members. It also serves to create a more positive environment for team discipline that can enhance rather than marginalize team member relationships. Stevenson (1975, p. 287) stated, "In the final analysis, it is the rationale of 'character-building,' of moral development, of citizenship development, of social development, that justifies the existence of . . . athletics in educational institutions." In today's sporting environment, the display of inappropriate (e.g., disrespectful, dishonest, and self-centered) behavior at all levels of athletic competition is becoming increasingly common.

Does restorative discipline and justice within the athletic environment represent a better solution to the growing malaise of our sports world? Based on the psychology and sociology of human achievement and relationships, it would seem that successful restorative discipline and justice processes within the athletic context may represent an enhanced description of achievement through successful relationships beyond our society's simple, culturally defined assessments of athletic achievement, which tend to focus primarily on winning and losing. The realities of competitive athletics are themed with an overarching goal of achievement. Unfortunately, most if not all social processes that are engaged, encouraged, and demanded within the athletic environment are done for the fundamental goal of winning athletic contests. The teaching of character and the desired beliefs that involvement on a sports team will automatically somehow teach its members the social skills necessary to navigate our relational world seem to have become secondary to the rationalized perceptions and beliefs that more is learned through victory than through defeat. The culturally acclaimed nobleness of the commonly believed virtues and benefits of competitive athletics, compared to the realities and tolerances of what society tends to accept in the processes of striving for athletic success, has possibly dulled our social senses in terms of our true understandings of "rightness" and "wrongness."

What do we want our children learning when they engage in athletic competition? What should they be learning when they become part of an athletic team? Enhanced social and psychological maturity should be the primary goal of the athletic experience. Upon further analysis, or "upon further review" as the NFL referee says when reviewing a call that is being challenged and that will either be determined as right or wrong, our current culture of sports needs more coaches that understand how to enhance the learning opportunities of our youth through the salient vehicle of competitive sports. Organized sports are one of the most powerful social influencers in our society. The experience of participating in sports has the ability to reinforce or teach any value we want it to, good or bad. Maybe with an accompanying model of restorative discipline and justice that is available when the inevitable team violation happens, good social teaching will occur.

17

Restorative Justice
in Disaster Management

Duane Ruth-Heffelbower

Disasters come in many forms: fire, flood, earthquake, volcano, mud-slide, civil war, invasion, bad government, economic collapse, famine, and on the list goes. One thing all these disasters have in common is people trying to help the victims. Individuals, government agencies, multinational agencies, and nonprofit organizations can all be involved in larger disasters. Human nature can often be seen at its best in these situations as people altruistically help in whatever way they can. Unfortunately, disasters can also bring out the worst in human nature.

Millions or even billions of dollars can be lost by ineptitude or diverted by corrupt people in the chaos of a major disaster. How best to help is a moving target, and decisions that look brilliant one week seem foolish the next. Money poured into Aceh on the northern tip of Sumatra after a tsunami devastated 120 miles (200 kilometers) of coastline and left more than 100,000 dead. The initial emergency response was to find shelter for hundreds of thousands of people. Tents, tarps, and shacks appeared quickly. Then the waiting began. Aceh being the site of a long-simmering civil war did not help.

Aid agencies converged on Aceh, somewhere between 250 and 300 of them at the peak. Some focused on emergency relief, others on reconstruction, and still others on rebuilding livelihoods. The latter saw some of the first visible ac-tion. Many of the people who lived in the devastated area earned their living from fishing or hauling freight down the coast by water. Their boats were all gone. The first to respond to the plight of the boat owners set up boat-building yards, hired local people, and built boats. Traditional wooden boats with up-turned ends began appearing—and sinking. It turned out that many of the real boat builders had been swept out to sea, leaving behind people who did not

Keywords: disaster management, justice, aid agencies

know how to build boats. Once that problem was addressed, nongovernmental organizations (NGOs) quickly went back into the boat business (Australian Council for International Development, 2005).

There was no coordination of NGO efforts in the beginning, although there were many attempts at coordination by the United Nations, the NGOs themselves, and the local government. It took several months for the BRR, the official government agency for reconstruction and rehabilitation, which had local authority, to begin real coordination efforts. With no coordination in place, agencies worked separately, promising people boats. After a while, it was discovered that twice as many boats had been promised as had originally existed, resulting in some people promised boats by two or more agencies. Some NGOs decided to leave the boat business, which left all the people they had promised without boats. Anti-NGO graffiti began to appear (Ruth-Heffelbower, 2006).

Everyone who visited the scene knew that housing had to be a top priority, and many NGOs began planning housing developments. Because international NGOs understandably want to have their own sign out front, these housing developments were not well coordinated, despite informal coordination among NGOs, the United Nations, and local governments. It quickly emerged that materials and building were not the only big problems; land ownership was another. Many people came back to their ruined or missing homes only to discover that their land was now part of the ocean (Mydans, 2005). Handmade signs planted in water proclaimed that the land was owned by a living person.

For those who made their living on the sea it was important to live near the shore, but no land was available for sale. Even for those willing to move far inland, title to land was a difficult thing to discern. Rebuilding progress slowed dramatically for some agencies, whereas others were successful in moving forward.

The second year after the 2004 tsunami saw a change in NGO activity. The slow pace of building new permanent homes left many people in makeshift shelters, so attention returned to temporary housing. One of the traditional ways for houses to be built by those who own land is to have a temporary house on the land and to build the permanent house as cash becomes available. NGOs were able to help those people. The people living in tents and shacks in refugee villages had no idea when their situation would change. The decision was made to build more temporary houses in dense blocks on land that could be acquired. Water and toilet facilities would all be communal, and the houses would consist of a single room. Low-lying land and even spits jutting into the ocean were used. Water lapped at new front doors.

How does one get the wood to build thousands of temporary little houses? Indonesia has vast lumber resources, but they tend to be export-oriented and far from Aceh. People forget that Indonesia is as wide east to west as the United States. If wood is imported, how will it get through customs, how much will it be delayed by that process, and how much will disappear? Items intended for relief were quickly a staple for street vendors in Sumatra and Java (Wallis, 2006).

When you manage to build the little houses, who will you consult in deciding how they should be shaped and sited?

A Japanese NGO solved the wood problem by prefabricating houses in Japan using metal for the frame. Delivery and setup on the site for each of these houses cost US$5,000.

A permanent house built of bricks and cement also costs US$5,000, and all the money goes to Indonesian workers and suppliers. The *Jakarta Post* reported on March 8, 2006, that "only 235 out of the estimated 16,000 temporary shelters needed for the 70,000 Acehnese living under canvas have been completed since the program began in September. About 12 percent of the around 120,000 new permanent homes required have been built" (BRR warns, 2006).

The local government was ill-prepared for the NGO onslaught. The nicer available housing was quickly snapped up by expatriates working for NGOs. Families were even known to move into temporary housing themselves so that they could rent their house to an NGO at a high rate. The rent on one home I visited would pay its full construction cost in two years. Most of the educated local people, particularly those who knew one of the NGO languages, were hired by NGOs for much more pay than they could expect from the Indonesian government or business employers. New Toyota Land Cruisers and other such vehicles with NGO logos on the side seemed to be everywhere. Tens of thousands of people were still living in tents and shacks (Ruth-Heffelbower, 2006).

These vignettes from one disaster suggest many opportunities for the application of restorative justice. Restorative justice practices have a role any time people believe that they have suffered injustice. The concept of injustice varies from culture to culture. Those who live in industrialized countries with functioning judicial systems see it quite differently from people who have never experienced a working judicial system and who have only begun to try moving from dictatorship to democracy. Indonesia is one of the latter places. Teaching about restorative justice in Indonesia and trying to use the Indonesian term for injustice, *ketidakadilan,* draws only blank looks. That changes when one uses the term *luka hati,* or "wound to the heart."

Restorative justice is about working with wounds to the heart. Whenever people have these wounds to the heart, they need a process to help them work through those feelings and begin to rebuild trust in the one who harmed them. Restorative justice can also provide a framework for systems and practices that avoid such wounds to the heart. Disaster management needs to take both into account.

An NGO, a government agency, or a multinational agency that plans a disaster response capability needs to include in its planning restorative processes for engaging the affected people in the creation of the plan, the execution of the plan, and conflict resolution. Avoiding revictimization needs to be an important consideration in planning. The Aceh scenario described offers good examples of the importance of all three areas.

Deciding what suffering people need and giving it to them without consulting the affected ones in the planning process is tantamount to revictimization. Disaster victims have had their ability to make meaningful choices stripped away. Many times, they have no resources to begin anew. The last thing they need is well-meaning responses to their plight that do not meet their real needs. A new fishing boat is great, but how about the nets and the gasoline? How about the marketplace to sell the fish? The marketplace was swept into the ocean, leaving nothing but a mud flat. An NGO working on boats would probably be happy to include those other things in its project, but without including their intended recipients in the conversation they do not recognize the needs; the result is wounds to the heart.

For victims of disasters, restorative justice means being empowered to begin making choices about what is necessary to rebuild their lives. Some researchers found that the "community organization['s] sense of community significantly predicted intrapersonal empowerment after controlling for demographics, participation, alienation, and other empowering organizational characteristic[s]" (Hughey et al., 2008, p. 651). The sense of community within the community organization is important and is an area where restorative practices indicate the inclusion of voices often excluded in the crush of disaster response.

Chittagong, Bangladesh, is an area of dense population that has been repeatedly flooded by cyclones. Organizing the community not only for disaster relief but also for risk management has been a critical task. A case study prepared by the Asian Disaster Preparedness Center says that

> the community empowerment approach for disaster management helped create a more proactive stance and attitude among the people. Community empowerment is a type of capacity development where its members decide on the goals and strategies for disaster risk management, contribute some (if not all) of the resources needed, and monitor their performance.[1]

Community empowerment is a restorative justice practice. Community development practitioners do not think in terms of restorative justice as they work, but their best practices are restorative. Phil Bartle's *Handbook for Mobilizers* was developed for use by United Nations Human Settlements Programme (UN-HABITAT) in Uganda. It says that

> empowering a community is not something that you can do to that community. Because the process of empowerment, or capacity development, is a social process, it is something that the community itself must undergo. Even members of a community, as individuals, can not develop their community, it is a growth process of the community as a whole, internally, as an organism (super organism or social organism).[2]

Bartle also points out that those responding to disasters or other situations requiring a relief/development response tend to think in terms of "projects." Each project is a discrete entity with its own workers and funding. This way of helping is not easily compatible with community empowerment and can lead to practices that are not restorative. A project organizer commonly has a short time frame within which to spend budgeted funds, "short" being a relative term. One agency with which I am familiar had US$13 million donated for tsunami relief. The decision was made to spend it over a three-year period. This proved to be daunting with all the delays described herein. Community empowerment tends to be front-loaded with time, something that project coordinators do not have.

There is a tension between pressures for control and pressures for support when outside people and money enter a community in an attempt to help. Restorative justice researchers have noted that the more restorative practices are those that marry high control and high support, rather than being permissive, punitive, or neglectful (Wachtel, 2003). People working in relief and development are aware of the need for recipients of aid to be involved but are equally aware of how quickly resources can disappear without strong safeguards. Indonesia worked hard at defeating what is known locally as KKN (corruption, collusion, and nepotism), but that is an uphill battle in the best of times. The sudden influx of money and outsiders not especially knowledgeable about the local setting created almost irresistible opportunities for self-enrichment.

Who gets hired to execute the plans that the NGOs develop? Educated, bilingual local people are hired for translation and management tasks. Is there a place for relatively uneducated people to gain employment in the project? Building boats and houses requires certain skills that only a few have, but any able-bodied person can carry things. Larger Indonesian construction projects tend to have brigades of people carrying wet concrete up a scaffold in a basket on their heads. Sometimes speeding up a work project by using skilled people and heavy equipment denies meaningful work to those who most need it. Were the intended recipients of aid consulted about balancing speed and employment? Revictimization can be the unintended consequence of failing to do so. For victims of disasters, restorative justice means being included in deciding how a project will be executed.

Conflicts between local people and aid providers are an inevitable consequence of disasters, no matter how carefully people try to avoid them. Local people are in competition for scarce resources. One definition of conflict is when one person perceives that another person is blocking him or her from having his or her needs met. In a case where many people's land simply disappeared, conflict over land ownership is inevitable. When an aid provider fails to live up to its promises, conflict is inevitable. When government agencies and better-funded NGOs are in competition for scarce resources, conflict is inevitable. This means that building a conflict resolution methodology into disaster planning is important.

Many of the large international NGOs collaborated with Mary Anderson to produce a process and a book called *Do No Harm: How Aid Can Support Peace—or War* (Anderson, 1999). Anderson recognized that any relief or development effort has within it the ability to either strengthen or weaken a society's connectors and dividers. Paying attention to this concept is difficult enough when one NGO is working with a group of people. The more NGOs and government agencies that are involved, the more difficult it becomes and the more likely aid providers will work at cross-purposes. The restorative process steps already mentioned, such as including recipients in planning and execution, go a long way toward alleviating the problem, but not far enough.

When an aid provider recognizes that its project has the potential to create division in the community rather than drawing the community closer together, it is incumbent upon it to work at the problem with the recipients. This may mean returning to the drawing board and including them in the new plan or, if conflict has already emerged, to offer a process for working through the conflict. The availability of people experienced in cross-cultural conflict resolution is a key element of the plan. Often an NGO or a government agency has no plan for dealing with conflict and seems surprised when it emerges. Having conflict resolution available on the ground at the time when it is needed is the preferable way.

The long-standing rebellion against the Indonesian government in Aceh meant that there was deep local mistrust of anything that came from Java, the seat of both the government and the dominant Javanese ethnic group, but that is where Indonesian technicians and technocrats come from. NGOs wanting to hire skilled people for the tsunami response needed to go to the source of such people on Java. The fact that most international NGOs working in Indonesia have their offices on the island of Java meant that relationships already in place were with people living on Java. The result was an influx of Javanese to Aceh.

When feelings of injustice or wounds to the heart have arisen in relation to disaster assistance, a restorative process requires that the person who is responsible for the offense acknowledge the hurt, work together with the offended one to figure out how to make things as right as possible, and clarify the parties' future intentions (Claassen, 2002). A facilitator is needed for this. One problem for people working across cultures is in understanding how this process can be done where face-to-face negotiation is not culturally appropriate.

Where mediation is taught in Europe and North America, it is the face-to-face model or shuttle negotiations that prevail. These models are certainly efficient and can have the most obvious results, but most of the world's people think they are wrong. Speaking directly with someone about a conflict maximizes the opportunity to lose face, and most people think that is either crazy or immoral. When one of these people is in conflict with someone else, the indirect method is necessary. For those who prefer the indirect method, the facilitator is a mutually accepted wise person who listens to each one separately and then gives advice. Because one cannot lose face by taking a wise person's advice, everyone is satisfied. Some cultures bring the parties together after the matter is resolved, and others never acknowledge that anything happened (Ruth-Heffelbower, 1999). Javanese use the latter model.

What this means for planners who will be working outside their home culture is that a system must be devised by a process with local people in the disaster area for handling conflicts before they arise. The book *Conflict and Peacemaking Across Cultures: Training for Trainers* (Ruth-Heffelbower, 1999) describes how to do this. The basic process includes having a person charged with implementing a conflict resolution process become part of the overall planning team. As local people are engaged, they are also challenged to think together with the outsiders involved how best to work through the conflicts everyone knows will arise.

The method described in *Conflict and Peacemaking Across Cultures* brings together a mixed group, including the stakeholders from local and outside groups. They begin by sharing how conflict is handled within their cultural groups through storytelling. They also talk about how they work with conflict among the different cultural groups that they commonly encounter. The next step is for a trained facilitator to show the group some of the conflict resolution methods developed in other places around the world. The third step is for the group to decide together how they want to work with the conflicts that develop among them, creating a unique methodology drawing from both their usual ways and the ways they have been exposed to.

On a personal note, the process described has usually taken me about three days to complete. Language issues are large because people use their most nuanced language when in conflict, and few interpreters are up to the task. The facilitator needs to deliberately work at language issues because that is how real understanding is usually found.

Groups that develop an agreement on how they will work at conflict are much less likely to have serious unresolved issues that prevent community empowerment. The group that works through the issues together will also have developed a level of trust that tends to prevent unresolved conflicts by bring issues to the surface long before they are a problem.

Restorative practices are found in many different disciplines and are not often labeled as restorative justice practices. Anderson's work provides an easy way to remember how it works. Any time a plan is being made or work is being done, simply ask whether the way it is being done strengthens or weakens community connectors and community dividers. If it is strengthening connectors and not strengthening dividers, it is on the restorative side of the scale. Even a process that is obviously strengthening dividers can be moved in a more restorative direction with thoughtful planning. That is the challenge for those who want to see restorative justice in unusual places.

One of the resource people who came from Java to Aceh had been trained in restorative justice principles and was familiar with my community empowerment model (Ruth-Heffelbower, 1999). His focus was trauma healing. He wrote, "In Aceh also, culture has the power to protect a community. We worked to bring psycho-social healing through community reunification, the recovery of symbols, and the use of rituals" (Kharismawan, 2009, pp. 4–5). His group rented buses and provided free transportation for people searching for relatives and other members of their communities. They helped clean up surviving mosques to provide community centers where people could come together for problem solving. They worked with people to determine the rituals they needed to begin the healing process. These are not the sort of activities usually found in a disaster response work plan. Kharismawan continues, "We found that psychosocial support for disaster survivors in a collective society must focus on the community rather than on individuals. When restoration of the community and its structure occurs, individuals will also recover" (Kharismawan, 2009, pp. 4–5).

Restorative justice tends to work with collectives as a way to reach individuals. It is difficult, if not impossible, to heal individuals without healing the community. Community conferencing, circles, and other dialogue processes—common restorative techniques—have at their core the belief that one heals individuals by healing community. Disaster response that focuses on helping individuals tends to divide communities as jealousy and feelings of injustice arise. Much of this bad feeling is avoided when responses focus on community needs first. Restorative justice works at prevention as well as responding to active conflicts. In disaster situations conflict is inevitable, and those who want to be helpful in any way will find restorative ways to approach all of their activities.

Restorative justice happens through a series of restorative processes. The processes described in this chapter can be effective in disaster management.

Notes

1. Asian Disaster Preparedness Center, "Community Empowerment and Disaster Risk Reduction in Chittagong City." Available at www.preventionweb.net/files/global platform/entry_bg_paper~SaferCities21.pdf (accessed July 14, 2009).

2. P. Bartle, "Handbook for Mobilizers." Available at www.scn.org/cmp/hbmob.htm (accessed July 14, 2009).

18

Hope and Reconciliation with Grief

Bonnie J. Redfern

When looking at grief through the lens of restorative justice, it is possible to identify common themes that exist when individuals experience conflict and loss. The pathway toward reconciliation and peace with loss seems to parallel the process of peacemaking in restorative justice. Bringing these common themes into focus makes it possible to envision a pathway to experiencing peace with loss, just as one can experience peace amid conflict. I believe a need exists to look at the journey of grief through this lens and consider a new model that companions those who mourn as they move toward peace. It is my hope that this chapter will expand the practice of peacemaking into the realm of grief and loss. It is my desire to see those who grieve experience peace.

Restorative Justice in Grief:
Looking at Loss Through the Lens of Peacemaking

Two California families will never forget the winter of 1996. One will remember with extreme joy, the other with profound grief.

After gathering mushrooms in the foothills near San Francisco the afternoon of February 3, 1996, a mother used the harvest in the family supper. Within hours of ingesting the mushrooms, she and her three teenage children became extremely ill. Examination of the mushrooms revealed that they were highly toxic. With massive doses of antibiotics, the woman and her two sons began to show improvement. But the thirteen-year-old daughter's health rapidly deteriorated and her liver began to fail. She was placed on the emergency transplant list.

Keywords: grief, mourning, loss, peace, hope, transformation, reconciliation, companioning, empowerment, conflict

On the morning of February 7, the family received news that a donor match was found for their daughter. That evening, she underwent a transplant graft; one-half of a healthy liver was attached to her failing liver. Within days, her liver regenerated, and she eventually made a complete recovery.

About 200 miles away, in a small community in central California, on the morning of February 5, a teenage boy made a grave mistake in the woodshop at his high school. He placed a wood file between a tool brace and the oak table-top that was spinning on the faceplate of a lathe. The file jammed and the table-top shattered.

Pieces of oak became projectiles in the woodshop. One 14-inch piece of wood hit the sixteen-year-old directly in the face. That blow left his family to contend with the realities of sudden death. After thirty hours on life support, the young man was declared brain-dead. His family made a decision that they never could have imagined; their precious son became an organ donor.

On February 7, the young man's liver, heart, kidneys, and pancreas were removed. That evening, a representative from the California Transplant and Donor Network gave the boy's family some preliminary information regarding the value of their decision. Although no identifying information was given, the representative noted that their son's liver went to a young girl in the San Francisco area who was near death after ingesting poisonous mushrooms.

I will never forget the winter of 1996. I remember it with profound grief. The young man in the woodshop was my only son, Scott.

The evening of February 7, just twenty-four hours after we said goodbye to our son, my husband and I lay awake; the late night news droned on in front of our sleepless eyes. We watched as cameras focused on a helicopter landing on the roof of the University Medical Center in San Francisco. Physicians stepped out with a small ice chest, and the news commentator said, "A liver match has been found for the young girl who ingested the poisonous mushrooms." We watched with disbelief as our son's liver was carried in that small ice chest to be transplanted into another human being.

The commentator then interviewed the girl's father, who waited outside the surgery room where his daughter received the gift of life. He announced with great joy, "Our prayers have been answered." My husband spoke the words that remained in our hearts, "And our prayers were not." Their family joyously celebrated the tremendous gift of life for their only daughter. Our family tearfully grieved the inconceivable loss of our only son.

Before my son's death, I viewed restorative justice as a process of peacemaking to recognize injustices and restore relationships broken by conflict or crime. As a graduate student of conflict and peace studies, a community mediator, a school teacher, and a parent, I knew the opportunity that restorative justice provided to transform individuals, restore relationships, and bring peace to conflictive situations.

Not long after the death of our son, I began to identify similarities in the process of restorative justice and my own journey of grief. I found that the practice of peacemaking often shed light on my experience with loss. I completed training in death and grief studies and found that the lens of peacemaking clarified common themes of conflict and loss. The pathway toward reconciliation and peace with loss seemed to parallel the process of peacemaking. I considered the potential the process of restorative justice could bring to individuals torn apart by loss to experience peace—found in the Hebraic notion of *shalom.*

Commonalities of Conflict and Loss

Conflict is a part of life—a characteristic of existence and relationships. Although one cannot avoid conflict, individuals can choose the effect that conflict has on their lives. If one chooses to suppress or deny the existence of conflict, tensions increase as the source of conflict becomes something or someone to be avoided. If one chooses to accept the reality of conflict, individuals can respond destructively, which escalates the conflict, or participate in a constructive process of peacemaking to reconcile the conflict and restore the relationship.

Likewise, it has been noted that death is perhaps the most inevitable part of life (Becvar, 2001). That may seem like an absurd statement. Yet, a French historian of science has noted that our Western society has become a death-denying society (Aries, 1981). Medical and technological advancements prolong life and delay death. Yet, death and loss cannot be avoided, no matter how much one may attempt to deny their inevitability or suppress their significance for those who remain. As in conflict, individuals can choose the effect that loss has on their lives. If one chooses to avoid the reality of loss, tensions increase as the need to grieve and mourn is suppressed or denied. If one chooses to accept the reality of loss, individuals can respond destructively, which complicates grief, or participate in a constructive process of grief work to reconcile the loss and transform the relationship.

In every conflict and in every loss, choices determine whether individuals will be destroyed or transformed. The restorative justice lens illuminates the need to recognize the reality of conflict and loss as part of the transformative pathway of peace. This lens also reinforces themes common to both conflict and loss, bringing new insight to how those who experience loss can experience peace in this most unexpected place.

The Theme of Relationship

Relationship is a connectedness to others through common interests, kinship, attractions, or goals. A clinical psychologist suggests that it is impossible to be in relationships without conflict, and therefore conflict becomes a reality of any relationship (Nadig, 2003). Besides blocking desires and goals, conflict has the potential to separate and destroy relationships. When the process of restorative justice is engaged, relationships can be restored and transformed.

Similarly, loss is embedded in the very nature of relationships and connectedness. With the capacity to love comes the necessity to grieve when someone loved dies (Wolfelt, 2002). Simply put, if we choose to love, we choose to grieve.

> Conflict and death can result in a loss of connectedness within a relationship.
> Relationship loss is the ending of opportunities to relate oneself to, talk with, share experiences with, make love to, touch, settle issues with, fight with, and otherwise be in the emotional and/or physical presence of a particular other human being. (Mitchell and Anderson, 1983, pp. 37–38)

Restorative justice clarifies the common theme of transforming relationships as a function of peacemaking and grief work. As does restorative justice in conflict, the adaptive work of grief includes recognizing a change in a relationship. A loved one is no longer present. Transforming the relationship from one of presence to one of memory, restoring rather than losing the relationship, is a transformative element of grief work.

The potential exists in conflict and loss to experience relationship loss. Restorative justice brings the hope of restored relationships.

The Themes of Forgiveness and Reconciliation

Two connected themes of restorative justice are forgiveness and reconciliation. As constructive pathways in conflict, forgiveness and reconciliation lead to the transformation of individuals and restored relationships. When we look through this lens, forgiveness and reconciliation become fundamental in transforming individuals who experience loss and provide pathways to experiencing peace with loss.

David Augsburger, considering the commonality of forgiveness in conflict and loss, writes that grief work seems to parallel the process of forgiving. In fact, he coins the term *forgrieving* to express how individuals who experience loss "gradually forgo the anger at injury, the rage of betrayal, and the resentment at duplicity, but without the aid of denial" (Augsburger, 1996, p. 68). He notes that in conflict, as in loss, there is the need to grieve the change in relationships, the hurt of injury, and the lack of resolution.

The restorative justice lens highlights forgiveness as a pathway to peace in loss. The death of someone can elicit negative emotions directed at the deceased, at those culpable for the death, or at one's self for thoughts and actions leading up to or contributing to the death. Forgrieving provides a pathway for the bereaved to release the negative emotions produced by the loss as they achieve "the capacity to mourn a loss, to grieve an injury, and to work through to healing" (Augsburger, 1996, p. 68).

Forgiveness moves one from being a victim to being a survivor (Zehr, 1995). *Survivor* is a common term used in the context of loss. However, the elements of grief and the pain of relationship loss often make the bereaved feel more like victims. I believe it is possible to conceive of forgiveness in loss as a means of transforming those who grieve and who feel like victims to become survivors in peace.

Likewise, the theme of reconciliation is rooted in the desire for continued relationship and becomes a transformative response to conflict. From the wisdom literature,[1] reconciliation is a pathway leading to a *healing place* "where truth and mercy have met, and where justice and peace have kissed" (Lederach, 1999, p. 53). Relationships and individuals, broken by conflict and torn apart by loss, are in need of a healing place. Each element of Lederach's healing place brings fresh perspective to the potential of achieving reconciliation and experiencing peace.

These elements—truth, justice, mercy, and peace—are foundational to the process of restorative justice. It is valuable to look at each element more fully—to comprehend its meaning in the context of the wisdom literature—to understand what each brings to the process of restorative justice in conflict as well as in grief.

Truth recognizes the reality that conflict and loss are a part of life. Truth does not deny the existence of conflict or repress the injury it can bring. Likewise, truth does not suppress grief or retreat from the sorrow of loss. Truth sees with striking reality that conflict and loss bring about pain, injury, and sorrow. Truth acknowledges that conflict and loss alter relationships. In the context of the wisdom literature, truth brings the notion of stability and continuance in the face of reality.

Mercy is the Hebraic notion of kindness, goodness, and forgiveness. When truth and mercy meet, the harshness of reality encounters the kindness of mercy. Mercy does not ignore what truth acknowledges, but sees the pain, the injury, and the sorrow through a lens that desires goodness and forgiveness. Mercy is reflected in Augsburger's notion of forgrieving—letting go of the injustice of pain and loss, and the anger and rage at injury, without the aid of denial.

Justice brings the notion of making things right to the realm of conflict and loss. As such, justice helps individuals communicate the criteria for reconciliation. As one seeks justice, one looks for opportunities to restore what was changed or redeem what was lost. It speaks to the needs illuminated by truth. It is often difficult to truly make things right in conflict and loss. How does one undo the injury of a criminal act or the injustice of the loss of one dearly loved? In restorative justice and peacemaking, the notion of justice communicates the criteria that will make things as right as possible and seeks to redeem and transform relationships.

Peace within the wisdom literature reflects both a passive and an active process to establish and maintain harmony, wholeness, and completeness. It implies a state or a condition within the individual that is not dependent on the absence or denial of conflict or loss. Through the lens of peacemaking, justice and peace come together in reconciliation. The physical, emotional, spiritual, and psychological elements illuminated with truth are seen as values, cognitions, and emotions that lead to transformation. It is in this healing place that those in conflict and loss can more fully understand what is central, what is essential to continuing to live.

It is possible to extend the concept of a healing place to the realm of loss. Truth, in the context of loss, is about what to remember and how to remember. Truth looks to the past, remembers the way it was before the loss, and underscores the value of restoring the past relationship. Justice is about what can be done now to restore wholeness and transform the relationship that has been separated by death. Justice looks to the present and recognizes the full weight of grief. Mercy and peace look to the future and ask, how will the bereaved learn to live with the loss? How can the relationship with the deceased be transformed from one of presence to one of memory? Mercy and peace cast their eyes toward the future and what it will be like because of this loss.

Through the lens of restorative justice, forgiveness and reconciliation bring new information to individuals experiencing loss. Forgiveness and reconciliation become pathways for the bereaved to transform negative emotions and cognitions, and reduce the factors that extend or complicate grief. As in conflict, forgiveness and reconciliation become processes for transforming relationships and experiencing peace with loss.

The Theme of Storytelling

The restorative justice process itself is essentially a storytelling process. Storytelling offers victims the opportunity to tell their side of injury and pain (Gehm, 1998). The important aspect of storytelling may not be merely the content of the story, but "the process the story ignites . . . they get us thinking about what is important; they communicate through symbol and metaphor deep truths about the mysteries of life" (Simpkinson and Simpkinson, 1993, p. 1). Storytelling helps individuals recognize the reality of the conflict. It provides individuals the opportunity to express the emotional and relational needs that contribute to and result from the conflict in order to establish the criteria for reconciliation.

Similarly, storytelling in loss is a way to integrate the loss into the world of the bereaved as they retell the circumstances of the death and the impact of the loss. Storytelling provides the opportunity to remember with truth the longed-for past, to cherish the relationship, and to move toward a future of hope.

In working with the bereaved, Wolfelt refers to this process of remembering as *storying,* which helps those who grieve bring meaning and purpose to life and death experiences by telling their stories (Wolfelt, 2002). In our death-denying society, both the bereaved and those around them attempt to put the loss behind them, get back to normal, and avoid the pain of grief and suppress the truth.

Storytelling encourages the recognition of the reality of the loss. The bereaved have the opportunity to contend with emotional needs, address spiritual needs, and verbalize their psychological needs through storytelling.

Moreover, the restorative justice lens views storytelling as an occasion for empowerment to occur. Empowerment—the awareness of one's own ability to seek solutions—leads to transformation in conflict and comes as one's story is heard and honored (Folger and Bush, 1994). In the same way, storytelling brings the possibility of empowerment to the realm of loss as the bereaved tell their story and as those who hear their story honor it. We actually become part of the audience, remaking ourselves as we listen to the story again and again (Gehm, 1998).

Furthermore, the more the bereaved tell their story and the circumstances surrounding loss, the more they begin to move from avoidance to recognition to reconciliation. Storytelling, as a process of restorative justice, promotes reconciliation as the bereaved look with truth to the past, examine and express the need for justice in light of this present loss, and articulate how mercy and peace merge for a life in the future without the physical presence of their loved one.

The power of storytelling and the notion of forgrieving are connected. In the many journeys back to the point of pain—to tell and retell various parts of the story—individuals revisit the past, rework the injury, and rebuild the loss, as they reinterpret the meaning it brings to life (Augsburger, 1996). Storytelling releases the story and reopens the future. Whether in conflict or loss, storytelling is a process of restorative justice and moves individuals toward experiencing peace.

A Restorative Justice Model in Conflict and Loss

This book presents a challenging notion: Can restorative justice be experienced in unusual places? Equally challenging is the thought of a single chapter addressing the prospect of restorative justice in the realm of grief and loss. With this limitation, I focus here on comparing the transformative mediation model of restorative justice with the companioning model of grief therapy.

Transformative mediation brings conflicting parties together. The parties' willingness to come together in this process demonstrates their recognition of conflict, a starting place in moving toward peace. Within this place, individuals come to listen and to be heard, to understand and to be understood, to recognize and resolve conflicts, and to find pathways to renew their relationship and live together in peace. The criteria for reconciliation are established to restore the relationship and experience peace.

The experience of being heard and understood, whether one is a victim or an offender, brings the potential for empowerment to occur. Empowerment allows individuals to gain clarity about their goals, resources, options, and preferences (Folger and Bush, 1996). They experience an awareness of their own self-worth and ability to deal with the difficulties they face, regardless of external constraints (Folger and Bush, 1994).

Within this transformative environment, mutual recognition—being willing and able to understand one another's position—often follows empowerment. Individuals are able to listen to and to respond to each other, increasing the potential for harmony and wholeness and renewed relationships.

The transformative mediation model of restorative justice closely parallels the companioning model of working with the bereaved. Alan Wolfelt developed the model of companioning the bereaved (see Appendix 18.A). When the similarities of these two models are brought into focus, companioning the bereaved emerges as a restorative approach to grief work. Just as transformative mediation encourages the victim and the offender to envision how to restore the relationship and move forward in the future, so too the companioning model encourages the bereaved to renew the relationship with the person who died—to transform it from one of presence to one of memory and embrace the potential of living with the loss.

The transformative mediation approach, where the mediator follows the parties around, allows the parties to clarify perceptions and explore options (Folger and Bush, 1994). Likewise, those who companion the bereaved follow the lead of the bereaved as they clarify their unique journey with grief and loss and explore the option of being transformed by the loss (Wolfelt, 1999).

Companioning the bereaved creates an environment in which individuals can express negative emotions, struggle to regain some sense of order, and search for meaning. Empowerment emerges through companioning, as those who grieve gain an awareness of their capacity to reconcile the physical, emotional, spiritual, and psychological elements of grief work and begin to see beyond the loss.

Transformative mediation in conflict and companioning the bereaved in loss capture the essence of restorative justice in several ways. Both reflect the notion that peace begins within the individual. Both emphasize the value of transforming relationships that have been broken by conflict or torn apart by loss. Both help the individual establish the criteria for reconciliation to be explored and expressed. Both become a holding place—creating a safe place where conflict can be recognized and relationships can be restored, or suspending the movement away from the pain of grief and allowing the bereaved to accept the reality of the loss and transform the relationship. As individuals face the overwhelming obstacles of conflict or the heavy burden of loss, empowerment creates a pathway through the obstacles and burdens to peace.

The transformative mediation and companioning models sustain the notion of bringing restorative justice to the unlikely place of grief and loss. Restorative justice brings the hope of transformation to those in conflict and those who experience loss.

A New Model in Loss

Out of my own personal desire to experience peace—*shalom*—after the death of my son, I searched for a pathway leading to peace with loss. My studies in peacemaking and conflict, and my training in death and grief, helped me envision such a path. Although many theoretical models and approaches exist to help the bereaved, a new model that looks at grief through the lens of restorative justice emerged from my own search. I believe this new model guides the bereaved through the painful but essential process of living with grief and helps them imagine a path toward peace with loss.

This new model, A Place Called Hope (Redfern, 2003), clarifies the needs of the mourner. It brings the hope of peace and transformation to those who live with grief and loss. The model incorporates current theories in the fields of death and grief studies and peacemaking in conflict. Specifically, it communicates the qualities of the companioning model developed by Wolfelt (Appendix 18.A) and elements of the peacemaking model of restorative justice developed by Ron Claassen (Appendix 18.B). I believe this model invites the mourner to enter the restorative, adaptive work of grief and mourning and provides an opportunity for the bereaved to be transformed rather than destroyed by the loss.

In addition, this new model allows those who companion the bereaved to become peacemakers as they journey with individuals torn apart by loss, peacemakers who bring the hope deeply rooted in the Hebraic traditions of *shalom*—the values of harmony, rest, wholeness, and a sense of being made one again. As peacemakers, those who companion the bereaved provide a safe place for empowerment and recognition to occur; present the potential of transforming relationships; and portray the hope that although loss and grief are part of life, it is possible to move toward experiencing peace with loss.

A Place Called Hope

A Place Called Hope communicates the many facets of the grief journey (see Figure 18.1). It speaks of a process through which the bereaved may embrace the hope of experiencing peace. It represents a location as it conveys the notion of a safe place, a holding place, where the bereaved come to do the adaptive work of grief. In addition, the model suggests an attitude or a position, a point in time when the bereaved embrace the spirit of hope.

Hope is both active and passive in nature—actively seeking a good yet to come, all the while passively waiting for the good to arrive. Hope, an integral element of the model, is brought into focus through the lens of restorative justice. The bereaved are given the prospect of being transformed by loss, as well as the permission to be suspended, supported, while waiting for transformation to occur.

Figure 18.1 A Place Called Hope

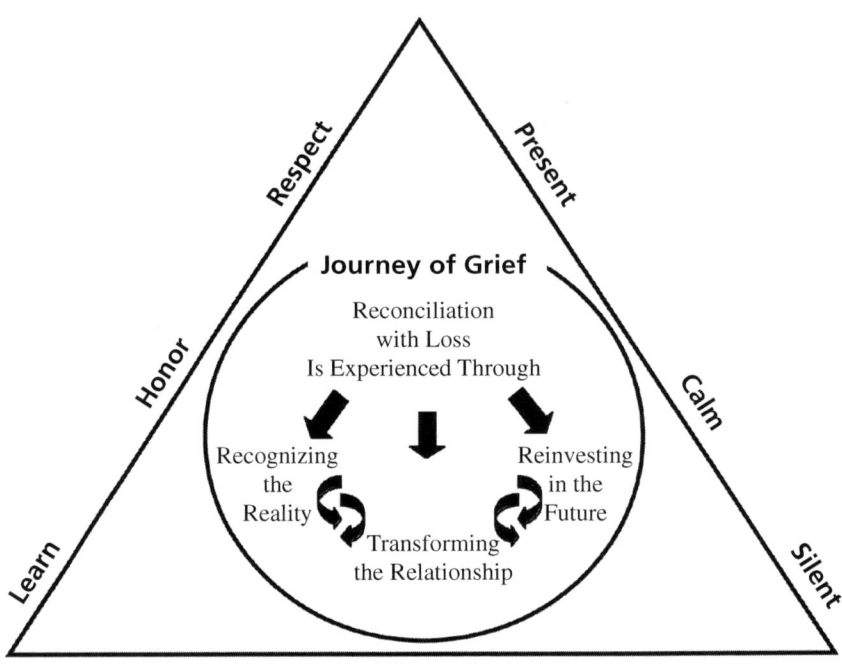

Commitment to be Constructive

Source: Redfern (2003).

A Place Called Hope communicates the intent of both the bereaved and those who companion the bereaved. The bereaved desire a safe place to grieve, a place where the elements of their grief are expressed, where empowerment is experienced, where the reconciliation needs are embraced, and where the hope of peace with loss is envisioned.

Commitment to Be Constructive

The triangular model rests upon the words *a commitment to be constructive.* The notion to establish this model on this principle comes directly from the context of peace studies. The value of being constructive was first cited in writings for the Harvard Negotiation Project, noting that an unconditional commitment to be constructive is pivotal to negotiations in peacemaking (Fisher and Brown, 1989). This value is a critical part of Claassen's peacemaking model wherein the commitment to be constructive is a starting point for dealing with injustices and violations (Claassen, 2003).

The death of a loved one often presents itself as an injustice or a violation to one's real and assumptive worlds. As such, the response to the injustice or violation of death can be expressed in destructive emotions, cognitions, and behaviors. A commitment to be constructive is an essential component of the model. A safe place where the bereaved can embrace their pain begins with a commitment to be constructive. It may be difficult to encounter the pain of loss all at once as the grief may indeed overwhelm the bereaved. Those who grieve need a safe place where they can embrace their pain in doses (Wolfelt, 1998b).

The Qualities of Restorative Justice in Loss

The words along the vertical lines of the triangle speak of attributes grounded in restorative justice. In conflict, these qualities bring to light what the victim and the offender bring to a place of reconciliation.

Likewise, these qualities are significant in the companioning model. Confusion may be present with the experience of grief and mourning. One must respect disorder and confusion in the adaptive work of grief. It is not about imposing order or logic (Wolfelt, 1998a). Respect for the disorder and uncertainty honors the story and brings normalcy to the confusion of grief. When one's world is shattered and thoughts do not make sense, one can feel powerless. Respect and honor offer the bereaved the opportunity to experience empowerment and help them to recognize their capacity to live with the loss. Honor acknowledges the spirit behind the expressed thoughts and emotions that may appear intellectually vague. It is not about the intellect. Honoring the spirit looks beyond the confusing thoughts and conflicting emotions to the expressions of the spirit.

Many theories of loss and grief portray the caregiver as the expert who leads the bereaved through a series of tasks or phases, as if to say, "Follow me. I will lead you out of the land of mourning." This could not be further from the truth, as each individual journey of grief is uniquely experienced in light of the circumstances of the death and of the relationship. Those who companion the bereaved display a willingness to learn. With companioning, the bereaved become the "teacher" with respect to their unique journey of grief and loss. The companion is not responsible for creating the map or finding the way out. Rather, the bereaved express their emotions, cognitions, and behaviors, and together with the companion, discover the pathway to peace.

The quality of presence communicates that grieving can be a lonely task and reconciling the loss may best be achieved with the presence of others (Mitchell and Anderson, 1983). With companioning, the opportunity to build a relationship exists through being present, both physically and emotionally, in the loneliness. The relationship developed through companioning provides security for the bereaved; individuals can grieve without the "fear of abandonment or condemnation" (Mitchell and Anderson, 1983, p. 117). Being present with those who grieve promotes and facilitates the adaptive work of grief and prepares the way for the journey toward peace.

The restorative justice model speaks of the quality of being present. Displaying a nonanxious presence produces what Heifetz calls a "holding environment," which serves to facilitate adaptive work (Heifetz, 1994, pp. 104–105). With the companioning model, the bereaved are suspended and supported to do the adaptive work of grief. It may be the desire of the bereaved to rush through the painful work of grief and mourning. Society may tell the bereaved to move on. Family and friends may encourage the return to some sense of normalcy. The companioning model brings a calm environment that promotes and facilitates the bereaved's desire to achieve reconciliation with loss. A nonanxious presence suspends time for those who need a place to mourn. As a virtue of peace, calm embodies the essence of *shalom* and becomes a refuge in the chaos of grief and loss.

In the context of grief and loss, one must understand the need for silence. "A listening presence comfortable with silence; bearing with individuals in their pain and confusion; responding encouragingly when strong feelings are expressed; and lending strength to people when they need an emotional 'prop'" are aspects of being supportive. "One must be able to listen without judging, hear without retreating, evoke without forcing, and understand without condescending" (Mitchell and Anderson, 1983, p. 117). Silence is not about waiting to speak. Rather, silence brings significance to listening. Silence demonstrates the immediacy of the nature of companioning and the value of the expression of grief and mourning.

A Place Called Hope brings the qualities of transformative mediation into the realm of grief and loss. It fosters empowerment as the bereaved are given a holding place to approach the adaptive work of grief and move toward peace.

The Journey of Grief

In my new model, the words within the top arc of the circle communicate that the adaptive work of grief is like a journey. The metaphor of a journey is supported with the notion that "griefwork is a lifelong task" (Augsburger, 1996, p. 68). The journey metaphor communicates the reality that one never completes the work of grief but learns to live with the loss and to move forward. The metaphor of a journey communicates several other notions. It speaks of traveling from one place to another, moving from how it was *before* the loss to how it is *now* with the loss, as well as how the *future* will be different in view of the loss.

Journeys are not always linear, indicating an unpredictable movement, as reconciliation with loss is not experienced sequentially or in any particular order. The movement may be forward or backward, as those who grieve can anticipate times of progress and times of retracing one's steps. The metaphor of a journey acknowledges that there will be interruptions. Periods of sorrow and times of darkness may make it difficult to continue. Within this safe place, the bereaved can be suspended to see their journey continue in the face of the unexpected. The metaphor indicates the uniqueness of the process. Variables of a journey cannot be controlled or duplicated. The nature of the death, the nature of the relationship with the deceased, and prior losses contribute to the uniqueness of one's journey of grief.

The lens of restorative justice makes it possible to focus on the goal of the journey—to companion the bereaved toward reconciliation and experiencing peace with loss. Reconciliation embraces the notion of acceptance, of contented submission, of bringing one's thinking consistent with a reality. It is a response to the change in relationship and is rooted in a desire for a restored relationship. It comes from a yearning for peace, both personally and relationally.

In loss, the practices of restorative justice and companioning the bereaved enlighten the goal of the journey. Reconciliation in loss helps the bereaved envision a new normalcy, where one is transformed to live with the loss.

The Dimensions of Experiencing Peace With Loss

Just as those who participate in the process of restorative justice in conflict, the bereaved move toward and experience peace through reconciliation. A Place Called Hope represents a safe place to move toward reconciliation with loss through the dimensions of grief.

Grieving accomplishes several goals: recognizing the reality of the loss, building cherished memories, beginning new investments and connections, and reconstructing one's paradigm of faith, often changed by loss (Mitchell and Anderson, 1983). The dimensions of this model incorporate these goals and represent recognized components of grief work within current theories on death and loss (Rando, 1993; Wolfelt, 2000; Worden, 1991). The lens of restorative justice provides insight into each dimension as one moves toward experiencing peace with loss.

Recognizing the Reality of the Loss

Recognizing the reality of the loss is a critical function to achieving reconciliation. If conflict is not acknowledged, there will be no movement toward reconciliation. Likewise, if the reality of the loss is denied, much of one's energy on the journey of grief is spent suppressing the elements of grief to avoid the reality. Reconciliation embraces the reality of the loss.

In current approaches to loss, Worden's four tasks of mourning begin with accepting the reality of the loss (Worden, 1991). Similarly, the bereaved's attempt to recognize the reality of the loss through acknowledging and understanding the death is part of the six processes of mourning (Rando, 1993). For reconciliation, the mourner needs to acknowledge the reality of the death as an essential component (Wolfelt, 2000).

Recognizing the reality of the loss produces physical, emotional, spiritual, and psychological elements of grief. Grieving is a process through which the profound emotions produced by the loss are acknowledged and expressed fully (Mitchell and Anderson, 1983). In this dimension, the truth of what happened is expressed and acknowledged. The needs created by one's emotions and cognitions are addressed. Recognizing the reality of the loss is integral to achieving reconciliation.

Transforming the Relationship

This dimension also gains clarity from the restorative justice lens. In conflict, reconciliation begins with an acknowledgment that relationships have been broken. A fundamental tenet of restorative justice is seeing the offense not only as the breaking of a law or a rule but, more important, the breaking of a relationship. Reconciliation emerges from a yearning for continued and renewed relationship—to be at peace, to experience harmony, and to be set at one again both personally and relationally. Reconciliation brings a restoring of connectedness (Tolliday, 1997).

Transforming the relationship in loss closely resembles the work of reconciliation through restorative justice. Motivated by a desire for continued relationship, it is possible to experience reconciliation with the loss as the bereaved transform the relationship that has been changed by loss. In loss, this becomes a way to restore connectedness.

> Literature on grief and grieving almost universally agrees that one major goal of grieving is to gain emotional release from the attachment to the lost person . . . but how is that emancipation to be achieved? There is a significant answer to this question: one gains emotional release from what is lost by actively making it a memory. (Mitchell and Anderson, 1983, pp. 125–126)

Although the death of the loved one separates the mourner from the deceased, that does not mean the end of their relationship (Rando, 1993). Many may counsel the bereaved to put the past behind them in order to move on with life. Embracing the potential of transforming the relationship means the relationship does not end. The relationship with the person who died continues through memory. "Embracing your memories—both happy and sad—can be a very slow and, at times, painful process . . . but remembering the past makes hoping for the future possible" (Wolfelt, 2000, p. 4).

Transforming the relationship is key to moving toward peace with loss. It can be painful, as it involves remembering the past. The qualities that surround the model provide a safe place to encourage the bereaved to do this adaptive work. It is important to note the nonsequential nature of these dimensions indicated by the new model, A Place Called Hope. I believe it is possible for the bereaved to journey from one dimension to another and back again. It is also possible for the bereaved to enter into the process of reconciliation at any dimension, as this is not a linear model.

While companioning, it may become evident that the bereaved are not yet willing or do not possess the capacity to recognize the reality of the loss. But there is great joy in remembering the relationship. In this instance, the value of storytelling becomes an integral part of the process. As one releases the stories, one moves closer to accepting the reality, as expressed in Augsburger's notion of forgrieving.

The nonlinear nature of the model provides for the lifelong journey of grief. One may believe the dimensions to be "completed" only to find the need to enter into a dimension when the pain of loss and the elements of grief arise with the passage of time.

Reinvesting in the Future

This dimension is a vital component of transformative theories of both conflict and loss. The restorative justice model suggests that making promises for the future and reinvesting in the relationship are important components of reconciliation. This lens brings the perspective of reinvesting in the future as an integral part of one's journey of grief.

The concept of a *healing place* speaks of reinvesting. As one wrestles with the search for meaning and tries to make sense of the loss, one grapples with how the future will look with the loss. Reconciliation brings the reality of the loss and the memory of the relationship into the perspective of the future. This part of grief work is *reintegration.* The bereaved are free to reintegrate in the future with the proper memory work to transform the relationship with the deceased. "Remembering and hoping are inextricably bound together. The future is opened to new relationships and new experiences to the degree that the past has been made a memory" (Mitchell and Anderson, 1983, p. 132).

It is important to remember that because this is a nonlinear model, it is possible for the bereaved to begin their journey by reinvesting in the future to find ways to bring value to the loss to foster healing. Recognizing the reality of the loss may come through a forward movement in life, where the absence of the loved one becomes painfully evident. As one reinvests in the future, the memories of the past may come to mind, and the value of remembering and transforming the relationship is embraced.

The model, therefore, illustrates the nonsequential path individuals may take on their journey of grief. Within the dimensions of the model, the bereaved retell the painful story as the reality of loss is recognized; they remember and value the relationship as it was before loss to transform it to one of memory and envision how to reinvest in the future. As loss and grief are expressed and the needs of the mourner are addressed and acknowledged along the journey, it is possible to experience transformation and move toward peace with loss.

Experiencing Peace with Loss

I believe the lens of restorative justice brings the hope of experiencing peace with loss for those who grieve. The companioning model of adaptive grief work brings a transformative approach to create a safe place where empowerment is found. In this holding place, the bereaved are able to articulate the criteria that must be addressed and met to achieve reconciliation.

Peace with loss does not mean that the bereaved will no longer grieve any more than experiencing peace in conflict means there will never be conflict again. Conflict and loss are inherent in relationships. To risk love is to risk loss. But through the transformative process of companioning, individuals can surrender to their grief and learn to live with it. Through the lens of restorative justice, individuals are transformed by the losses of life.

Conclusion

Although I will always remember the winter of 1996 with profound grief, I can say that I have been transformed through my personal journey with loss. I have looked through the lens of restorative justice at the loss of my son and have found a place of hope and reconciliation. I have surrendered to my loss with the reality that the death of my son has forever changed the world as I knew it.

For me, the beauty of the restorative justice model, in both conflict and loss, is that the journey does not end with surrender. The restorative elements embedded in transformative mediation in conflict and companioning the bereaved in loss offer the hope that reconciliation and restored relationships will come from surrender. There is the potential to transform the pain and sorrow and envision a future that acknowledges the reality that death and loss are inevitable. Certainly, my future will always include the pain of the loss of Scott, but there is an opportunity for me, for my family, and for all who grieve to journey a restorative pathway toward experiencing peace with loss.

Appendix 18.A The Companioning Model

I continue to advocate in my writings and teachings that caregivers to the bereaved (i.e., "to be torn apart" or "to have special needs") should "companion" not "treat" people in grief. I appreciate the support and enthusiasm many of you have given me as I teach this philosophy throughout North America. For those of you not familiar with "companioning," I invite you to consider the philosophy that undergirds my work with bereaved people as well as my writings. I believe in "companioning" the bereaved instead of "treating" them.

I have taken liberties with the noun "companion" and made it into the verb "companioning" because it so well captures the type of counseling relationship I support. Actually, the word companion, when broken down into its original Latin roots, means *com* for "with" and *pan* for "bread." Someone you would share a meal with—a friend, an equal.

Companioning is about honoring the spirit;
  It is not about focusing on the intellect.
Companioning is about curiosity;
  It is not about expertise.
Companioning is about learning from others;
  It is not about teaching them.
Companioning is about walking alongside;
  It is not about leading or being led.
Companioning is about being still;
  It is not about frantic movement forward.
Companioning is about discovering the gifts of sacred silence;
  It is not about filling every painful moment with talk.
Companioning is about listening with the heart;
  It is not about analyzing with the head.
Companioning is about bearing witness to the struggles of others;
  It is not about judging or directing those struggles.
Companioning is about being present to another person's pain;
  It is not about taking away or relieving the pain.
Companioning is about respecting disorder or confusion;
  It is not about imposing order and logic.
Companioning is about going to the wilderness of the soul with another
      human being;
  It is not about thinking you are responsible for finding the way out.

Source: Alan Wolfelt, *Companioning the Bereaved* (Bishop, CA: Companion Press, 2005).

Appendix 18.B The Peacemaking Model: When Agreements Are Made and Kept, Trust Grows

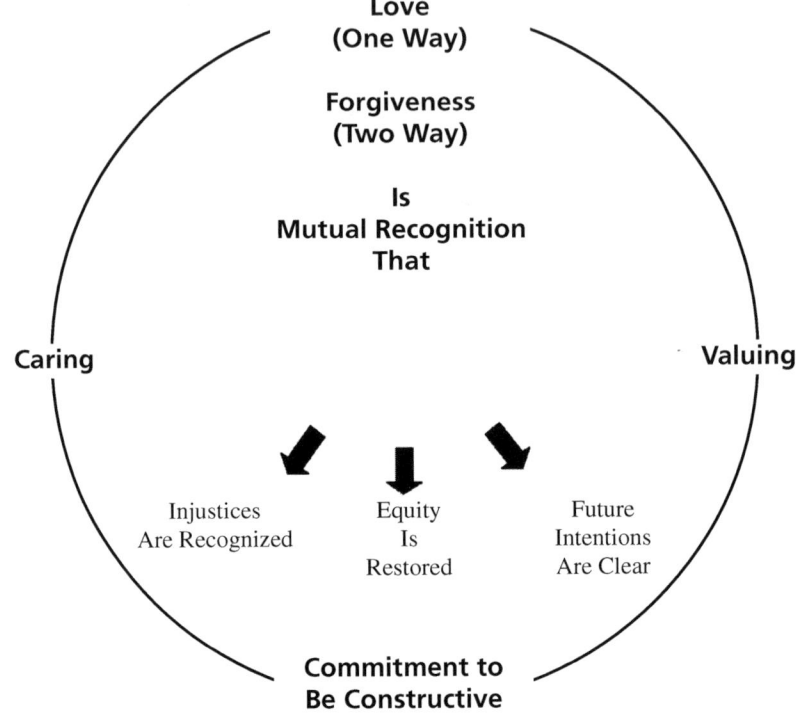

Source: Ron Claassen and Roxanne Claassen, *Discipline That Restores: Strategies to Create Respect, Cooperation, and Responsibility in the Classroom* (Charleston, SC: BookSurge Publishing, 2008).

Note

1. "One of the more notable products of the ancient Hebrew religious culture consisted of that group of compositions known as the wisdom literature. In the canonical writings it included the books of Proverbs, Job, Ecclesiastes, and certain of the psalms, particularly those dealing with the topic of wisdom" (Harrison, 1969, p. 1004).

References

Abril, J. C. (2004). *Final report to the Bureau of Justice Statistics from the Southern Ute Indian Community Safety Survey.* Award No. 2001-3277-CA-BJ U.S. Washington, DC: Department of Justice/Office of Justice Programs/Bureau of Justice Statistics.

Abril, J. C. (2005). The relevance of culture, ethnic identity, and collective efficacy to violent victimization in one Native American Indian tribal community. PhD diss., University of California, Irvine. ProQuest/UMI No. 3167918.

Abril, J. C. (2007). Native American Indian identity and violent victimization. *International Perspectives in Victimology, 3*(1), 22–28.

Abril, J. C. (2008). Cultural conflict and crime: Violations of Native American Indian cultural values. *International Journal of Criminal Justice Sciences, 2*(1), 44–62.

Abril, J. C. (2009). Negotiation of tertiary power in a Native American Indian tribal community. In K. Jaishankar (Ed.), *International perspectives on crime and justice.* Newcastle-upon-Tyne, UK: Cambridge Scholars Publishing.

Ahmed, R., Seedat, M., van Niekerk, A., and Bulbulia, S. (2004). Discerning community resilience in disadvantaged communities in the context of violence and injury prevention. *South African Journal of Psychology, 34*(3), 386–408.

American Bar Association (2003). Guidelines for the appointment and performance of defense counsel in death penalty cases. Retrieved on September 19, 2007, from http://www.nacdl.org/sl_docs.nsf/issues/ABADPGuidelines/$FILE/ABA_DPGuidelines2003.pdf.

Anderson, M. B. (1999). *Do no harm: How aid can support peace—or war.* Boulder, CO: Lynne Rienner Publishers.

Aries, P. (1981). *The hour of our death.* New York: Alfred A. Knopf.

Asmal, K., Chidester, D., and James, W. (Eds.). (2003). *Nelson Mandela: In his own words.* New York: Little, Brown.

Augsburger, D. (1996). *Helping people forgive.* Louisville, KY: Westminster John Knox Press.

Australian Council for International Development (2005). Third quarterly NGO report on the Asian tsunami. Retrieved on October 9, 2007, from http://www.reliefweb.int/library/documents/2005/acfid-sasia-30sep.pdf.

Bain, P., and Spencer, C. (2007). *Fact sheet 2, World Elder Abuse Awareness Day.* Prepared for Federal/Provincial/Territorial Ministers Responsible for Seniors in Canada.

Bazemore, G., and Umbreit, M. (1997). *Balanced and restorative justice for juveniles: A framework for juvenile justice in the 21st century.* St. Paul, MN: Center for Restorative Justice and Mediation.

Beck, E., Britto, S., and Andrews, A. (2007). Reaching out. In Beck, Britto, and Andrews (Eds.), *In the shadow of death: Restorative justice and death row families* (pp. 177–196). New York: Oxford University Press.

Becroft, A. (2006, May). Restorative justice in the youth court: A square peg in a round hole? *Restorative Justice Online.* Retrieved on June 14, 2009, from http://www.restorativejustice.org/editions/2006/may06/becroft.

Becvar, D. S. (2001). *In the presence of grief: Helping family members resolve death, dying and bereavement issues.* New York: Guilford Press.

Biermans, N. (2002, October). Restorative justice and the prison system. Papers from the Second Conference of the European Forum for Victim-Offender Mediation and Restorative Justice, Oostende, Belgium. Retrieved on July 27, 2009, from http://www.euforumrj.org/readingroom/Oostendeconf.pdf.

Bitel, M., Thurlow, J., Roberts, L., Sseruma, W. S., and Gross, T. (2005). *The national evaluation of restorative justice in schools.* London: Youth Justice Board. Available from http://www.yjb.gov.uk/Publications/Scripts/prodView.asp?idProduct=207&eP=PP.

Bowers, S., and Wells, L. (1986). *Ways and means.* Kingston, UK: Kingston Friends Workshop Group.

Boynton, G. (1997). *Last days in Cloud Cuckooland.* New York: Random House.

Braithwaite, J. (1989). *Crime, shame and reintegration.* Cambridge,UK: Cambridge University Press.

Braithwaite, J. (1999). A future where punishment is marginalized: Realistic or utopian? *UCLA Law Review, 46*(6), 1727, 1750.

Braithwaite, J. (2002). *Restorative justice and responsive regulation.* New York: Oxford University Press.

Braithwaite, V., Ahmed, E., Morrison, B., and Reinhart, M. (2003). Researching the prospects for restorative justice practice in schools: The Life at School Survey 1996–9. In L. Walgave (Ed.), *Repositioning restorative justice* (pp. 169–190). Devon, UK: Willan Publishing.

Bredemeier, B. (1993). Moral psychology in the context of sport. In R. N. Singer, M. Murphey, and L. K. Tennant (Eds.), *Handbook of research on sport psychology* (pp. 587–599). New York: Macmillan.

Bredemeier, B., and Shields, D. (1985). Values and violence in sport. *Psychology Today, 19,* 22–32.

Bredemeier, B., and Shields, D. (1986). Game reasoning and interactional morality. *Journal of Genetic Psychology, 147,* 257–275.

Bridges to Life (BTL) (2009). *Recidivism and other evaluation studies.* Unpublished report.

BRR warns it may take over unfinished contracts (2006, March 8). *The Jakarta Post.*

Bureau of Justice Statistics (2007). Criminal offenders statistics. Retrieved on October 24, 2009, from http://www.ojp.gov/bjs/crimoff.htm.

Burford, G., and Pennell, J. (1998). *Family group decision making project: Outcome report* (vol. 1). St. John's, Canada: Memorial University of Newfoundland, School of Social Work.

Burr, R. (2006, December). Expanding the horizons of capital defense: Why defense teams should be concerned about victim survivors. *The Champion,* 44–48.

Caley, D. (1998). *The expanding prison.* Toronto: House of Anansi.

California General Election Official Voter Information Guide (2006). Retrieved on October 16, 2007, from http://www.voterguide.sos.ca.gov/pdf/prop83_text.pdf.

California Youth Authority (2002). *Impact of crime on victims classes/panels for offenders*. Sacramento: California Youth Authority.

Canadian Conference of Mennonite Brethren Churches (2008). Confession of Faith. Retrieved on March 31, 2009, from Article 13, http://www.mbconf.ca/home/products_ and_services/resources/theology/confession_of_faith/detailed_version/#13.

Carceral, K. C., and Bernard, T. J. (2005). *Prison, Inc.: A convict exposes life inside a private prison*. New York: NYU Press.

Carney, A. G., and Merrell, K. W. (2001). Bullying in schools: Perspectives on understanding and preventing an international problem. *School Psychology International, 22*(3), 364–382.

Carson, D. K. (1995). American Indian elder abuse: Risk and protective factors amongst the oldest Americans. *Journal of Elder Abuse and Neglect, 7*(1), 17–39.

Carter, J. (2006). *Palestine: Peace not apartheid*. New York: Simon and Schuster.

Chankova, D. (1996). Mediation as an innovation in the criminal procedure. In L. Kornezov, S. Margaritova, and D. Chankova (Eds.), *A century of criminal code and current issues of criminal legislation 1896–1996*. Sofia, Bulgaria: Ministry of Justice (in Bulgarian).

Chankova, D. (2002). *Victim-offender mediation*. Sofia, Bulgaria: Feneya (in Bulgarian).

Chankova, D. (2006). Applicability of victim-offender mediation in Bulgaria according to the law enforcement authorities. *Scientific Proceedings of Law and History Faculty at South-West University "N. Rilski"-Blagoevgrad, 2*(1) (in Bulgarian).

Chankova, D., Georgieva, E., and Bakalov, G. (2008). Findings of surveys on applicability of victim-offender mediation in Bulgaria. *Legal Tribune, 1* (in Bulgarian).

Chankova, D., and Staninska, E. (in press). Bulgaria on the road to restorative justice and victim-offender mediation. In D. Miers and I. Aertsen (Eds.), *Regulating restorative justice: A comparative study of legislative provisions in European countries*. Frankfurt: Verlag für Polizeiwissenschaft.

Chinova, M., and Ivanova, M. (2005). The crime victim at the stage of pre-trial proceedings. *Contemporary Law, 4* (in Bulgarian).

Claassen, R. (1996a). *Restorative justice—Fundamental principles*. Paper presented at the May 1995 meeting of the National Commission for Protection of Children's Rights (NCPCR), Minneapolis; revised at the May 1996 meeting of the UN Alliance of NGOs Working Party on Restorative Justice, New York.

Claassen, R. (1996b). Restorative justice principles. Retrieved on July 27, 2009, from http://peace.fresno.edu/docs/rjprinc2.html.

Claassen, R. (2001). Copyrighted training materials. Center for Peacemaking and Conflict Studies, Fresno Pacific University.

Claassen, R. (2002). A peacemaking model. Fresno, CA: Center for Peacemaking and Conflict Studies. Retrieved on October 13, 2009, from http://peace.fresno.edu/docs/APeacemakingModel.pdf.

Claassen, R. (2003.) A peacemaking model: A Biblical perspective. Retrieved on September 22, 2008, from http://peace.fresno.edu/docs/APeacemakingModelBP.pdf.

Coakley, J., and Bredemeier, B. (1988). Youth sports: Development of ethical practices. Manuscript.

Cowie, H. (2000). Bystanding or standing by: Gender issues in coping with bullying in English schools. *Aggressive Behavior, 26*, 85–97.

Crowe, F. (1997). Quantifying conflict resolution styles among prison inmates. *Journal of Offender Rehabilitation, 25*(3–4), 131–146.

Daly, K. (2003). Mind the gap: Restorative justice in theory and practice. In A. von Hirsch, J. V. Roberts, A. E. Bottoms, M. Schiff, and K. Roach (Eds.), *Restorative justice and criminal justice: Competing or reconcilable paradigms?* (pp. 219–236). Oxford, UK: Hart Publishing.

Daniels, G. (writer), and McDougall, C. (director) (2006). Conflict resolution [television series episode]. In G. Daniels (executive producer), *The office*. New York: NBC Universal.

Deloria, D. J., and Weikart, D. P. (1970). *Longitudinal results of the Perry Preschool Project*. Ypsilanti, MI: High/Scope Educational Research Foundation.

Dignan, J. (2005). *Understanding victims and restorative justice*. Maidenhead, UK: Open University Press.

Dignan, J., and Marsh, P. (2001). Restorative justice and family group conferences in England: Current state and future prospects. In G. Maxwell and A. Morris (Eds.), *Restoring justice for juveniles: Conferences, mediation and circles* (pp. 85–102). Oxford, UK: Hart Publications.

Dison, J. (2007). Restorative justice in prison. Manuscript.

Dorne, C. (2008). *Restorative justice in the United States*. Upper Saddle River, NJ: Pearson Prentice Hall.

Durkheim, E. (1933). *The division of labor in society* (translated from the French). New York: Free Press.

Edgar, K., O'Donnell, I., and Martin, C. (2003). *Prison violence: The dynamics of conflict, fear and power*. Portland, OR: Willan Publishing.

Eleven secondary school students were arrested (2003, December 23). *Singtao Daily*, A2 (in Chinese).

Elias, R. (1993). *Victims still: The political manipulations of crime victims*. London: Sage.

English, S. J., and Crawford, M. (1989). *Victim awareness education is basic to offender programming: A model course*. Sacramento: California Youth Authority.

Erez, E., and Laster, K. (1999). Neutralizing victim reform: Legal professionals' perspectives on victims and impact statements. *Crime and Delinquency, 45*(4), 530–553.

Evans, B. (2002). *You can't come to my birthday party! Conflict resolution with young children*. Ypsilanti, MI: High/Scope Press.

Evje, A., and Cushman, R. (2000). A summary of the evaluations of six California victim offender reconciliation programs. The Judicial Council of California Administrative Office of the Courts. Retrieved on October 12, 2009, from http://www.courtinfo.ca.gov/programs/cfcc/pdffiles/vorp.pdf.

Ex Parte KAN-GI-SHUN-CA (otherwise known as Crow Dog), 109 U.S. 556 (1883).

Fisher, R., and Brown, S. (1989). *Getting together: Building relationships as we negotiate*. New York: Penguin Books.

Five bullies beat a form-one boy (2001, June 9). *Apple Daily*, A13 (in Chinese).

Folger, J. P., and Bush, R. A. B. (1994). *The promise of mediation*. San Francisco: Jossey-Bass.

Folger, J. P., and Bush, R. A. B. (1996). Transformative mediation and third-party intervention: Ten hallmarks of a transformative approach to practice. *Mediation Quarterly, 13*(4), 263–278.

Folger, J. P., Poole, M. S., and Stutman, R. K. (2005). *Working through conflict* (5th ed.). Boston: Pearson/Allyn and Bacon.

Form-two boy chopped his classmates (2001, November 8). *Ming Pao*, A6 (in Chinese).

Four offenders were sentenced to life imprisonment (1999, January 31). *Apple Daily*, A2 (in Chinese).

Frankel, P. (2001). *An ordinary atrocity: Sharpville and its massacre*. New Haven, CT: Yale University Press.

Fung, A. L. C., and Tsang, S. M. (2007). Anger coping method and skill training for Chinese children with physically aggressive behaviors. *Early Child Development and Care, 177*(3), 259–273.

Fung, A. L. C., Wong, J. J. P., and Chak, Y. T. C. (2007). Who are the true "bullies" and the "victims"? *Journal of Youth Studies, 10*(1), 3–13.

Gaboury, M. T., and Ruth-Heffelbower, D. (2007). Corrections-based victim services and restorative justice programs. In L. J. Moriarty and R. A. Jerin (Eds.), *Current issues in victimology research* (2nd ed., pp. 289–308). Durham, NC: Carolina Academic Press.

Gaboury, M. T., and Sedelmaier, C. M. (2007). Impact of crime on victims (IOC) curriculum development project: Final evaluation report. Retrieved on October 24, 2009, from https://www.ovcttac.gov/victimimpact.

Gaboury, M. T., Sedelmaier, C. M., Monahan, L., and Monahan, J. (2008). A preliminary evaluation of behavioral outcomes in a corrections-based victim awareness program for offenders. *Journal of Victims and Offenders, 3*(2), 217–227.

Gallager, E., and Pittaway, E. (1995). *A guide to enhancing services for abused older Canadians.* Victoria, Canada: Centre for Aging, University of Victoria.

Gartrell, D. (1994). *A guidance approach to discipline.* Albany, NY: Delmar Publishers.

Gartrell, D. (1995). Misbehavior or mistaken behavior. *Young Children, 50,* 27–34. Available from the High/Scope website: (US) http://www.highscope.org; (UK) http://www.high-scope.org.uk.

Gehm, J. R. (1998). Victim-offender mediation programs: An exploration of practice and theoretical frameworks. *Western Criminology Review, 1*(1). Retrieved on March 12, 2003, from http://wcr.sonoma.edu/v1n1/gehm.html.

Gibson, J. (2004). *Overcoming apartheid: Can truth reconcile a divided nation?* New York: Russell Sage Foundation.

Goldfarb, M. A. (2004). What they're reading: The power and potential of mediation. *About Campus 9*(3), 27–29.

Graybill, L. S. (2002). *Truth and reconciliation in South Africa: Miracle or model?* Boulder, CO: Lynne Rienner Publishers.

Green, S. (2007). "The victims" movement and restorative justice. In G. Johnstone and D. W. Van Ness (Eds.), *Handbook of restorative justice* (pp. 171–191). Cullompton, UK: Willan Publishing.

Groh, A. (2003). *A healing approach to elder abuse and mistreatment: The restorative justice approaches to elder abuse project.* Waterloo, Canada: Community Care Access Centre of Waterloo.

Groh, A. (2005). Restorative justice: A healing approach to elder abuse. In R. Gordon and E. Elliott, *New directions in restorative justice: Issues, practice, evaluation* (pp. 175–192). Cullompton, UK: Willan Publishing.

Guadalupe, J. L., and Bein, A. (2001). Violence and youth: What can we learn? *International Journal of Adolescence and Youth, 10*(1/2), 157–176.

Hanson, R. K., and Bussiere, M. (1998). Predicting relapse: A meta-analysis of sexual offender recidivism studies. *Journal of Consulting and Clinical Psychology 66*(2), 348–362.

Harrison, R. K. (1969). *Introduction to the Old Testament.* Grand Rapids, MI: Eerdmans Publishing.

Heifetz, R. A. (1994). *Leadership without easy answers.* Cambridge, MA: Belknap of Harvard University Press.

Hohmann, M., and Weikart, D. P. (1995). *Educating young children.* Ypsilanti, MI: High/Scope Press.

Hopkins, B. (2004). *Just schools: A whole school approach to restorative justice.* London: Jessica Kingsley Publishers.

Hughey, J., Peterson, N., Lowe, J., and Oprescu, F. (2008). Empowerment and sense of community: Clarifying their relationship in community organizations. *Health Education and Behavior, 35*(5), 651–653.

Hugh-Jones, S., and Smith, P. K. (1999). Self-reports of short- and long-term effects of bullying on children who stammer. *British Journal of Educational Psychology, 69,* 141–158.

INPEA (International Network for the Prevention of Elder Abuse) (2007). Community guide to raise world awareness on adult abuse: A "tool kit" for taking action: Step by step. Retrieved on March 31, 2009, from http://inpea.net/weaad/weaad2008/downloads/community_guide_toolkit_07.pdf.

IRA. (2005, July 28). Full text of the IRA statement issued on Thursday, July 28, 2005. *Times Online.* Retrieved in December 2007 from http://www.timesonline.co.uk/tol/news/uk/article548962.ece.

Jackson, A. J. (2009). The impact of restorative justice on the development of guilt, shame, and empathy among participants in a victim impact training program. *Journal of Victims and Offenders, 4*(1), 1–24.

Johnstone, G. (2002). *Restorative justice: Ideas, values, debates.* Cullompton, UK: Willan Publishing.

Johnstone, G. (Ed.) (2003). *A restorative justice reader: Texts, sources, and contexts.* Cullompton, UK: Willan Publishing.

Johnstone, G., and Van Ness, D. (Eds.) (2006). *Handbook of restorative justice.* Cullompton, UK: Willan Publishing.

Judicial Council of California (2006). *Balanced and restorative justice: An information manual for California.* San Francisco: Judicial Council of California/Administrative Office of the Courts.

Karmen, A. (2007). *Crime victims: An introduction to victimology.* Belmont, CA: Wadsworth.

Kazura, K., Temke, M., Toth, K., and Hunter, B. (2002, February). Building partnerships to address challenging social problems. *Journal of Extension, 40*(1). Ideas at Work. Retrieved on October 11, 2009, from http://www.joe.org/joe/2002february/iw7.php.

Kharismawan, K. (2009, July–September). Culture and healing. *Peace Office Newsletter, 39*(3), 4–6. Published by the Mennonite Central Committee.

Kidd, J. (2006). Restorative social work. Master's thesis, University of Queensland, Brisbane, Australia.

Kraybill, D. (2006, October 11). Why the Amish forgive: Tales of redemption at Nickel Mines. Retrieved on October 20, 2006, from Eastern Mennonite University website, http://www.emu.edu/news/index.php/1246.

Krikler, J. (2005). *White rising.* New York: Manchester University Press.

LaFond, J. Q. (2005). *Preventing sexual violence: How society should cope with sex offenders.* Washington, DC: American Psychological Association.

Leaders from two Koreas sign peace declaration. (2007, October 4). Retrieved in December 2007 from http://www.korea.net/news/news/newsview.asp?serial_no=20071004022.

Lederach, J. P. (1999). *The journey toward reconciliation.* Scottdale, PA: Herald.

Lehman, J., Beatty, T. G., Maloney, D., Russel, S., Seymour, A., and Shapiro, C. (2002). *The three R's of reentry.* Washington, DC: Justice Solutions. Retrieved on October 13, 2009, from http://www.appa-net.org/eweb/docs/appa/pubs/RRR.pdf.

Leonard, P. (2006, December). All but death can be adjusted: Recognizing victims' needs in death penalty litigation. *The Champion,* 40–43.

Limper, R. (2000). Cooperation between parents, teachers, and school boards to prevent bullying in education: An overview of work done in the Netherlands. *Aggressive Behavior, 26,* 125–135.

Linden, R., and Groh, A. (in press). Addressing elder abuse: The Waterloo Restorative Justice Approach to Elder Abuse. *Journal of Elder Abuse and Neglect.*

Lord, J. H. (1990). *Victim impact panels: A creative sentencing opportunity.* Dallas, TX: MADD.

Mandela, N. (1994). *Inaugural address.* Retrieved in December 2007 from Washington State University, http://www.wsu.edu:8080/~wldciv/world_civ_reader/world_civ_reader_2/mandela.html.

Marshall, T. F. (1995). Restorative justice on trial in Britain. *Mediation Quarterly, 12*(3), 217–231.

Masten, A. S., and Coatworth, J. D. (1998). The development of confidence in favorable and unfavorable environments: Lessons from research on successful children. *American Psychologist, 53*(2), 205–220.

McGoldrick, D., Rowe, P., and Donnelly, E. (Eds.) (2004). *The permanent International Criminal Court: Legal and policy issues.* Oxford, UK: Hart Publishing.

Mediation UK (1998). *Mediation works! Conflict resolution and peer mediation manual for secondary schools and colleges.* Bristol, UK: Mediation UK.

Mentoring + Befriending Foundation (2005). Retrieved on August 14, 2005, from http://www.mandbf.org.uk.

Miers, D., Maguire, M., Goldie, S., Sharpe, K., Hale, C., Netten, A., et al. (2001). *An exploratory evaluation of restorative justice schemes.* London: Home Office Policing and Reducing Crime Unit Research, Development and Statistics Directorate, Clive House, Petty France. Retrieved on August 6, 2009, from http://www.homeoffice.gov.uk/rds/prgpdfs/crrs09.pdf.

Miers, D., and Willemsens, J. (Eds.) (2004). *Mapping restorative justice: Developments in 25 European countries.* Leuven, Belgium: European Forum for Victim-Offender Mediation and Restorative Justice.

Miller, R. (1996). *Cloudhand, clenched fist: Chaos, crisis and the emergence of community.* San Diego, CA: Laura Media.

Mirsky, L. (2006). The Sefton Centre for Restorative Practice: A restorative community in the making. Retrieved on March 22, 2006, from http://www.realjustice.org/library/sefton.html.

Mitchell, K. R., and Anderson, H. (1983). *All our losses: All our griefs.* Philadelphia: Westminster Press.

Monahan, L. H., Monahan, J. J., Gaboury, M. T., and Niesyn, P. A. (2004). Victim voices in the correctional setting: Cognitive gains in an offender education program. *Journal of Offender Rehabilitation, 39,* 21.

Morrison, B. (2002). Bullying and victimization in schools: A restorative justice approach. *Australian Institute of Criminology: Trends and Issues, 219,* 1–6.

Morrison, B. (2005a). *Building safe and healthy school communities: Restorative justice and responsive regulation.* Paper presented at the IIRP Sixth International Conference on Conferencing, Circles and Other Restorative Practices, Penrith, NSW, Australia.

Morrison, B. (2005b). Restorative justice in schools. In E. Elliott and R. M. Gordon (Eds.), *New directions in restorative justice* (pp. 26–52). Cullompton, UK: Willan Publishing.

Morrison, B. (2007). Schools and restorative justice. In G. Johnstone and D. W. Van Ness (Eds.), *Handbook of restorative justice* (pp. 325–350). Cullompton, UK: Willan Publishing.

Mydans, S. (2005, April 6). In tsunami area, relief is very slow in coming. *New York Times.* Retrieved on November 17, 2007, from http://www.nytimes.com/2005/04/06/international/asia/06aceh.html?_r=1&pagewanted=print&position=&oref=slogin.

Nadig, L. A. (2003). Relationship conflict: Healthy or unhealthy. Retrieved on March 14, 2003, from http://www.drnadig.com/conflict.html.

National Institute of Corrections (2004). *Corrections-based services for victims of crime.* Longmont, CO: U.S. Department of Justice, National Institute of Corrections

Information Center. Retrieved on July 27, 2009, from http://www.nicic.org/pubs/2004/019947.pdf.

NAVSS (National Association of Victims Support Schemes) (1984). *The victim and reparations.* London: NAVSS.

Neimeyer, R. A., Prigerson, H. G., and Davies, B. (2002). Mourning and meaning. *American Behavioral Scientist (46),* 235–251.

Nerenberg, L. (2008). *Elder abuse prevention: Emerging trends and promising strategies.* New York: Springer Publishing.

O'Brien, S., Maloney, D., Costello, D., and Landry, D. (2003, Summer). Bringing justice back to the community. *Juvenile and Family Court Journal,* 35–46.

O'Connell, P., Pepler, D., and Craig, W. (1999). Peer involvement in bullying: Insights and challenges for intervention. *Journal of Adolescence, 22,* 437–452.

O'Connell, T., Wachtel, B., and Wachtel, T. (1999). *Conferencing handbook: The new real justice training manual.* Pipersville, PA: Piper's Press.

Olweus, D. (1993). *Bullying at school: What we know and what we can do.* Oxford, UK: Blackwell.

Olweus, D. (1997). Bully/victim problems in school: Knowledge base and an effective intervention program. *Irish Journal of Psychology, 18*(2), 170–190.

O'Moore, A. M., and Minton, S. J. (2005). Evaluation of the effectiveness of an anti-bullying programme in primary schools. *Aggressive Behavior, 31,* 609–622.

Ortega, R., and Lera, M. (2000). The Seville anti-bullying in school project. *Aggressive Behavior, 26,* 113–123.

Panev, B. (2008). About applicability of mediation in criminal proceedings. *Legal Tribune, 1* (in Bulgarian).

Petersilia, J. (2003). *When prisoners come home: Parole and prisoner reentry.* New York: Oxford University Press.

Pollock, F. (1899). The king's peace in the Middle Ages. *Harvard Law Review, 13,* 177–189.

Pranis, K., Stuart, B., and Wedge, M. (2003). *Peace making circles: From crime to community.* St. Paul, MN: Living Justice Press.

Price, M. (1995). Comparing victim-offender mediation program models. *VOMA Quarterly, 6*(1), 1–6.

Public Safety Canada (2006). Dangerous offender designation. Available from http://www.publicsafety.gc.ca.

Putnins, A. L. (1997). Victim awareness programs for delinquent youths: Effects on moral reasoning maturity. *Adolescence, 32,* 709–715.

Rando, T. A. (1993). *Treatment of complicated mourning.* Champaign, IL: Research Press.

Rawlings, A. (1996). *Ways and means today: Conflict resolution, training, resources.* Kingston, UK: Kingston Friends Workshop Group.

Recidivism of sex offenders (2001). Retrieved on December 5, 2007, from http://www.csom.org/pubs/recidsexof.html.

Redfern, B. J. (2003). *Experiencing peace with loss.* Fresno, CA: Fresno Pacific University.

Restorative justice: Values and principles (2005). Retrieved from the Crime Safety and Crime Prevention Council website, http://www.preventingcrime.net/library.

Restorative justice city. (2004). Retrieved January 2007 from http://www.restorativejustice.org/articlesdb/articles/5774/.

Rigby, K. (1996). *Bullying in schools: And what to do about it.* London: Jessica Kingsley Publishers.

Rigby, K. (1999). Peer victimization at school and the health of secondary school students. *British Journal of Educational Psychology, 69,* 95–104.

Robinson, G., and Maines, B. (1997). *Crying for help: The no blame approach to bullying*. Bristol, UK: Lucky Duck Publishing. Retrieved in 2003 from http://www.luckyduck.co.uk.

Roche, D. (2006). Dimensions of restorative justice. *Journal of Social Issues, 62*(2), 217–238.

Rojek, D. G., Coverdill, J. E., and Fors, S. W. (2003). The effect of victim impact panels on DUI rearrest rates: A five-year follow-up. *Criminology, 41,* 1319–1340.

Roland, E. (2000). Bullying in school: Three national innovations in Norwegian schools in 15 years. *Aggressive Behavior, 26,* 135–143.

Ruth-Heffelbower, D. (1999). *Conflict and peacemaking across cultures: Training for trainers*. Fresno, CA: Center for Peacemaking and Conflict Studies.

Ruth-Heffelbower, D. (2006). Private interviews with expatriate aid workers in Banda Aceh.

Ruth-Heffelbower, D. (2007). Learn about victim-offender mediation. Retrieved on April 19, 2009, from the Victim Offender Mediation Association (VOMA) website, http://www.voma.org/abtvomshtml.

Ruth-Heffelbower, D., and Gaboury, M. (2008). Victim-offender programs in correctional settings: Can they effectively bridge divergent perspectives? In L. J. Moriarty (Ed.), *Controversies in victimology* (2nd ed., pp. 133–146)). Newark, NJ: Matthew Bender.

Rutter, M. (1987). Psychosocial resilience and protective mechanisms. *American Journal of Orthopsychiatry, 57*(3), 316–331.

Salkova, E. (2008). Is a question of discussion the applicability of mediation in penal matters in Bulgaria? *Legal Tribune, 1* (in Bulgarian).

Salmivalli, C. (1999). Participant role approach to school bullying: Implications for interventions. *Journal of Adolescence, 22,* 453–459.

Sampson, R. J., Raudenbush, S. W., and Earls, F. (1997). Neighborhoods and violent crime: A multi-level study of collective efficacy. *Science, 277,* 918–924.

Schiebstad, I. (2003). An evaluation of victim impact classes. Manuscript. Saint Ambrose University, Social Work Program, Davenport, IA.

School Councils UK (2005). Retrieved on August 14, 2005, from http://www.schoolcouncils.org.

Schrag, L. (2003). Restorative justice in Northern Ireland: An outsider's perspective. Paper presented at the Sixth International Conference on Restorative Justice. Retrieved on December 8, 2007, from http://www.sfu.ca/cfrj/fulltext/schrag.pdf.

Schwartz, E. (2008, February 7). "Mental health courts: How special courts can serve justice and help mentally ill offenders." *U.S. News and World Report.* Retrieved on July 30, 2009, from http://www.usnews.com/articles/news/national/2008/02/07/mental-health-courts.html.

Seymour, A. (1989). *Victim services in corrections*. Washington, DC: Office for Victims of Crime, US Department of Justice.

Shah, Z. (2006, May). Kirklees mediation. *Mediation UK Education and Youth Steering Committee (EYSC) Newsletter,* pp. 5–9.

Sharp, S. (1996). Self esteem, response style and victimization: Possible ways of preventing victimization through parenting and school based training programs. *School Psychology International, 17,* 347–357.

Sharpe, S. (1998). *Restorative justice: A vision for healing and change*. Edmonton, Canada: Victim Offender Mediation Society.

Sherman, L., and Strang, H. (2007). *Restorative justice: The evidence*. London: Smith Institute.

Simpkinson, C., and Simpkinson, A. (Eds.) (1993). *Sacred stories: A celebration of the power of stories to transform and heal.* New York: HarperCollins.

Smith, J. D., Schneider, B. H., and Smith, P. K. (2004). The effectiveness of whole-school anti-bullying programs: A synthesis of evaluation research. *School Psychology Review, 33*(4), 547–560.

Smith, M. D. (1975). The legitimation of violence. In R. S. Gruneau and J. G. Albinson (Eds.), *Canadian sport: Sociological perspectives.* Don Mills, Canada: Addison-Wesley.

Smith, P. K., Morita, Y., Junger-Tas, J., Olweus, D., Catalano, R., and Shee, P. (1999). *The nature of school bullying: A cross-national perspective.* New York: Routledge.

Smith, P. K., and Sharp, S. (Eds.) (1994). *School bullying: Insights and perspectives.* London: Routledge.

Steinmetz, M. (1990). Elder abuse: Myth or reality. In T. H. Brubaker (Ed.), *Family relationships in later life* (pp. 193–211). Newbury Park, CA: Sage.

Stevenson, C. L. (1975). Socialization effects of participation in sport: A critical review of the literature. *Research Quarterly, 46,* 287.

Stormy teenagers (1999, October 15). *The Sun,* A1 (in Chinese).

Stuart, B. (1997). *Building community justice partnerships: Community peacemaking circles.* Ottawa, Canada: Department of Justice.

Teen gangsters sexually assaulted a 13-year-old girl for 3 hours (1999, February 5). *Ming Pao,* A3 (in Chinese).

Thompson, D., Arora, T., and Sharp, S. (2002). *Bullying: Effective strategies for long-term improvement.* London: Routledge/Falmer.

Thompson, M., Osher, F., and Tomasini-Joshi, D. (2007). *Improving responses to people with mental illnesses: The essential elements of a mental health court.* Bureau of Justice Assistance, Office of Justice Programs, US Department of Justice. Retrieved on July 30, 2009, from http://www.ojp.usdoj.gov/BJA/pdf/MHC_Essential_Elements.pdf.

Thorsborne, M., and Vinegrad, D. (2002). *Restorative practices in schools.* Buderim, Queensland, Australia: Marg Thorsborne.

Thorsborne, M., and Vinegrad, D. (2004). *Restorative practices in classrooms.* Buderim, Queensland, Australia: Marg Thorsborne.

Tkachuk, B. (2002). Criminal justice reform: Lessons learned, community involvement, and restorative justice. HEUNI Papers. Retrieved on April, 6, 2009, from http://www.heuni.fi/uploads/hl5y98fikdy.pdf.

Tolliday, P. (1997). A definition of reconciliation. Retrieved on January 8, 2003, from the Australia STAR website, http://www.australianstars.com.au/history.html#definition.

Tonja, R. N., Overpeck, M., Pilla, R. S., Ruan, W. J., Simons-Morton, B., and Scheidt, P. (2001). Bullying behaviors among US youth: Prevalence and association with psychosocial adjustment. *Journal of the American Medical Association, 285,* 2094–2100. Available at http://jama.ama-assn.org/cgi/gca.

Trendafilova, E. (2001). *The Amendments to Criminal Procedure Code from 1999: Theoretical grounds, legislative decisions, tendencies.* Sofia, Bulgaria: Ciela (in Bulgarian).

Tutu, D. P. (1999). *No future without forgiveness.* New York: Doubleday.

Umbreit, M. (1995). *Mediating interpersonal conflicts: A pathway to peace.* West Concord, MN: CPI Publishing.

Umbreit, M. (2007). Humanistic mediation: A transformative journey of peacemaking. *Conflict Resolution Quarterly, 14*(3), 201–213.

Umbreit, M. S., Vos, B., and Coates, R. B. (2006). *Restorative justice dialogue: Evidence-based practice.* St. Paul: Center for Restorative Justice and Peacemaking, University of Minnesota.

United Nations (2000, July 27). *Basic principles on the use of restorative justice programmes in criminal matters* (ESCO Res. 2000/14 U.N. Doc. E/2000).

US Department of Justice (1998). *New directions from the field* (1998-432-163/95263). Washington, DC: US Government Printing Office.

US Department of Justice (2005). Victim impact panels. *Restorative Justice Fact Sheet.* Washington, DC: Office for Victims of Crime.

US Postal Service (2007). REDRESS statistics. Retrieved on December 5, 2007, from http://www.usps.com/redress/stats.htm.

Van Ness, D., and Strong, K. H. (1997). *Restoring justice: An introduction to restorative justice.* Cincinnati: Anderson Publishing.

Van Ness, D. W. (2005). *An overview of restorative justice around the world.* Vancouver, Canada: International Centre for Criminal Law Reform and Criminal Justice Policy. Retrieved on October 24, 2009, from http://www.icclr.law.ubc.ca/Publications/Reports/11_un/Dan%20van%20Ness%20final%20paper.pdf.

Van Ness, D. W., Morris, A., and Maxwell, G. (2003). Introducing RJ. In A. Morris and G. Maxwell (Eds.), *Restorative justice for juveniles: Conferencing, mediation, and circles* (pp. 1–16). Oxford, UK: Hart Publishing.

Wachtel, T. (1997). *Real justice.* Pipersville, PA: Piper's Press.

Wachtel, T. (2003). Reclaiming children and youth. *Journal of Strength-Based Interventions, 12*(2), 83–87.

Wahl, J. (2000). *Elder abuse: The hidden crime.* Toronto: Advocacy Centre for the Elderly and Community Legal Education Ontario.

Wallis, D. (2006). After the tsunami in Aceh Province. Retrieved on July 13, 2009, from http://www.magbaztravels.com/content/view/338/30.

Warren, C. (2004). *Restoring the balance: A guide to restorative approaches to behaviour management in schools.* London: Lewisham Action on Mediation Project.

Whitney, I., and Smith, P. K. (1993). A survey of the nature and extent of bully/victim problems in junior/middle and secondary schools. *Educational Research, 35,* 3–25.

Wilson, R. J. (2007). Circles of support and accountability: Empowering communities. In D. S. Prescott (Ed.), *Knowledge and practice: Challenges in the treatment and supervision of sexual abusers* (pp. 280–309). Oklahoma City: Wood 'N' Barnes Publishing.

Wilson, R. J., Cortoni, F., and Vermani, M. (2007). *Circles of support and accountability: A national replication of outcome findings.* Ottawa: Correctional Service of Canada.

Wilson, R. J., Picheca, J. E., and Prinzo, M. (2005). *Circles of support and accountability: An evaluation of the pilot project in south-central Ontario.* Ottawa: Correctional Service of Canada.

Wolf, R. S., and Pillemar, K. A. (1989). *Helping elderly victims: The reality of elder abuse.* New York: Columbia University Press.

Wolfe, R. (2009, April 19). From tragedy to forgiveness, with a stop at San Quentin. *The Press Democrat.* Retrieved on July 27, 2009, from http://www.pressdemocrat.com/article/20090419/ARTICLES/904199938?Title=From-tragedy-to-forgiveness-with-a-stop-at-San-Quentin.

Wolfelt, A. (1998a). Companioning vs. treating: Beyond the medical model of bereavement—Part One. *The Forum Newsletter, 24*(4), 1 and 10.

Wolfelt, A. (1998b). Companioning vs. treating: Beyond the medical model of bereavement—Part Two. *The Forum Newsletter, 24*(6), 3 and 15.

Wolfelt, A. (1999). *Comprehensive bereavement skills training manual.* Fort Collins, CO: Center for Loss and Life Transitions.

Wolfelt, A. (2000). *Afterwords: Helping yourself heal.* Fort Collins, CO: Companion Press.

Wolfelt, A. (2002). The awesome power of telling the story. Retrieved on October 26, 2002, from http://www.centerforloss.com/library/centerforloss/showarticle.asp?Article= awesomepower.htm&AudienceID=127.

Wong, D. S. W. (1999). Culturally specific causes of delinquency: Implication for juvenile justice in Hong Kong. *Asia Pacific Journal of Social Work, 9*(1), 98–113.

Wong, D. S. W. (2001). Pathways to delinquency in Hong Kong and Guangzhou (South China). *International Journal of Adolescence and Youth, 10*(1/2), 91–115.

Wong, D. S. W. (2003). *School bullying and responding tactics: A life education approach.* Hong Kong: Arcadia Press.

Wong, D. S. W. (2004). School bullying and tackling strategies in Hong Kong. *International Journal of Offender Therapy and Comparative Criminology, 48*(5), 537–553.

Wong, D. S. W., and Lee, S. T. (2005). Strategies for tackling school bullying: A whole-school approach. In W. L. Lee (Ed.), *Working with youth-at-risk in Hong Kong* (pp. 39–52). Hong Kong: Hong Kong University Press.

Wong, D. S. W., and Lo, T. W. (2002). School bullying in secondary schools: Teachers' perceptions and tackling strategies. *Educational Research Journal, 17*(2), 251–272 (in Chinese).

Wong, D. S. W., Lok, P. P., Lo, T. W., and Ma, S. K. (2002). *A study of school bullying in primary schools in Hong Kong.* Hong Kong: Department of Applied Social Studies (in Chinese).

Wong, D. S. W., Ngan, M. H., Cheng, H. K., and Ma, S. K. (2007). *The effectiveness of restorative whole-school approach in tackling bullying in secondary schools.* Hong Kong: City University of Hong Kong.

Worden, J. W. (1991). *Grief counseling and grief therapy* (2nd ed.). New York: Springer.

WRCEA (Waterloo Region Committee on Elder Abuse) (2008). *Elder abuse: What you need to know.* Waterloo, Canada: WRCEA.

Wright, M. (2006). Restorative justice and the victim: The English experiences. *International Perspectives in Victimology, 2*(1), 6–24.

Zehr, H. (1990). *Changing lenses: A new focus for crime and justice.* Scottdale, PA: Herald Press.

Zehr, H. (1995). *Changing lenses: A new focus for crime and justice* (3rd ed.). Scottdale, PA: Herald Press.

Zehr, H. (2001). *Transcending: Reflections of crime victims.* Intercourse, PA: Good Books.

Zehr, H. (2002). *The little book of restorative justice.* Intercourse, PA: Good Books.

Zehr, H., and Leonard, P. (2006). *Defense-initiated victim outreach training notebook.* Atlanta: Council for Restorative Justice, Georgia State University School of Social Work.

The Contributors

Zenebe Abebe received his doctorate in higher education administration, with a special emphasis in student development and international education, from Southern Illinois University-Carbondale, his MA in counseling psychology from Northern Illinois University, and his BA in psychology from Goshen College. Most recently, he was vice-president for the Office of Equity and Inclusion at Marian University. Before that, he held numerous positions in institutions of higher education in both multicultural education and study abroad programs and was also a professor of psychology. Through the years, he stayed active in his community consulting and conducting workshops for private businesses, churches, and government organizations regarding the issues of multicultural education, antiracism process, and workplace diversity. In addition, he has made numerous professional presentations at the regional and national levels. Zenebe has continuously contributed to academic and scholarly works and has authored several publications. His most recent publication was *The Two Faces of Racism,* published in 2008.

Julie C. Abril received her PhD in criminology, law, and society at the University of California, Irvine. Currently, she is assistant professor of sociology and criminal justice at Eastern New Mexico University. She has published widely in the areas of Native American Indians, violent victimization, crime, prisoner issues, and identity. She was recently elected to the Executive Board of the Division on People of Color and Crime of the American Society of Criminology (2007–2009). Her research is basic and empirical in nature. Abril has received numerous awards and honors, including a National Research Service Award from the US Department of Health and Human Services National Institutes of Health in 2006. She is also a consultant to the US Department of Justice on matters related to crime and violence among Native American Indians.

Dobrinka Ivanova Chankova is a pioneer in introducing restorative justice practices to Bulgaria's criminal justice system. She is professor of criminal procedure law of the Faculty of Law and History at South-Western University in Blagoevgrad, Bulgaria. Currently, she is also executive director of the Institute for Conflict Resolution, Sofia. Her professional interests and concentrations in law studies include human rights, European integration, alternative conflict resolution, victim-offender mediation, the rights of crime victims, and restorative justice systems. She received her law training at Sofia University and has worked and conducted research at many institutions, including the Directorate of Human Rights at the Council of Europe (Strasbourg), the European University Institute (Florence), the University of Cambridge and Civil Service College (London), the Central European University (Budapest), and the Austrian Study Centre for Peace and Conflict Resolutions (Stadtschlaining). She participated in the working group that developed the Bulgarian Mediation Act 2004 and is currently a member of the European Forum for Restorative Justice, the Union of Bulgarian Scientists, and the Union of Bulgarian Lawyers. She also serves on the editorial board of the *Law Without Borders Journal.*

Ron Claassen, MA, M.Div., D.Min., is director of the Center for Peacemaking and Conflict Studies at Fresno Pacific University. He teaches several courses in the MA Peacemaking and Conflict Studies Program and provides training, consultation, and intervention services in the community. He is founder and former director of the Fresno County Victim Offender Reconciliation Program, the first victim-offender rehabilitation program in California. Claassen has extensive experience in mediation, including victim-offender (ranging from petty theft to negligent homicide), contract disputes, racial and sex discrimination, employee disputes, wrongful termination, school site disputes (parents, teachers, administrators), church disputes, and public policy issues. A trainer of thousands in conflict resolution and mediation training events, he has also written numerous articles and training manuals related to the constructive management of conflict, including "Restorative Justice Fundamental Principles," which was adopted in May 1996 by the UN Alliance of NGOs' Working Party on Restorative Justice. With his wife, Roxanne (an eighth-grade teacher), he has coauthored "Making Things Right," a mediation training curriculum for students in grades 4–12 and *Discipline That Restores,* a step-by-step book for implementing restorative justice in the classroom.

John Dussich has degrees in clinical psychology (BS), corrections and criminology (MS), and criminology and sociology (PhD), all from Florida State University. He served twenty-nine years in the US Army's Military Police Corps, retiring at the rank of colonel in 1993. For the past thirty-four years he has been working mostly in the field of victimology, specializing in victim services. He is creator and founder of the National Organization for Victim Assistance

(NOVA), which he launched in Fresno, California, in 1976 at the Second National Conference on Victim Assistance. He served as its first executive director for four years. He has also been active in the American Society of Victimology and in the World Society of Victimology, serving as its founding secretary-general for two terms and recently for another three-year term; he has just completed a three-year term as its president. He recently finished ten years teaching criminology, victimology, and victim services in Japan and continues there as director of the Tokiwa International Victimology Institute (TIVI) and as editor of its journal, *International Perspectives in Victimology.* He is currently professor of victimology at California State University, Fresno, Department of Criminology, where he coordinates victim services internships and teaches victimology, victim services, legal issues in victim services, criminology, family violence, elder abuse, and international victim services. His writings have centered on abuse of power, victimological research, disaster victimization, victimological theory, coping theory, international victimology, and victim services—focusing on Asia, Latin America, and Europe. He is a trained disaster crisis responder and has logged many hours as a volunteer working with victims in numerous disasters around the world: Bosnia, El Salvador, Japan, Indonesia, the United States (for victims of the September 11 terrorist attack), and, most recently, China (for victims of the massive earthquake).

Mario Thomas Gaboury, PhD, is associate dean of the Henry C. Lee College of Criminal Justice and Forensic Sciences at the University of New Haven. He is also professor and chair of the Department of Criminal Justice and directs the University of New Haven Crime Victim Study Center. In 2007, he was named to a three-year appointment as the first Oskar Schindler Humanities Foundation Endowed Professor, focusing on humanitarianism and specifically addressing human trafficking issues. His current research centers on victimology, victims' rights, global human trafficking, victim impact education in correctional settings, restorative justice, and mental health in Vietnam. Gaboury is currently president of the American Society of Victimology and an executive board member of the Joint Center on Violence and Victim Studies. He is formerly deputy director of the Office for Victims of Crime at the US Department of Justice. His most recent scholarly articles have appeared in the following journals: *Victims and Offenders, Forensic Nursing, Offender Rehabilitation, Traumatic Stress,* and *International Perspectives on Victimology.*

Arlene Groh, RN, BA, an elder abuse restorative justice consultant at Healing Approaches to Elder Abuse and Mistreatment, Waterloo, Ontario, gives presentations and workshops internationally, nationally, and locally on the complex issue of elder abuse. Her topics include how to respond to elder abuse, with restorative justice as a resource option, and how to mobilize a community to identify and prevent elder abuse. She was formerly a case manager for in-home health services funded by Canada's Ministry of Health. She pioneered and co-ordinated the Restorative Justice Approaches to Elder Abuse Project, was a founding member of the Waterloo Region Elder Abuse Response Team, and was the elder abuse/restorative justice resource consultant for the team. Groh, whose innovative approaches to elder abuse have received national and international attention, is a volunteer for the Waterloo Region Committee on Elder Abuse and a board member of Victim Services of the Waterloo Region. She has been a working group participant of the Round Table for Ontario's Elder Abuse Strategy of the Provincial Elder Abuse Faith Interest Group and a board member of Focus for Ethnic Women. She is author of *A Healing Approach to Elder Abuse and Mistreatment: The Restorative Justice Approaches to Elder Abuse Project,* contributor to *New Directions in Restorative Justice: Issues, Practice, Evaluation,* edited by E. Elliott and R. Gordon, and coproducer of the video *A Healing Approach to Elder Abuse.* She is the recipient of many awards for her outstanding contribution to seniors and her dedication to the prevention of elder abuse.

Dennis Janzen is director of athletics and head women's volleyball coach at Fresno Pacific University. He holds a PhD in psychology of sport from the University of Southern California and is considered an expert in the field of character development and moral reasoning in the area of athletic competition. He has had coaching experience that ranges from elite world-class Olympic athletics to elementary-age youth sports. His volleyball teams at Fresno Pacific University have won three National Association of Intercollegiate Athletics (NAIA) national championships and have established themselves as a perennial power in college volleyball. He has recently been involved in the NAIA Champions of Character Initiative, leading two major character conferences designed specifically for high school–age student-athletes and their coaches. He is a frequent speaker at community groups and major coaching clinics. He is a member of the American Volleyball Coaches Association's Curriculum and Education Committee, which focuses on the development of educational materials and programs for coaches. His research interests include aggression in sports, the effects of athletic competition on character development and moral reasoning levels, and leadership development in athletics.

Marian Liebmann has a degree from Oxford University and qualifications in teaching, art therapy, and social work. She was a teacher and an educational writer before her long involvement in criminal justice. She has worked at a day center for ex-offenders, has provided victim support, and has served in the probation service. She was director of Mediation UK for four years and projects adviser for three years, working on restorative justice issues. Since 1998, she has been a freelance consultant and trainer with youth offending teams and mediation services in the United Kingdom and in several African and Eastern European countries, including a three-year project in Serbia and Montenegro in which she trained 180 victim-offender mediators. Liebmann has been involved with restorative justice initiatives in several prisons. She has worked with teenagers and trained them as peer mediators in school. She is also an art therapist in the mental health service and runs Art and Conflict and Art Therapy and Anger Management workshops. In 2005, she received a special merit award of the Longford Prize for outstanding contribution to social and penal reform for her pioneering work in art therapy, restorative justice, and mediation. She has authored or edited ten books, contributed twenty chapters to other books, and written numerous journal articles.

Shannon Moroney, BA, BEd, MA, was born and raised in Ontario, Canada, and has worked as a teacher, counselor, and social justice advocate for many years. In 2005, her life was traumatically altered when her husband committed several violent sexual assaults on two strangers and acts of voyeurism on her and others. Following a lengthy court process, he was sentenced to an indeterminate period of incarceration and declared a dangerous offender. Moroney now speaks publicly about her painful and eye-opening experiences as both a victim of crime and the spouse of an offender, advocating for restorative justice and sharing her personal journey of hope and forgiveness. She has presented to international audiences that include lawyers, judges, restorative justice facilitators, police, victim service providers, students, social workers, correctional officers, victims of crime, and prison inmates. She lives in Toronto.

Bonnie J. Redfern works as a mediator, trainer, and grief counselor with her husband, Tony, at the New Path Center, the California nonprofit organization they cofounded. As an educator in California public schools for twenty-five years, she has been a mentor and master teacher who successfully implements restorative justice theories, skills, and practices into the classroom. She proves that concepts of grace, forgiveness, restoration, and respect are workable and motivating themes for students in the primary grades, in parent and school intervention, and in training new teachers to create classrooms where respect nurtures a positive learning environment. She brings her undergraduate work in psychology, the experience of reconciling the death of her sixteen-year-old son, and her master's work in peacemaking and conflict studies together in her thesis work, *Experiencing Peace with Loss: Looking at Grief Through the Lens of Peacemaking.*

Clare Ann Ruth-Heffelbower is program director of Circles of Support and Accountability (COSA) at the Center for Peacemaking and Conflict Studies of Fresno Pacific University. She has been involved in restorative justice work for more than twenty years with the Victim Offender Reconciliation Program (VORP) of the Central Valley and is a member of the Association for the Treatment of Sexual Abusers. She brings years of experience with church and community-based organizations, both in the United States and in Indonesia, having served as a pastor, an administrator, and a board member. She has taught on both the graduate and undergraduate level. She received her D.Min. from the San Francisco Theological Seminary.

Duane Ruth-Heffelbower is an attorney and counselor-at-law, a mediator, an arbitrator, and a facilitator in all disputes; a member of the Fresno Pacific University School of Business faculty in the Leadership and Organizational Studies MA program; director of graduate academic programs at the Center for Peacemaking and Conflict Studies; faculty member in the Criminology and Restorative Justice Studies degree completion program; administrator for the Victim Offender Reconciliation Program of the Central Valley, Inc.; and supervisor of the Dispute Resolution Program Act (DRPA) civil court mediation project. He has trained thousands of people on five continents in dispute resolution and handled more than 3,000 North American cases as advocate, mediator, arbitrator, and facilitator. His writing draws on these practical applications.

Jill Schellenberg, MA, PhD, is professor in the School of Humanities, Religion, and Social Sciences at Fresno Pacific University and director of the Criminology and Restorative Justice Studies Program. She teaches courses in restorative justice, conflict management, conflict transformation, victimology, victim recovery, and criminology statistics. She is a mediator with the Victim Offender Reconciliation Program of the Central Valley, Inc., and a board member of Kings View Corporation dealing with mental and developmental disabilities. She is a member of the Association for Conflict Resolution (ACR) and the American and World Societies of Victimology.

Mark S. Umbreit is director of the Center for Restorative Justice and Peacemaking at the University of Minnesota. He is also author of *Facing Violence: The Path of Restorative Justice and Dialogue.*

Arthur Wint, JD, is professor of criminology and coordinator of the Peace and Conflict Studies Program at California State University, Fresno. He teaches courses on juvenile delinquency, criminal law, legal policy in victim services, and peace studies. He serves on the board of the Fresno Victim Offender Reconciliation Program and as a VORP mediator. In addition, he serves on the Ethics Committee of the Central Valley Children's Hospital and previously served on the Fresno County Juvenile Justice Commission. He has written articles on various subjects, including people trafficking, euthanasia, victims' attitudes toward crime, and police liability for use of deadly force. He has served as a core faculty member for the National Victim Assistance Academy (NVAA) since 1997, when he was the Fresno site coordinator. His NVAA teaching responsibilities have included hate crimes, restorative justice, diversity/underserved populations, victims with disabilities, and international issues in victim services.

Dennis Wong received social work undergraduate training in the early 1980s and is currently a registered social worker. He received his MA in social policy (York, UK) in 1986 and his PhD in social work (Bristol, UK) in 1996. Before joining City University of Hong Kong as an academic in 1989, he worked as a social worker in the fields of youth services, outreach, and residential services for delinquents. He is currently associate professor in social work and criminology and program leader of BSocSc (criminology) at the City University of Hong Kong. Over the past twenty years he has been involved in many large-scale studies commissioned by governmental and nongovernmental organizations. His research interests include juvenile delinquency, restorative justice, and school bullying. In addition to publishing a number of articles in local and international journals, he has recently published five textbooks related to youth values, juvenile delinquency, school bullying, mediation, and restorative justice.

Howard Zehr is professor of restorative justice at the Center for Restorative Justice at Eastern Mennonite University in Harrisonburg, Virginia. His book *Changing Lenses: A New Focus for Crime and Justice* is considered a foundational work in the restorative justice field. His other publications include *Doing Life: Reflections of Men and Women Serving Life Sentences* (1996), *Transcending: Reflections of Crime Victims* (2001), *The Little Book of Restorative Justice* (2002), *Critical Issues in Restorative Justice* (2004; coedited with Barb Toews), *The Little Book of Family Group Conferencing, New Zealand Style* (2004; coauthored with Allan MacRae), and *The Little Book of Contemplative Photography*. His awards include the International Peace Award 2006, Community of Christ; the Lifetime Achievement Award, Journal of Law and Religion, 2006; the Annual Peacebuilder Award, New York Dispute Resolution Association, 2003; and the Restorative Justice Prize, Prison Fellowship International, 2003. He lectures and consults internationally on restorative justice. He is also on the Fulbright Senior Specialist Roster and in 2007 lectured and consulted in New Zealand in this capacity. He received his PhD from Rutgers University.

Index

Abebe, Zenebe, 196
Accountability: athletic team
relationships, 208–213; Circles of
Support and Accountability, 2, 33–34;
defining crime in terms of victims, 55;
offender family reconciliation, 24;
organized sports, 8; sex offenders,
93–94, 98–99
Aceh, Sumatra, 219–222
Active listening, 167, 238
Adam Walsh Child Protection and Safety
Act (2006), 28
Adams, Gerry, 146, 151
Adult-child conflict, 168
Adversarial legalism, 6
African National Congress (ANC),
147–149
Afrikaner Weerstandsbeweging
(AWB), 148
Aid for Victims of Crime, 66
Alfred P. Murrah Federal Building,
Oklahoma City, 5, 133
American Parole and Probation
Association (APPA), 18–19
Amish school shooting, 59
Ancient civilizations, 67–69
Anderson, Mary, 223–224
Art therapy, 76, 97, 103
Asperger's syndrome, 172
Assimilative Crimes Act (1898), 109
Ataxic cerebral palsy, 57

Athletics, college: acceptable behavior
and notion of justice, 207–208;
benefits and disadvantages of
restorative discipline, 209–210; game
reasoning, 207–208; implementation
of restorative discipline and justice,
213–216; model for restorative
discipline and justice, 210–213; need
for restorative discipline and justice,
208–209; restorative justice and
discipline concept, 205–206; rule-
setting, 203–205
Australia: victim-offender dialogue
programs, 18
Autonomy of abused elders, 43

Bad Medicine, 116–117
Balance, social and moral, 210
Banishment from the Ute community,
111
Bartle, Phil, 222
Bay Area Women Against Rape, 66
Bear Dance, 108, 110–111
Beck, Elizabeth, 134, 140
Behavior paradigm of criminal
justice, 70
Boal, Augusto, 53(n9)
Boat building, Indonesia, 219–220, 223
Braithwaite, John, 155
Branham, Mickell, 134, 140
Bridges to Life (BTL) program, 22–23

265

About the Book

The increasing popularity of restorative justice has prompted new and varying applications of its core principles. The authors of *The Promise of Restorative Justice* highlight the ways that these new ideas now spark innovations both throughout the criminal justice system and in arenas as diverse as business, education, athletics, and the aftermath of ethnic conflict. They offer fresh approaches to addressing the problems of crime and other human conflicts in ways that productively incorporate the values of mutual respect, accountability, and ultimately reconciliation between offenders and victims.

John P. J. Dussich is professor of victimology and criminology at California State University, Fresno. **Jill Schellenberg** is a faculty member at Fresno Pacific University, where she directs the Criminology and Restorative Justice Studies Program.